Studies in
Modern French History

Mutinous memories

Manchester University Press

Studies in
Modern French History

Edited by
David Hopkin and Máire Cross

This series is published in collaboration with the UK Society for the Study of French History. It aims to showcase innovative short monographs relating to the history of the French, in France and in the world since c.1750. Each volume speaks to a theme in the history of France with broader resonances to other discourses about the past. Authors demonstrate how the sources and interpretations of modern French history are being opened to historical investigation in new and interesting ways, and how unfamiliar subjects have the capacity to tell us more about the role of France within the European continent. The series is particularly open to interdisciplinary studies that break down the traditional boundaries and conventional disciplinary divisions.

Recently published in this series
Emile and Isaac Pereire: Bankers, Socialists and Sephardic Jews in nineteenth-century France   Helen Davies
From empire to exile: History and memory within the pied-noir and harki communities, 1962–2012   Claire Eldridge
The stadium century: Sport, spectatorship and mass society in modern France   Robert W. Lewis
Nobility and patrimony in modern France   Elizabeth C. Macknight
The republican line: Caricature and French republican identity, 1830–52   Laura O'Brien
In pursuit of politics: Education and revolution in eighteenth-century France   Adrian O'Connor
Terror and terroir: The winegrowers of the Languedoc and modern France   Andrew W. M. Smith
Robespierre and the Festival of the Supreme Being: The search for a republican morality   Jonathan Smyth

The Society for the
Study of French History

Mutinous memories

A subjective history of French military protest in 1919

MATT PERRY

Manchester University Press

Copyright © Matt Perry 2019

The right of Matt Perry to be identified as the Author of this work has been asserted by him in accordance with the Copyright, Designs and Patents Act 1988.

Published by Manchester University Press
Oxford Road, Manchester M13 9PL

www.manchesteruniversitypress.co.uk

British Library Cataloguing-in-Publication Data
A catalogue record for this book is available from the British Library

ISBN 978 1 5261 1410 5 hardback
ISBN 978 1 5261 1411 2 paperback

First published 2019
Paperback published 2021

The publisher has no responsibility for the persistence or accuracy of URLs for any external or third-party internet websites referred to in this book, and does not guarantee that any content on such websites is, or will remain, accurate or appropriate.

Typeset by
Deanta Global Publishing Services

Contents

Preface	vi
Acknowledgements	ix
List of abbreviations	x
Introduction	1
1 Sensing mutiny	25
2 Mutinous emotion	54
3 A mutineers' world: transnationalism and the sense of place	83
4 Age, time and personal memory	115
5 Associational memory	145
Conclusion	173
Bibliography	188
Index	205

Preface

From his vantage of the factory council movement in Turin, surveying the 'revolutionary tide' across the globe in June 1919, Antonio Gramsci pointedly referred to the French army as being 'shot through with the threatening spasm of rebellion'.[1] This book is an account of that revolt as a microcosm of the turbulence that Gramsci himself experienced. It is concerned with the subjectivity of these French mutineers, just as Gramsci himself was preoccupied with the consciousness of the revolutionary subjects in his formulation of the theory of hegemony.

This book follows on from my research into the novelist of the Black Sea Mutiny, César Fauxbras. Though he was not a crew member of one of the mutinous vessels, Fauxbras was stationed in the Tunisian port of Bizerte when the battleship *Voltaire* mutinied and where the battleship *France* anchored on its return from Sevastopol, having launched the Black Sea Mutiny six weeks earlier. Others have also been drawn to this Black Sea Mutiny as an outstanding example of internationalism and revolutionary courage. William Zak, a British communist furniture maker, wrote a 216-page manuscript about the event, which resides undated in the People's History Museum (in Manchester). The puzzle of when it was written and why it was not published spotlights some of the problems that my research interrogates. First, the manuscript is highly reliant upon the research of communist mutineer-historian André Marty. Seeing past Marty as the solitary tribune of the participants to the mutineers themselves is difficult. Second, the date of writing unwittingly says much about the afterlife of the mutiny, with its cycles of interest and neglect within French and revolutionary political culture, as well as the shifting uses to which the mutiny was put. A couple of clues mark the scent of a trail. Zak wrote his manuscript 'within recent years' of the Invergordon Mutiny, when Royal Navy warships rebelled against the cuts of Ramsay MacDonald's National Government in late 1931. Zak also referred, in his conclusion, to the 'war plans of British imperialism' with no mention of fascism, US imperialism, the Soviet Union's Great Patriotic War or the anti-fascist resistance movements. Two options therefore make sense: shortly before the turn to the Popular Front (1934–35) or between the Ribbentrop-Molotov Pact and the invasion of the Soviet Union (August 1939–June 1941).[2] These opportunities for publication remained open only briefly, after which anti-militarist agitation within the British Armed Forces was strictly off the British Communist Party's agenda. So Zak's untimely manuscript began to gather a thick layer of dust symptomatic of the complex afterlife of the mutiny.

The aim of the book is to rediscover the subjectivity of the mutineers, thereby illuminating the context of 1919. The mutiny should be situated at the highpoint of what Mike Davis calls the 'Third European Revolution' (1916–21) in his periodisation of the long waves of class struggle from 1838 to 1921. Naval mutiny was integral to this phase, with the roles played by the Kronstadt naval fortress and the battleship *Aurora* during the October Revolution as well as the Kiel Mutiny, which transformed war into revolution in Germany.[3] For Davis, this points to how warships provided the weakest link to the armed forces, being akin to floating factories that scions of the aristocracy officered and recruited proletarians below deck. Those attempting to contain the French mutinies were acutely aware of German and Russian precedents. Indeed, French military intelligence possessed the radio intercepts of mutinying German sailors as they spread their revolution from ship to ship and ship to shore.[4]

This book does not plot the narrative of revolt. Neither does it outline the structural forces that prepared it. Instead, it is more interested in conjuncture, namely the moment of 1919, and focuses on the intensity of mutineer experience through an interrogation of the component parts of their consciousness: their visions, their sounds, their feelings, their world and how this panoramic subjectivity persisted in their memory.

Notes

1 Antonio Gramsci, *Selections from Political Writings 1910–1920* (London: Lawrence and Wishart, 1977), p. 61.
2 People's History Museum (henceforth PHM) CP IND MISC 3 1 William Zak, Unpublished account of the Black Sea Mutiny.
3 Mike Davis, *Old Gods, New Enigmas: Marx's Lost Theory* (London: Verso, 2018), pp. 31–3, 136.
4 Service Historique de la Defence, Vincennes (henceforth SHD) 6 N 54 radio intercepts, November 1918.

Acknowledgements

I am indebted to colleagues at Newcastle University for their support, especially those in the Labour and Society Research Group: Máire Cross, Joan Allen, Sarah Campbell, Claudia Baldoli and Bruce Baker. I would like to thank Emma Brennan of Manchester University Press and the anonymous referees who read the script. I am grateful for the funding for the project from the faculty of Humanities and Social Sciences. The archivists at the *Archives Départementales de la Seine-Saint Denis* (Bobigny) and at the *Service Historique de la Défense* (Vincennes) deserve special appreciation. Frédérick Genevée kindly granted permission over conditions of consultation to the papers of André Marty. Special thanks to MLG.

To Claudia, and all my brothers and sisters.

List of abbreviations

ADSSD	*Archives Départementales de la Seine-Saint-Denis*, Bobigny.
AFAMNA	*Association Fraternelle des Anciens de la Mer Noire et de leurs Amis* (Fraternal Association of the Veterans of the Black Sea and their Friends).
CGT	*Confédération Générale du Travail* (General Confederation of Labour).
CGTU	*Confédération Générale du Travail Unitaire* (United General Confederation of Labour).
CHSP	*Centre d'Histoire de Science Po*, Paris.
FFI	*Forces Françaises de L'Intérieur* (Free French Forces, the resistance army).
FTP	*Francs-Tireurs et Partisans* (Sharpshooters and Partisans, the military-wing of the Communist resistance movement).
NCO	Non-Commissioned Officer.
PCF	*Parti Communiste Française* (French Communist Party).
RMA	*Regiment de Marche d'Afrique* (African Infantry Regiment).
SFIO	*Section Française de l'Internationale Ouvrière* (French Section of the Worker's International).
SHD	*Service Historique de la Defence*, Vincennes.
SR	*Section Russe* (Russian Section of French military intelligence).

Introduction

Prompted by the centenaries of the Great War and Russian Revolution, scholars are reassessing the place of 1919 in French and global history. Tyler Stovall recently deemed this year to be the high point of French labour militancy and a revolutionary moment with regard to Parisian workers, tenants and consumers.[1] As such, he challenged the convention that 1920 signalled the apogee of post-war unrest with the rail workers' strikes and the foundation of the French Communist Party (PCF) at the Congress of Tours.[2] Given his focus upon France's capital, it is unsurprising that Stovall should only have given scant consideration to the mutinies of the French Army and Navy of that year. the mutinies belonged to the traditional narrative of the PCF, for which these mutinies constituted a foundational myth.[3] Nevertheless, these military revolts underline the new emphasis upon 1919 as pivotal in the re-stabilisation of the French political order.[4] At a global scale, 1919 makes the case for renewed scrutiny, being a year of revolution, counter-revolution, race riots, labour militancy, women's enfranchisement and expulsion from the workplace, anti-imperial insurgency and the redrawing of borders. Understandings of its wider chronological context are also being revised. Thus, historians of the First World War argue that global conflict began in 1911 and only achieved final closure in 1923 and, therefore, that the 1914–18 periodisation is highly misleading.[5]

This research into the French military protest dovetails with scholars investigating the events of 1919 from below, or what might be called the global underside of the 'Wilsonian moment'.[6] Until 28 June 1919, the Allies remained at war with Germany, despite the Armistice of

11 November 1918. During that period, the Great Powers redrew the map of the world at the Treaty of Paris and established the League of Nations, intending to prevent future war. However, what is often missed is that 1919 was a complex threshold between war and peace that a variety of social and political forces contested and that that contestation, like the war itself, was on a global scale. Powerful surges of contentious politics, including revolutions in Germany and Hungary, constituted a transnational wave of rebellion. This process began prior to the war ending, with mutinies and labour and consumer unrest, in addition to colonial revolt, reaching a high point in 1919. Most obviously, the Russian Revolutions of 1917 (which should not be seen as an exclusively European affair) continued into 1919, which signalled a decisive year for the Bolshevik regime. Unrest was more widespread than a Eurocentric or Russo-centric approach suggests. Labour unrest was widespread with general strikes in Barcelona, Belfast, Buenos Aires, Glasgow, Peru, Seattle and Winnipeg, as well as miners' and steel strikes in the US and metalworkers' strikes in France. The colonial dimension complicates traditional narratives of the events of 1919: the Irish Republic was declared; Afghanistan gained independence. Indeed, this year witnessed the emergence of anti-colonial insurgency and movements across Europe's colonies and beyond (notably Egypt, India, Afghanistan, Algeria, Morocco, Korea, China and Ireland). In the metropolitan centres of the British Empire, race riots took place. Racial violence was also witnessed in Chicago and in twenty-five other locations during the 'red summer' in the US. Counter-revolution in Central and Eastern Europe had a murderously anti-Semitic dimension, as did the unrest in Argentina, the bloody repression of the tragic week that followed militant strikes. Further scrutiny is also needed to examine the gender dynamics of the year. For women, 1919 had a contradictory international balance sheet, being an important moment of political enfranchisement but also featuring their expulsion from the wartime labour force.[7]

The year of 1919 has many legacies. It signalled the first Arab spring, with the awakening of anti-colonial Arab nationalism in the Wilsonian and Bolshevik context. As a consequence of the Jallianwala Bagh massacre, Britain definitively lost its moral claim to India. Race riots brought to public attention the presence of Black communities in the UK. Demobilisation brought the great reversal of wartime women's participation in skilled occupations in the belligerent states, largely restoring the pre-war pattern of exclusion and discrimination. The first Fascist movement was founded, as was the Communist International.

If this book is a social history of one particular strand of 1919, namely, that of French military protest, it seeks to transcend older conventions of history from below in two ways. First, this book aims to assemble mutineer consciousness through its constituent parts: the senses, emotions, spatial understandings and memory. It therefore draws upon and combines insights from the history of emotions, of the senses, of the mnemonic and spatial turns. Second, it seeks to transcend the methodological nationalism of the classic works of history from below, conceived as the people's history of Britain, France and elsewhere.

'The Black Sea Mutiny': a single and plural contentious sequence

As regards the revolts themselves, the Black Sea Mutiny became shorthand for a wider cycle of contestation with its roots in French intervention in Russia at war's end. Initially, as a consequence of Russian withdrawal from the war, French armed forces were stationed in the former Romanov Empire to the north at Archangel and Murmansk, and to the south in the Black Sea.[8] The intervention clearly took on a counter-revolutionary character, seeking to extend French spheres of influence, imperial power and economic interests. A brief outline of the sequence of mutinies illustrates the scale and pattern of the revolt. Generally overlooked in the historiography, the first mutiny began shortly after the arrival of French armed forces on 21 November 1918, when soldiers of the 21st Colonial Infantry stationed in Archangel refused to fight.[9] This isolated rebellion, without any apparent connection to other mutinies, anticipated three waves of protest.

The epicentre of the wave of mutinies was the Black Sea. On 23 November 1918, the Allies decided to send the French fleet and Royal Navy to Sevastopol. With the transport of troops proving slow, the news of the armed movements of the Ukrainian nationalists (led by Petlioura), the anarchists (led by Makhno) and the Bolsheviks (led by Grigoriev) alarmed Allied commanders. The occupations of Odessa and Sevastopol were seemingly in keeping with the terms of the Armistice, allowing, as they did, the withdrawal of German troops. In January and February 1919, the French-Allied occupation extended to Kherson and Mykolaiv (Nikolaev).

The first phase of mutiny began with the 58th Infantry at Tiraspol, in the Ukraine, between 30 January and 8 February 1919. The 58th Infantry had been fighting against Bulgarian troops in Bessarabia.[10] On 2 February 1919, they received orders to take Tiraspol on the River Dniester, which was in Bolshevik hands. When the French troops advanced on the town, artillery and machine gun fire pinned them down. They had been told that there were only a few Bolsheviks and that the local population would welcome them with open arms. That evening the Bolsheviks sent out a sortie, resulting in several French troops being killed and injured. In light of the Armistice and the absence of a declaration of war on Russia, the troops held a meeting and decided to disobey orders ('*nous ne marcherons plus*'). On 7 February, officers reminded the men of their duty and furthermore the consequences of disobedience. The men remained calm and did not appear to be shaken. On 8 February, 467 men refused to cross the Dniester.[11] After their officers' persuasive powers had failed, the mutineers were taken to Bender, where they were kept imprisoned for three days and court-martialled for disobeying an order in the face of the enemy. From there, they went by boat to Istanbul (Constantinople), then Oran, Casablanca and the penal colony of Meknes, where they served sentences of hard labour: road-building in the Moroccan sun.

On the night of 1–2 March, Jeanne Labourbe's arrest and murder occurred. Labourbe was a French emigré who had joined the Bolsheviks and was disseminating revolutionary propaganda amongst French troops. This event became synonymous with the wave of mutinies for two reasons. First, the murder acted as a 'moral shock' or 'injustice frame' for mutineers, which official denial compounded.[12] Second, she achieved martyr status within the French left as the 'first French communist'. Despite official denial, the rumour persisted that the French authorities, particularly Colonel Trousson, alongside White Russian allies participated in her torture, mutilation and execution.[13]

This first phase of mutiny occurred against the backdrop of humiliating Allied retreat. The threat to Kherson rendered the occupation of Mykolaiv impossible. A battle for Kherson took place between 2 and 9 March. Mutinies affected the 176th Infantry and a detachment of sailors of the battleship *Justice* at Kherson between 4 and 9 March. General Philippe d'Anselme decided to evacuate on 9 March. The following day, d'Anselme telegraphed General Henri Berthelot with news that two French units that had arrived from Kherson the previous day had refused orders. Moreover, the local population was hostile to their presence.[14]

The withdrawal continued with the evacuation of Greek troops from Mykolaiv that occurred on 12 March under the supervision of the battlecruisers *Du Chayla* and the *Bruix*. The last Greek troops left the following day. A month later, on 5 April, mutinies broke out at Odessa with the 7th Engineers as well as the 19th Artillery at Coilendorf. Two days later, in the north, the 21st Colonial Infantry regiment mutinied once more at Archangel.[15]

With the second phase of contestation, the mutinies passed from the Army to the Navy.[16] On 16 April, the authorities discovered André Marty's conspiratorial preparations and clandestine contacts with Rumanian Social Democrats. Marty was an engineer officer aboard the destroyer *Protet* then stationed in Galați (Galatz), a port city on the Danube in eastern Romania.[17] Three days later on 19 April the revolt aboard the battleship *France* at anchor in Sevastopol harbour began, quickly spreading to other battleships, including the *Jean Bart*, the *Justice*, the *Vergniaud* and the *Mirabeau*, as well as smaller ships, gunboats *Algol* and *Escaut*. On the second day of protests, 20 April (Easter Sunday), a notorious incident took place: the Morskaïa Road 'ambush' or 'massacre'. Greek troops under French command opened fire with machine guns on a demonstration of the local population and French mutineers in Sevastopol. Although historians have sometimes downplayed this event and at other times (in the case of Marty's history of the mutiny) struggled to ascertain the truth, this much is clear: there were several French injuries and one fatality.[18] In his report on the affair, Lieutenant Vaublanc identified the victim of the shooting as Raymond Firmin Morvan, a third-class sailor and apprentice quarter-master of the *Vergniaud*.[19] Motivated by a desire for demobilisation, a crucial compounding grievance for the crew of the *France* was the order to perform coal loading duties on the Easter holiday. Under pressure from the revolt, the Commander agreed the *France* could return home and postponed coal duties. These were performed without supervision of the officers on Tuesday, 22 April, and the *France* set sail the following day. The mutineers aboard the *France* believed that they had secured victory with their Commander's word of honour as its guarantee. It was not until their arrest in Bizerte on 1 May that they realised the ephemeral nature of their victory.

As news of the Sevastopol rebellion spread, the mutinies recommenced elsewhere in the Black Sea. The battlecruiser *Waldeck-Rousseau* was in Odessa. Marty's presence awaiting court martial precipitated the movement aboard. On 23 April, the crew learned that an officer accused of conspiracy from the *Protet* was on the ship. Two days later, sailors from the supply boat *Suippe* told of the events of Sevastopol. On 26 April, Admiral Caubet hastily removed Marty from the ship, shortly before the first assemblies of men, who sang the *Internationale*, and elected delegates. Their demands resembled those of the previous mutinies. Playing for time, the Admiral made concessions and said that he would do all he could to return swiftly to France and that there would be no punishments. The outbreak of unrest took hold on the nearby torpedo boats *Mameluk* and *Fauconneau*.[20] The battlecruiser sailed to Tendra, apparently en route to Istanbul. At Tendra, the mutiny spread to the battlecruiser *Bruix*. However, having bided his time, the Admiral was able to arm his officers and restore order on the *Waldeck-Rousseau* and then threaten the mutineers of the *Bruix*. In the final episode in this sequence of revolts in the Black Sea, the torpedo boat *Dehorter* at Kertch mutinied between 1 and 10 May.

What followed was a third more expansive stage of revolt spread across the Mediterranean to France, involving sailors, soldiers and workers in port cities, in which the desire for demobilisation and military grievances mixed on the streets with the demands of labour. At Istanbul (Constantinople), on 2 May, the battlecruiser *Ernest Renan* joined the movement upon which three days of effervescence took place. On 20 May, 117th Heavy Artillery disobeyed orders in Toulouse, followed by the 4th and 37th Colonial regiments on 27 May, in Bender, Bessarabia.

The movement reached the home of the Mediterranean Fleet during the second week of June. The Toulon agitation took its most serious turn on 10 June aboard the battleship *Provence*, when a group of 200 sailors attempted to seize weapons and roughly handled officers.[21] The *Jean Bart*, the *Démocratie*, the *Courbet*, the *Diderot*, the *Lorraine*, the *Jules Ferry* and the *Pothuau* were caught up in the mood of insubordination, as were the naval depots, 112th Infantry and 143rd Colonial Infantry. Huge street demonstrations occurred in Toulon on 12 and 16 June.

By now, in France, the Black Sea Mutiny had become common knowledge and was debated in the Chamber of Deputies from 12 to 17 June. Whereas left-wing deputies read letters from war-weary troops, the Minister of the Navy, Georges Leygues, denounced the mutiny as a German plot, a criminal intrigue, a product of revolutionary propaganda designed to undermine victory and an act of madness.[22] With the knowledge of the mutinies spreading to the public and within the armed forces, the agitation moved from port to port, from the Mediterranean to the Atlantic. During 14–15 June, sailors stationed in

Rochefort protested. Two days later, the movement spread to sailors and soldiers in Brest, leading to violent clashes with police on horseback sent from Nantes.[23] On 19 June, Lorient witnessed demonstrations, as did Cherbourg on 24 June.

During this final phase of military protest, the mutinies returned to the warships on the north African coast, the Black Sea, the eastern Mediterranean and the Baltic. On 13 June, noisy protests began during the inspection of plates aboard the Danton-class battleship *Condorcet*, which had arrived at Tendra, near Odessa, in the Black Sea. Further refusals of orders ensued, as well as the election of delegates who would present the demands of the crew. In the Tunisian port of Bizerte, the agitation on the Danton-class battleship *Voltaire* began on 16 June, when the Commander Captain Stabenrath received two anonymous letters from the crew demanding demobilisation and leave, both referring to the Black Sea Mutiny. Indicative of how protest circulated, men joining the crew from Toulon communicated news of events in the Black Sea. The mutiny proper broke out on 19 June after Rear-Admiral de Margerie inspected the crew and announced that the ship was to leave for the eastern Mediterranean. As the Rear-Admiral went ashore, fifty men leant over the railings and shouted 'Demobilisation! Leave! To Toulon!' After the evening meal, a large assembly of men began a protest on the deck of the ship. The following morning, graffiti announced another meeting at 7.30 a.m., which elected delegates (Georges Wallet, Henri Alquier, Pierre Vottero and Le Bras). They met with the Commander, who promised to look into their demands, thereby calming the situation. Another mutinous assembly gathered on the evening of 20 June. The Commander waited three days to restore order through a wave of arrests.

A pattern of insubordination was now spreading to all compass points with a similar pattern of grievances, arguments and tactics. The demands for demobilisation or leave, knowledge of the Black Sea Mutiny, unofficial gatherings, protests during inspections or refusals to cooperate with orders and arguments about the constitutional nature of the intervention connected the movement. Unrest reached the French patrol boats in the Baltic Sea between 21 and 23 June. With demobilisation, leave and the return to France featuring as principal demands, the *Dunois* and *Intrépide* witnessed protests, perhaps spreading to other ships in the area. On 26 June, sailors aboard the cruiser *Guichen* seized the ship in the Greek port of Itea, only to have it recaptured via the rapid deployment of Senegalese riflemen. On 1 August, in Tendra, all but one of the crew of the torpedo boat *Touareg* signed a protest letter after receiving news that their service was to continue. Two days later, the crew refused to be inspected but the arrest of their leader and intimidation persuaded them to return to normal duties. The cruiser *D'Estrées* was also the scene of protests by the crew on 13 and 14 August in Vladivostok.[24] On this occasion, their demands for demobilisation led to the repatriation of reservists.

The final act of mutiny took place on board the Danton-class battleship *Diderot* on 5 October, ending the generalised phase of military protest that stretched from June to October. From late September to early October, a series of incidents occurred on the *Diderot*. The visit of Admiral de Bon and his inspection of the crew precipitated protests on 24 September at Beirut. By 2 October, 200 of the crew listened to Page give a militant speech, who was then arrested for his efforts. Three days later, a similar number of men assembled and decided to storm the ship's cells to liberate Page. The bugle call to action and the intervention of the Commander-in-Second thwarted their plans and Page was escorted away on a launch, thereby defusing the situation. By this time, peace with Germany had been signed, demobilisation continued to relieve the crisis, and the coming elections of November offered the prospect of change in the political situation.

If the mutinies of the infantry are included, the wave of military protest lasted nearly a year, beginning in November 1918 and lasting until early October of the following year. Its extensive geography ranged from Archangel and Vladivostok, via the Baltic to the Atlantic ports of metropolitan France, across the Mediterranean to the Black Sea. Hundreds of mutineers faced courts martial. This was very much more than the 'two days of madness' or 'two bad days' as Leygues described it in the Chamber of Deputies.[25]

The historiography of a mutiny

This book proposes a fundamental reassessment of these events and their significance in cycles of transnational contention, French collective memory and political culture. The existing historiography of the mutinies is deficient in this regard. André Marty dominated early versions of the mutinies (which was to be expected given that he was a prominent member of the PCF by the time these assessments were made). He produced a series of pamphlets, articles and the multi-volume *La Révolte de la Mer Noire* (1927–29). The latter entered the literary canon of the

French labour movement and new editions followed in 1932, 1939, 1949, 1970 and 1999. He produced a shortened text *Les Heures Glorieuses de la Mer Noire* in 1932 (which was, like *La Révolte*, republished on the thirtieth anniversary).

Marty was earnest about his history and perhaps his scholarship ought to be taken more seriously.[26] He went to great lengths to find material for his book, describing it at one stage as a *collective* work under his editorship. At the same time, Marty was under contradictory pressures, between scholarship and filling gaps in the narrative, between searching for the truth about what had happened and the political conclusions to be drawn from the events. His book was a party history, a foundational text of French Communism. Despite amnesties for mutineers in 1921 and 1923, legal guilt and innocence shaped mutineer narratives, including Marty's own. For Marty then, the need to write a carefully researched rebuttal of court-martial charges complicated the assertion of the heroic status of the mutineers. He had to deal with official denial and a lack of access to official documents. Despite considerable efforts to find French or Russian sources, he never discovered the identity of the sailor shot on 20 April 1919 on Morskaïa Road, as that information could only be found in the Ministry of the Navy files.[27] Finally, Marty had to write in the midst a virulent campaign conducted by members of the extreme-right, for whom the mutineers were a handful of traitors in league with (even in the pay of) foreign powers.[28]

As a consequence of the two Marty 'affairs' (1919 and 1952), the campaign for his release (likened at the time to the Dreyfus Affair) and his publications, André Marty has, more than anyone else, shaped the memorialisation of the mutiny. A corrective to this imbalance is needed. Albert Cané initiated the *Comité des Marins* (Sailors' Committee) that led the campaign for the amnesty of mutineers, and toured the country in public meetings in 1920 and 1921.[29] Cané claimed that he had not heard of Marty's case until September 1920.[30] Though this may be an exaggeration, Marty only became synonymous with the mutiny in retrospect. Cané insisted that the Committee of Social Defence was responsible for Marty's celebrity rather than the other way around.

Reactions to Marty's book are unhelpfully polarised; all sides have missed its significance as a consequence of partisanship. With typical hyperbole, when Marty was in favour with the *Parti Communiste Français* (PCF, French Communist Party), it did its best to assert the factual credentials and historical value of Marty's historical work, which provided 'a passionate account, careful to re-establish the truth deformed by reaction'. Marty was a 'remarkable' Marxist historian, substantiating every fact with 'authentic testimonies, official reports, letters or accounts of soldiers and sailors'.[31] In the main, traditionalist historians and those of the right disparaged Marty's literary efforts, stressing its omissions, errors and political bias.[32] Raphael-Leygues and Barré criticised Marty's 'memoirs' for being revised and corrected many times (being a sign of weakness rather than sustained research). For them, Marty lacked the credibility of another mutineer Charles Tillon's memoirs.[33] There was also criticism from the left. Writing in 1953, the mutineer Le Roux complained about Marty's interpretation of the events in Sevastopol, downplaying its libertarian character. However, the toll of the years upon Le Roux's memory left giveaway clues that betrayed the certainty of his assertions. Le Roux had to backtrack to render his own account consistent, having forgotten to explain how the mutiny spread from the landing party to the ship: 'I forgot to say that two of us were sent aboard to be disciplined and they spread the rumour that we were in revolt. This contact had an influence over the action of those on board.'[34] This exchange reveals a danger: the goal of moving away from Marty in favour of the restoration of mutineer dialogue can be lost in point-scoring contentions.

While Marty clearly lacked a professional historian's training, his *Révolte* is a valuable and in some ways methodologically innovative text. He took the project seriously. So, for instance, he battled with the party press to ensure that the publication was presentable, angrily sending seventeen pages of corrections to his second edition.[35] Writing in June 1936 to Chorokhov, who had been a Bolshevik negotiator with the French Admiral Exelmans, Marty asserted his history of the mutiny as its 'most complete and verified' account in the French language. Fascinatingly from a methodological viewpoint, he described it as a collective enterprise of 112 participants that he simply 'edited and coordinated'.[36] This perspective ought to be situated within the Comintern policy of workers-as-correspondents ('*rabcors*') in revolutionary newspapers. A 1932 issue of *L'Humanité* illustrates this *rabcors* approach with its round-up of witnesses from the mutinies of 1917, 1919 and the Christmas truce of 1914.[37]

If Marty established the landmark text, others followed. Charles Tillon, another mutineer and communist who had held a ministerial post in the post-Liberation government, wrote *La Révolte Vient de Loin* (1969) the fullest personal memoir of the wave of naval mutiny based on his personal experiences on board the *Guichen* which mutinied at

Itea, Greece, on 26 June. Three years after Tillon's memoir, the PCF published a collection of two eyewitness accounts, documents and a historical introduction, Jean Le Ramey and Pierre Vottero's *Mutins de la Mer Noire* (1973).

From a more conservative perspective, the Minister of the Navy Georges Leygues's grandson, Jacques Raphael-Leygues, and Jean-Luc Barré produced a history of the mutiny that drew on the minister's personal papers. It sought to provide a popular narrative of events to bring the mutiny to the public eye and to offer an alternative perspective to Marty's communist narrative. Despite drawing on some interesting sources, including interviews with Charles Tillon and Admiral Peltier, the authors' sympathies lay too obviously with the authorities and took the official interpretation of the events more or less at face value and therefore routinely attempted to discredit Marty. Problematically, the work sympathises with Georges Legyues's pathologising dismissal of the revolt as 'two days of madness'.[38] Indeed, Raphael-Leygues cites the far-right *Action Française* leader Charles Maurras on the need for reform in the Navy, noting the hostility of the officer class to the Third Republic for 'the noblest of reasons'.[39] This text sits therefore in the wider nostalgic literature glossing over the naval hierarchy's affinity with *Action Française*, Vichy and the Empire.[40]

The most substantial text on this topic remains Philippe Masson's monograph *La Marine Française et la Mer Noire, 1918–1919* (1982).[41] As might be expected from the Head of the Historical Service of the Navy and a professor of maritime history at the School of Naval Warfare, he frames the mutiny very much within the institutional language and mindset of the French Navy. He also draws on the conventional interpretation of the mutinies of Chemin des Dames of 1917 as akin to a breakdown in industrial relations rather than an act of political or anti-war radicalism.[42] There is no denying that it is a scholarly and rigorous work, drawing on the full documentation of the naval and national archives and it does not indulge in political apologia. That said, the empiricist assumptions and official status of the work means that it cannot be the last word, especially on the agency of the mutineers. My research aims to go back to the sources that Masson used, somewhat amplified where possible, and read them through a different lens. This research is concerned less with the reconstruction of events from the official documentation than understanding the mindset of the officer class, the military elites and the government in their struggle against the mutiny.

Evidence and subjectivity: privileging mutineer sources

From the evidentiary perspective, this new research privileges mutineers' subjectivity through their own accounts of the events. Ironically, the materials revising Marty's account come largely from the former PCF central committee member's archive. In the preparation of *La Revolte*, Marty used his contacts from the prisons, the navy and the PCF to elicit testimony from mutineers, usually via correspondence. He compiled fragments of biographical information on around 200 mutineers of 1919 (from both the Army and Navy as well as from the Black Sea and beyond).[43] Claiming to base his history on the testimony of 112 mutineers, the testimonies of around fifty mutineers survived in his personal papers both from the French Army intervening in the Russian Civil War and the Navy (as well as additional ones from the mutinies of 1917). This provides a rich and underutilised resource allowing the kind of scrutiny of senses, emotions and memory more typically reserved for those of a more elevated social status.[44]

Several documentary sources allow access to mutineer understandings of 1919. Surveying Marty's archive requires consideration in turn of the following forms: correspondence, court-martial reports, letters with memoirs attached, artefactual discussion, events-based discussion and personal reflection. Each form has its specificity and, within that, each instance possesses its own peculiarities. Perhaps most significantly, temporal and spatial distance from the events shaped testimony. For example, in Marty's papers, there are two examples of a *carnet de route* (campaign journal) written as a perfectly contemporaneous diary.[45] The account of Lucien Godin, a sailor aboard the battlecruiser *Bruix*, covers 30 March–22 May 1919, and details the day-to-day events across the entire cycle of protest in the Black Sea. The notebook of Marius Jules Cyrille of the *Ernest Renan*, however, runs from 25 February to 23 June 1919. This form avoids the filters of memory and the distance of time present in other evidence.

Many testimonies take the epistolary form, which offers interesting additional insights into the relationships between these former mutineers: their modes of address, the use of language, shifting degrees of formality, their emotional bonds, their sense of shared experience and dialogues with past selves. The Marty papers have an abundance of mutineers' letters. Complex contexts of authorship, addressee, timing and the nature of the author's participation in events require careful consideration. Ernest Duport's letter to his parents provides a case in point. It is lengthy, rich in description and emotional detail, as well as being written almost contemporaneously to the mutiny, within only a couple of weeks of the events. A tension between his assertion of manhood through participation in epic events and an anxiety about parental response highlights the ambivalence of his account. Marty was also ambivalent about Duport, wrestling with the paradox that he was politically suspect but provided the richest source of information. In Marty's papers, a handwritten note glued to a typed comment described Duport as *'une ordure'* (a piece of refuse) for his cowardly double role – 'white for the officers, black for the sailors', as the note put it. The note alleged that Duport even stated that if the Commander could not make the men accept orders, then he would himself, with a revolver in his hand. The note also claimed that Duport failed to refute the Commander-in-Second's deposition at the court martial on this count.[46]

While Marty collected letters that appeared in the press or those to other addressees (as with the one that Duport forwarded to him), in the main he was the intended recipient. The letters therefore reflect the mutineers' verdict on Marty and his endeavours to write their history. To these letters several more could be added from the papers of Charles Tillon, who after the Second World War played a prominent role in the association of former mutineers. These testimonies allow for new insights into the subaltern experience of the mutiny. Although mediated through the filter of retrospection, they contain the emotions, memories, understandings, knowledge and thought processes of the mutineers. This subjectivity is almost entirely missing in previous accounts of the mutinies.

The contrast with court-martial testimony is revealing. Where the latter produced a divisive constraint upon mutineer subjectivity, letters in both Marty's and Tillon's papers were essentially solidaristic: assisting Marty in the writing of *La Révolte* or connected to Tillon's work in the mutineers' veteran association. They were private and bilateral. They allowed an emotional refuge in hostile environments, allowing the author to express himself with an emotional freedom more difficult for veterans to do in public. In effect, Marty and Tillon acted as nodal points for network construction. They fostered emotional bonds, mutual services and a shared reading of the mutiny, rebuilding what repression had fragmented.

Marty was at some disadvantage regarding the accrual of testimonies. He had been on a smaller ship and had been relatively isolated, being imprisoned before the main events of Easter 1919. The mutineers were scattered to the prisons and penal colonies of the French empire and were thus difficult to contact. Marty himself was imprisoned until July 1923. He amassed his archive because several veterans were able to provide him a name or two from whom he could get more information – usually these were people from the towns or areas the veterans belonged to and people with whom the veterans had kept in touch.

In addition to letters, memoirs provide another major source of the mutineers' views of events. Both published and unpublished accounts of the mutinies exist.[47] Marty's papers contain several unpublished memoirs that mutineers appended to letters sent to Marty.[48] Song (and to a lesser extent poetry) offers insight into mutineer subjectivity. Singing played a major part in the events, and analysis of the content, timing and function of the songs has rich analytical potential, though equally song might be politically instrumentalised retrospectively, thereby affecting our reconstruction of events. Beyond these sources of evidence, other materials – photographs, leaflets, novels, posters, newspapers, parliamentary debates, Ministry of the Interior and of the Navy records – could enhance the research in two distinct ways. First, the official documentation allows access to how the authorities comprehended the mind of the mutineers and the moment of 1919. Second, these and other sources permitted the event to persist in French political culture, constituting the mutiny's sedimentary layers of artefact upon which even the mutineers themselves drew.

Theory and concepts: reaching out for mutineer subjectivity

From a theoretical viewpoint, this book is conceived as a reconstruction of mutineer subjectivity, integrating various components that make up consciousness: the senses, emotions, reasoning and cognition, language and memory. The approach is informed theoretically by three fields of scholarship. First, the intention is to recover fruitful elements of Marxist theory and historiography. The result connects into an earlier generation of Marxists who were preoccupied with consciousness, thought and language, namely Vygotsky, Volosinov, Bakhtin, Gramsci, Lukacs, Benjamin and Lefebvre, whose thought was in no small way prompted by the experience of 1919. The virtue of these thinkers is that they challenge the conventions of structural and post-structuralist linguistics regarding human consciousness. Thus, Valentin Volosinov embeds language within social contestation through the concept of multi-accentality.⁴⁹ For current purposes, Henri Lefebvre's major contribution to Marxism lies in his elaboration of the 'social production of space' being a major influence on social constructivist understandings of the organisation of space and the sense of place.⁵⁰ Developmental psychologist Lev Vygotsky proposes an understanding of consciousness as a dialectic of thought and language rather than reducing the former to the latter. In addition, he critiques the dominant Jamesian notion of emotions within psychology.⁵¹ Bakhtin supplies a dialogical version of language apt to understanding the heterogeneity of subaltern thought as well as the effort of the authorities to homogenise thought into an official monologue.⁵² Through the concepts of contradictory consciousness and good versus common sense, Antonio Gramsci allows a dynamic model of how thought responds in social conflict. His notion of hegemony also provides a sensitive and culturally aware framework of the influence of dominant ideas.⁵³ Gramsci's contemporary Walter Benjamin gained recognition for his theorisation of temporality in revolutionary ferment with regard to how agents experience time, reconfiguring past, present and future. As well as this, his diverse writings encompass memory, photography and the ruins of capitalist progress.

Overall, then, given that Vygotsky, Volosinov, Bakhtin, Gramsci, Lukacs, Benjamin and Lefebvre adopted a Marxist framework, consciousness was for them a shared category, if viewed from different perspectives, and thus allows a coherent integration of their insights. Taken together, these thinkers offer coordinates of subjectivity, thereby refreshing the Marxist historiography of consciousness that has centred on a defence or revision of E. P. Thompson's conceptualisation of class consciousness.⁵⁴ It also provides an alternative to the language-centred conceptualisation of phenomenology drawing on Heidegger that has been so influential via the post-structuralisms of Foucault and Derrida, sometimes known as the 'linguistic turn'.⁵⁵

The second intellectual field that furnishes theoretical shape to the project is social movement theory. Through such scholars as Charles Tilly, Sidney Tarrow, Doug MacAdam and Donatella Della Porta, social movement theory has done more than Marxism to codify the processes and mechanisms of social protest and social movements. Their categorical precision proves invaluable to comprehending the course of the mutiny through cycles of protest, protest repertoires, political opportunity structures, injustice frames and dynamics of contestation.⁵⁶ Moreover, the collection of essays *Silence and Voice in the Study of Contentious Politics* (2001) mapped out a renewal of social movement theory's conceptual toolkit (voice and silence, emotions, space and time), coinciding with new directions in social and cultural history. Social movement theory also acts as a bridge to transnational reinterpretations of history, allowing us to situate the mutiny in a global pattern of contestation.

The third optic offering theoretical insight into this research is the cross-disciplinary dialogues of memory, senses, emotions and consciousness. After Lucien Febvre's injunction to historians to take seriously the historical reconstruction of emotions, the historiography of emotions emerged in earnest with the work of Peter and Carol Zisowitz Stearns.[57] They were concerned with the time-specific norms directing emotional life, or as they put it, the 'emotionology'. They considered the history of the modern US from the successive viewpoints of anger, sadness, jealousy and the emergence of 'cool' as the predominant American emotional style.[58] Their assumptions and those of other modern historians of emotions flowed from Norbert Elias's *Civilizing Process* (2000), in which modernity led to progressively greater emotional self-control in the public sphere.[59] In response to this modernisation thesis, Barbara Rosenwein has challenged the grand narrative of affective patterns, arguing that it misunderstands pre-modern emotional styles.[60] As an expert in Medieval Europe, she proposes instead a multiplicity of emotional communities.

Within the historiography of emotions, William Reddy's work is rightly influential. Drawing insight into consciousness from outside history, Reddy argues that what we learn from the disciplines of neuroscience and experimental psychology is that a Saussurean understanding of language as an autonomous higher system is untenable. For Saussure, a sequential, linear process from lower order functions of the mind (such as sight and hearing) crosses a threshold into the independent higher-order realm of language. This flawed model of language is shared by post-structuralism.[61] Instead, Reddy observes that the relationship between language and lower order functions is not linear and strictly hierarchical but multiple, and that the neuroscientists prefer centre-surround or cascade models of brain dynamics. In practical terms, this suggests an integrated approach to consciousness, paying attention to its many facets, moving away from self-sufficient textual or discursive approaches that privilege language. Reddy thus problematises the relationship between words and feeling, proposing the concept of the 'emotive' as speech expressing emotions. For Reddy, at a societal level, governments and elites regulate 'emotional regimes' of rules of articulation and repression of emotions. These regimes are not all-encompassing, as nonconformist emotional refuges (namely sites of 'emotional liberty') challenge such emotional regimes. Reddy has, more than anyone else, engaged in a multidisciplinary dialogue and attempted to theorise the nature of emotions. Nevertheless, in identifying emotion as a 'new underlying structure', it is hard to see how Reddy escapes the charge of exchanging one reductionism for another.[62]

Echoing this cross-disciplinary stance from the scientific side of the fence, Steven Rose's work on memory bears similarities to Reddy's intervention. Rose's appeal to move beyond the Cartesian dualism of brain and mind prompts us (as Reddy has done) to think of the implications of the revolutionary insights of recent years into consciousness, the composition and functioning of the *brain* and what this can mean for those concerned with the *mind* in the study of memory.

Ultimately, this book seeks to reconceptualise how historians might think about consciousness. Scholars from different disciplines have declared successive paradigmatic shifts in aspects of, or related to, consciousness and this research aims to encompass these sensory, spatial, emotional, linguistic and cognitive 'turns' into a holistic approach to individual and collective consciousness. Consciousness therefore offers a terrain to reintegrate the fragmentary dynamics and advances of the scholarship in these fields. This is not to assert that this is the only way that such a connectivity can be established, but it is the one that is appropriate to the source material available in this study.

Signposting mutiny

Each chapter scrutinises one aspect of mutineer consciousness in the following instalments: the senses, emotions, place and space, personal memory and collective mnemonic practice. Chapter 1 therefore probes the first dimension of mutineer subjectivity: the senses. The opening problem when interrogating mutineer testimony from this perspective is why some senses (vision and hearing) registered but others were strangely absent. The sights and sounds of mutiny divulge much about the experience of the participant. A visual language, notably the red flag, communicated and disseminated mutiny as well as contesting the visual order of the authorities. This disruption in the visual realm made a powerful impression on all sides. More fundamentally, the epistemological relationship of sight and truth features in mutineer accounts and requires consideration. Mutineers tested the claims of their superiors with their own eyes: seeing was disbelieving. The mutiny also entailed a soundscape tantamount to an auditory contest comprising silences, the overwhelming volume of modern warfare, laughter, murmuring, slang and song. The senses nourished mutineer subjectivity as intermediaries with the 'outside world'.

Chapter 2 investigates the inner world of emotions. The armed forces (and particularly the Navy) expected recruits to conduct themselves according to emotional conventions. Mutiny broke those norms of emotional behaviour. To understand mutineer subjectivity then, it is necessary to outline military emotionology and the role of emotions in the mutiny. Fear and anger emerge at the breaking point of mutiny and feature as the most common emotions cited in mutineer accounts. These two emotions highlight the need to consider emotions as a relationship of mind and body, with mutineers recording the corporeal effects of these emotions. If fear and anger punctuate the course of the mutiny at specific points, a broader emotional sequence underpins the cycle of protest and its aftermath. The pattern of hope, joy and despair is discernible and this evolution has considerable importance for the turn of events themselves and their afterlives.

Chapter 3 inspects the mutiny in the wider world, in the dynamics of space and place. Transnational circulations (of information, ideas, contention, mutiny, disease and people) shaped the experience of 1919. In this year more than any other, territorial divisions of the globe were not fixed or stable. Military service meant travel and the need to make sense of unfamiliar lands and peoples. Moreover, military authorities relied upon the place-bound ideology of nationalism and perceived mutiny as a contravention of this very specific place attachment. In the age of imperialist war, national, ethnic and racial identities interacted with nationalism in complex ways. Furthermore, one feature of the transnational experience of 1919 was the act of fraternisation, which mutineers understood in political, internationalist or universalist terms. Yet, given colonial assumptions and the strategies of the French military, there were racial limits to mutineer internationalism and fraternisation. On their part, the French authorities sought to exploit colonial troops to repress the mutinies as part of their response to the emergency of 1919.

Chapter 4 discusses the personal memory and forgetting of mutineers. Mutineers reflected upon this process, allowing analysis of the dynamics of memory within mutineer consciousness. Some mutineers sought to compensate for the frailty of memory with material objects such as photographs, press cuttings, printed songs or letters. Ageing and the passage of time meant that memory constituted a potentially troubling negotiation between a present and a past self, ultimately a self-awareness of one's own loss of vitality.

The final chapter broaches how these personal dynamics of memory converge in collective commemoration and the capacity of these practices to shape the historical reception of the mutiny. In particular, the chapter scrutinises the Fraternal Association of the Veterans of the Black Sea and their Friends set up in 1949, with its last act in 1973. The precarious history of the Association amounts to a contest to assert the significance of the 1919 mutinies against powerful forces of oblivion, revealing the way in which 1919 stayed with the mutineer generation.

Overall then, the senses, emotions, space and memory combine to constitute the world of the mutineer. Through their subjectivity of thought and deed, the mutineers could in turn attempt to transform that world. This book proposes that the actions, feelings, sights, sounds and places that jumble together in mutineer memory enrich our understanding of 1919, taking us beneath the diplomacy and peacemaking of high politics, helping us to comprehend the century's most unruly year, giving us a glimpse of the torrid complexity of its global underside.

Notes

1 Tyler Stovall, *Paris and the Spirit of 1919: Consumer Struggles, Transnationalism, and Revolution* (Cambridge: Cambridge University Press, 2012).
2 Adrian Jones, 'The French railway strikes of January–May 1920: new syndicalist ideas and emergent communism', *French Historical Studies*, 12, 4 (1982), pp. 27–42.
3 Matt Perry, *Memory of War in France, 1914–45: César Fauxbras, the Voice of the Lowly* (Basingstoke: Palgrave Macmillan, 2011), pp. 42–4.
4 Charles S. Maier, *Recasting Bourgeois Europe: Stabilization in France, Germany and Italy in the Decade after World War I* (Englewood Cliffs, NJ: Prentice-Hall, 1974).
5 Robert Gerwarth and Erez Manela, 'The Great War as a global war: imperial conflict and the reconfiguration of the world order, 1911–23', *Diplomatic History*, 38, 4 (2014), pp. 786–800. Robert Gerwarth and Erez Manela (eds), *Empires at War: 1911–1923* (Oxford: Oxford University Press, 2014).
6 Erez Manela, *The Wilsonian Moment: Self-determination and the International Origins of Anticolonial Nationalism* (Oxford: Oxford University Press, 2007).
7 David F. Krugler, *1919, The Year of Racial Violence: How African Americans Fought Back* (New York: Cambridge University Press, 2015). Jan Voogd,

Race, Riots and Resistance: The Red Summer of 1919 (New York: Peter Lang, 2008). Erez Manela, 'The Wilsonian moment and the rise of anticolonial nationalism: the case of Egypt', *Diplomacy and Statecraft*, 12, 4 (2001), pp. 99–122. Erez Manela, 'Imagining Woodrow Wilson in Asia: dreams of east-west harmony and the revolt against empire in 1919', *American Historical Review*, 111, 5 (2006), pp. 1327–51. Jacqueline Jenkinson, 'Black sailors on Red Clydeside: rioting, reactionary trade unionism and conflicting notions of "Britishness" following the First World War', *Twentieth Century British History*, 19, 1 (2007), pp. 29–60. Jacqueline Jenkinson, *Black 1919: Riots, Racism and Resistance in Imperial Britain* (Liverpool: Liverpool University Press, 2008). Robert Gerwarth, 'The Central European counter-revolution: paramilitary violence in Germany, Austria and Hungary after the Great War', *Past & Present*, 200, 1 (2008), pp. 175–209. Stéphane Audoin-Rouzeau and Christophe Prochasson (eds), *Sortir de la Grande Guerre-Le Monde et l'Après 1918* (Paris: Tallandier, 2015).

8 Michael Jabara Carley, 'The origins of the French intervention in the Russian Civil War, January–March 1918: a reappraisal', *Journal of Modern History*, 48 (1976), pp. 413–39; Michael Jabara Carley, *Revolution and Intervention: The French Government and the Russian Civil War, 1917–1919* (Buffalo: McGill-Queen's University Press, 1983). Peter Kenez, *Civil War in South Russia, 1919–1920* (Berkeley: University of California Press, 1977).

9 SHD 7N 393 telegram, 24 November 1918. P. Facon, 'Les mutineries dans les corps expéditionnaires français en Russie Septentrionale (décembre 1918–avril 1919)', *Revue d'Histoire Moderne et Contemporaine*, 24 (1977), p. 463.

10 *L'Humanité*, 21 August 1919.

11 SHD 7 N 800 Note on the affair of the 58th Infantry in southern Russia, n.d. On 10 February, first sanctions were imposed and then, on 18 April, the Ministry of War decided that they would be sent to Morocco; ultimately, 180 were repatriated to France and 225 sent to Morocco.

12 Mobilisation scholar Jasper's concept of 'moral shock' encompasses both a cognitive or learning dimension as well as a sudden emotionally charged dénouement as the catalyst for a protest frame. James M. Jasper, *The Art of Moral Protest* (Chicago: University of Chicago, 1997), p. 106. For instance, Archives Départementales de la Seine-Saint-Denis, Bobigny, Fond André Marty (henceforth ADSSD AM) 281J IV E2.22 Mauence (*Justice*) to Marty, 31 August 1924.

13 For an example of the widespread nature of the rumour see the song, ADSSD AM 281J 2 C76 'Pour la liberte!'

14 Philippe Masson, *La Marine Française et la Mer Noire, 1918–1919* (Paris: Publications de la Sorbonne, 1982), p. 177.

15 SHD 7N 393 telegram no. 394–8, 2 March 1919; SHD 7N 393 Telegram no. 601–3, 4 March 1919; SHD 7N 393 Telegram no. 2319 B3/3, 6 March 1919.

16 Christopher M. Bell and Bruce A. Elleman, 'Naval mutinies in the twentieth century and beyond', in Christopher M. Bell and Bruce A. Elleman (eds), *Naval Mutinies of the Twentieth Century: An International Perspective* (London: Frank Cass, 2003), pp. 264–76. Jane Hathaway (ed.), *Rebellion, Repression, Reinvention: Mutiny in Comparative Perspective* (Westport, CT: Praeger, 2001). Philippe Masson, 'The French naval mutinies of 1919', in Bell and Elleman (eds), *Naval Mutinies*, pp. 106–22, p. 119.

17 SHD SS Ed 30 Commander (*Captaine de Frégate*) Garnier to Contre-Amiral Commandant DNBO, 27 April 1919. 'André Marty' (6 November 1886–23 November 1956), *Dictionnaire Biographique du Mouvement Ouvrier Français*, www.maitron-en-ligne.univ-paris1.fr (last accessed 12 April 2018).

18 Masson, *Marine*, p. 267; with the author claiming no fatalities on 21 April (sic), Andrew Orr, 'The myth of the Black Sea Mutiny: communist propaganda, Soviet influence and the re-remembering of the mutiny', *French History*, 32, 1 (2018), p. 91.

19 SHD SS Ed 30 Vessel Lieutenant Vaublanc's report, 24 April 1919.

20 SHD SS Ed 30 Enseign de Vaisseau Durand to Commandant (*Mameluk*), 7 May 1919.

21 SHD SS Ed 30 telegrams of Maritime Prefect (Toulon) to Ministry of the Navy, 7–19 June 1919. Jean-Jacques Antier, 'Révolte des équipages de la flotte à Toulon', *Les Dossiers Histoire de la Mer* (February–March 1980), pp. 73–86.

22 *Journal officiel de la République française. Débats parlementaires. Chambre des députés*, 13 June 1919, p. 2679.

23 SHD SS Ed 30 telegrams of Maritime Prefect (Toulon) to Ministry of the Navy, 18–21 June 1919.

24 SHD SS Ed 30 Captaine de Vaisseau Thomine to Commandant (*Condorcet*), 16 June 1919; Captaine de Vaisseau to Commandant (*Vergniaud*), 16 July 1919; Captaine de Corvette Valat to Captaine de Vaisseau (*Dehorter*), 13 May 1919; Vice-Amiral de Bon's report on *Touareg* court martial, 4 November 1919.

25 Jacques Raphael-Leygues and Jean-Luc Barré, *Les Mutins de la Mer Noire* (Paris: Plon, 1981), pp. 63–4 and 220.

26 Orr, 'The myth', pp. 86–105. Paul Boulland, Claude Pennetier and Rossana Vaccaro (eds), *André Marty: l'Homme, l'Affaire, l'Archive* (Paris: CODHOS Editions, 2005).

27 ADSSD AM 281J III D2.12 Lachurie, *Vergniaud: Souvenirs d'un ancien matelot du cuirassé Vergniaud*. ADSSD AM 281J A4 2.2 Marty to the Military Revolutionary Council of the Black Sea Fleet, 4 November 1932.

28 *Action Française*, 10 June 1919, 12 June 1919, 13 June 1919, 17 June 1919, 18 June 1919, 19 June 1919.

29 Amnesty laws relating to different categories of military prisoners were passed on 24 October 1919 and 29 April 1921. *L'Humanité*, 26 August 1922.

30 *Le Libertaire* seems to suggest as much, announcing Cané's second round of public meetings in Troyes, Epinal, Belfort, Nancy, Metz, Reims, *Le Libertaire*, 11 February 1921; announcing another round of meetings along the Atlantic coast, *Le Libertaire*, 1 April 1921; featuring an article from André Marty, *Le Libertaire*, 24 October 1922.
31 A.Y., 'André Marty: Les heures glorieuses de la mer Noire', *Pensée*, 23 (April–May 1949), pp. 133–5.
32 Masson, *Marine*, pp. 626–7.
33 Raphael-Leygues and Barré, *Mutins*, p. 112. Tillon suffers guilt by association with Marty for Orr, 'The myth', p. 92. 'Charles Tillon' (3 July 1897–13 January 1993), *Dictionnaire Biographique du Mouvement Ouvrier Français*, www.maitron-en-ligne.univ-paris1.fr (last accessed 12 April 2018).
34 Centre d'Histoire de Science Po Fond Charles Tillon (henceforth CHSP CT) 1 *Contre-Courant*, n.d., 1953, p. 7.
35 *Archives Départementales de Seine-Saint-Denis* (ADSSD) AM 281J I A7 4–19 Marty to Bureau d'Éditions, 13 July 1933.
36 ADSSD AM 281J III D 3.1 letter Marty to Chorokhov, 28 June 1936.
37 *L'Humanité*, 25 August 1932.
38 Raphael-Leygues and Barré, *Mutins*, pp. 64–5.
39 Raphael-Leygues and Barré, *Mutins*, p. 19.
40 Ronald Chalmers Hood III, 'The French Navy and parliament between the wars', *International Historical Review*, 6, 3 (1984), pp. 386–403. Ronald Chalmers Hood III, *Royal Republicans: The French Naval Dynasties between the Wars* (Baton Rouge, LA: Louisiana State University Press, 1985). Robert O. Paxton, 'Darlan, un amiral entre deux blocs: réflexions sur une biographie récente', *Vingtième Siècle*, 36 (October–December 1992), pp. 3–19. Martin Thomas, 'After Mers-el-Kébir: the armed neutrality of the Vichy French navy, 1940–43', *English Historical Review*, 112, 447 (1997), pp. 643–70.
41 Masson, *Marine*.
42 Guy Pedroncini, *Les Mutineries de 1917* (Paris: Presses Universitaires de France, 1967). For ensuing historiography of the 1917 mutinies, Leonard V. Smith, *Between Mutiny and Obedience: The Case of the French Fifth Infantry Division during World War I* (Princeton: Princeton University Press, 1994). André Loez, 'Les mots et cultures de l'indiscipline: les graffiti des mutins de 1917', *Genèses*, 59, 2 (2005), pp. 25–46. André Loez and Nicolas Mariot (eds), *Obéir/Désobéir: les Mutineries de 1917 en Perspective* (Paris: La Découverte, 2008).
43 *Dictionnaire Biographique du Mouvement Ouvrier* has details of several mutineers, www.maitron-en-ligne.univ-paris1.fr (last accessed 12 April 2018).
44 Reddy makes the point of the danger of the history of emotions being confided to a cultured literary milieu, Jan Plamper, 'The history of emotions:

an interview with William Reddy, Barbara Rosenwein, and Peter Stearns', *History and Theory*, 49, 2 (2010), pp. 237–65.
45 ADSSD AM 281J VI D2.89–98 Lucien Godin (*Bruix*), 28 rue D'Aboukir, Courbevoie, Extract of a travel diary (*Carnet de route*), 30 March–22 May 1919. ADSSD AM 281J III D2.5 Marius Jules Cyrille (*Ernest Renan*) Extracts of a notebook of the journey, *Cahier de route*, 25 February–23 June 1919.
46 ADSSD AM 281J IV D2 3 notes, (n.d.). Marty also used Duport's letter to the latter's wife: André Marty, *La Révolte de la Mer Noire* (Paris: Editions sociales, 1949), p. 337.
47 Jean Le Ramey and Pierre Vottero, *Mutins de la Mer Noire* (Paris: Éditions Sociales, 1973).
48 ADSSD AM 281J VI D2.18–23 François Perrone, *Memoire de la Mer Noire: Bord du Waldeck-Rousseau*, 28 January 1920. VI D2. 63–74 R. Nouveau, *De Toulon à Calvi par Odessa*, n.d.
49 Valentin Nikólaievich Volosinov, *Marxism and the Philosophy of Language* (Cambridge: Harvard University Press, 1986), p. 71.
50 Henri Lefebvre, *The Production of Space* (Oxford: Blackwell, 1991).
51 Lev S. Vygotsky, *Thought and Language* (Cambridge: MIT Press, 1986), pp. 210–56.
52 Mikhail Mikhaïlovich Bakhtin, *The Dialogic Imagination: Four Essays* (Austin: University of Texas Press, 2010).
53 Antonio Gramsci, *Selections from the Prison Notebooks of Antonio Gramsci* (New York: International Publishers, 1971).
54 Harvey J. Kaye, *The British Marxist Historians: An Introductory Analysis* (Basingstoke: Palgrave Macmillan, 1995). Geoff Eley and Keith Nield, *The Future of Class in History: What's Left of the Social?* (Ann Arbor, MI: University of Michigan Press, 2007).
55 Timothy Brennan, 'Subaltern stakes', *New Left Review*, 89 (2014), pp. 67–87. Bryan D. Palmer, *Descent into Discourse: The Reification of Language and the Writing of Social History* (Philadelphia: Temple University Press, 1990).
56 Marco Guigni, Doug McAdam and Charles Tilly, *How Social Movements Matter* (Minneapolis, MN: University of Minnesota Press, 1999).
57 Lucien Febvre, 'Sensibility and history: how to reconstitute the emotional life of the past', in Peter Burke (ed.), *A New Kind of History: From the Writings of Lucien Febvre* (New York: Harper & Row, 1973), pp. 12–26. Joanna Bourke, 'Fear and anxiety: writing about emotion in modern history', *History Workshop Journal*, 55, 1 (2003), pp. 111–33. Peter N. Stearns and Carol Z. Stearns, 'Emotionology: clarifying the history of emotions and emotional standards', *American Historical Review*, 90, 4 (1985), pp. 813–36.
58 Carol Zisowitz Stearns and Peter N. Stearns, *Anger: The Struggle for Emotional Control in America's History* (Chicago: University of Chicago Press, 1986). Peter N. Stearns, *American Cool: Constructing a*

Twentieth-Century Emotional Style (New York: New York University Press, 1994). Peter N. Stearns, *Jealousy: The Evolution of an Emotion in American History* (New York: New York University Press, 1989). Peter N. Stearns and Jan Lewis (eds), *An Emotional History of the United States*, Volume 4 (New York: New York University Press, 1998).

59 Norbert Elias, *The Civilizing Process: Sociogenetic and Psychogenetic Investigations* (Oxford: Blackwell Publishers, 2000). Johan Huizinga, *The Waning of the Middle Ages: A Study of the Forms of Life, Thought and Art in France and the Netherlands in the XIVth and XVth Centuries* (London: Edward Arnold, 1937).

60 Barbara H. Rosenwein, 'Worrying about emotions in history', *American Historical Review*, 107, 3 (2002), pp. 821–45.

61 William M. Reddy, 'Saying something new: practice theory and cognitive neuroscience', *Arcadia-International Journal for Literary Studies*, 44, 1 (2009), pp. 8–23.

62 Plamper, 'The history of emotions', p. 235.

1

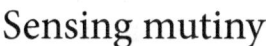

Sensing mutiny

To understand the consciousness of mutineers is to rethink how they constructed their world. Mutineer subjectivity (in both thought and action) formed 'from the outside in', through sensory perception, and 'from the inside out', through the cognitive-affective process. Mediated traces of both processes register in their testimony. This chapter draws together and examines these traces of the world 'from the outside in' that refracted through the senses for the insights that they might yield into mutineer subjectivity. Generally speaking, historians tend to specialise in either the senses or the emotions, these two fields having developed independently of each other, both claiming pioneer status at the new historiographical frontier. Instead, the approach adopted here is to amalgamate the senses and emotions in the clearing house of consciousness, with memory and language facilitating that interaction.

Mutineers' testimonies offer glimpses of how they rendered their sensuous environments comprehensible. These texts can be scrutinised for the mutiny's sights, smells, touch, taste and sounds. In *Les Cinq Sens* (1985), philosopher Michel Serres upended the assumptions of the linguistic turn, proposing scrutiny of the 'Empire of the Senses' to replace what Roland Barthes called the 'Empire of the Signs'.[1] For Serres, though all-encompassing texts and narratives might find affinity with the urban-literary world of academics, these linguistic forms denied the significance of sensuous connections to the world beyond the text. Serres thereby launched what David Howes called a 'sensual revolution' in the humanities and social sciences. While adopting a materialist approach to the mind, these scholars avoid the false opposition of neuroscience and culture, stressing the cultural mediation of the senses or 'culture tunes our neurons'.[2] Within history, too, this approach had already taken root. Thus, for instance, Alain Corbin has shown the profound associations between revolution and smell in the social imagination.[3] Such works announced the increased historiographical interest in the senses that went beyond the 'conceptually flaccid' allusion to the senses for purposes of literary embellishment.[4] The aim of this chapter is to demonstrate the conceptual advance that the sensory dimension adds to mutineer subjectivity, revealing how mutineers exercised agency within this realm and considering its wider significance.

The relations between sight, hearing, smell, touch and taste and their distinctive purchase upon memory are revealing. The sensory register of mutineer odysseys, their destinations and their battleships do more than provide colour to their narratives, forming a crucial element of their subjectivity tangling together affective and cognitive processes.

The mutiny of the senses: vision, hearing and the missing senses

Arising in the eighteenth century as a rejection of religious authority in knowledge, empiricism proposed that all knowledge derives from what the senses render observable. Mutineers attributed the senses a somewhat analogous role prompting a cognitive process wherein trusting their senses, the mutineers rejected what their officers told them about the war of intervention against Russia. The senses acted, at least in the accounts of those in the subordinate ranks, as a cognitive catalyst, the departure point for learning and reasoning about the situation. Mutineers asserted that first-hand sensory experience gave access to the truth. 'A young socialist' stressed to *La Vague* the veridical quality of sight in his account of the atrocities of the French intervention into the Russian Civil War, entitling his letter 'What I *saw* in Russia'.[5] Equally, decades later, Marcel Tondut appealed to fellow mutineers to establish a facticity that 'what they had *seen*' provided (my italics for emphasis).[6] This followed the powerful Great War trope of the unquestionable truthfulness of authentic combat experience, which relied upon the senses, especially sight. Thus, Jean Norton Cru distinguished between the combatant and the non-combatant so that 'the most contagious legends will not contaminate the defensive witness and his incomplete but faithful vision of war'.[7]

Historians of the senses have noted the considerable difference in the frequency and quality of the traces of senses in the historical record.[8] Moreover, a cultural and historical specificity exists in the value, 'ratio', enumeration and definition of particular senses.[9] In the case of the mutinies of 1919, witnesses certainly do not give attention to each sense in equal measure. Calibrating the ratio of the senses in mutineer testimony, sight and hearing were most prominent, almost to the complete exclusion of smell, taste and touch. The balance between sight and hearing mitigated modernity's 'exchange of an ear for an eye' as McLuhan puts it, in which written forms of communication (notably print) displace a premodern predominantly oral culture.[10]

Why certain senses are missing is in itself significant. Given that David Howes identifies touch and taste as the senses of proximity, their absence might plausibly imply that the mutiny was sensed not so much at the scale of personal space but in a shared one, within earshot or as far as the eye could see.[11] It might imply a certain distance from events that is not just physical but also temporal. As time passes, the immediacy of the senses as a whole is lost, being reduced to what is seen and heard. Another reason for the absence of certain senses in memory is that habituation filters sensory information from consciousness in the first place, in the same way that sensitivisation alerts consciousness to the unfamiliar.[12] Corbin offers an alternate interpretation. The reports of naval hygiene experts deemed that the senses were a mark of social distinction. The sailors' taste, hearing and touch had lost their refinement through chewing tobacco, hearing artillery and working with their hands.[13] Without ruling out the possible desensitivisation of naval labour, this may have said more about the officers' view of the inferiority of the sailors than being the reason for the absence of these senses from testimony.

The sense of touch surfaced rarely and was confined to the cold: the cold of the Crimea, of Galați, of a night of coaling duties, or the lack of adequate clothing. In one or two cases, taste cropped up in relation to the 'vile' or 'rotten' quality of food, such as the time when the crew of the Danton-class battleship *Condorcet* were fed 'detestable' mussels without salt, mutineer Albert Cornier believing this antagonised spirits significantly.[14] Complaints about tinned meat (known as *singe* (monkey)) appeared in the narratives too, but these had a routine quality.

Sometimes, the references in mutineer testimony to the senses are metaphoric. Thus, the strikes in Istanbul were not to Commander of the Army of Orient, General Franchet d'Espèrey's, 'taste', demonstrating the strong link between the emotion of disgust and gustatory metaphors. This also connects to the well-documented relationship between feelings of disgust for those in supposedly inferior class locations.[15] This is why Marty took great exception in his court martial when the prosecution alleged that 'his tastes were alienated by the debauchery' of the sailors on the destroyer *Protet*.[16] He wrote in his notebook that he had only one word for his shipmates: comrade [sic]. All this bears out the proposition of the parallel circuitry of senses, emotions and reason and their instantaneous pathways and connections: our testimonies subsume one within another, metaphorise one for another or combine them indissolubly.

Seeing mutiny

A few mutineer testimonies recognise modern warfare as sensory overload. Helping to frame this, cultural theorist Walter Benjamin classically challenged the liberal-capitalist ideology of progress through his metaphor of the angel of history's horror as it surveyed the civilisational ruins of the early twentieth century.[17] The destruction of a massive stockpile of munitions on Berezan Island in the Black Sea prompted mutineer Lucien Godin to reflect upon France's role in the Russian Civil War in his journal.[18] He vividly described erupting volcanoes, raining iron, shooting flames, sinister marsh fires, black veils with red flashes, jets of water and the death rattle of an agonising earth. His aestheticised attempt to convey the scene gives the impression of his senses being overpowered. This apocalypse in sound and vision corresponded in his narrative to a moral decadence of the political and military elites and a civilisational crisis of France itself. This destruction was performed 'in the name of law and civilisation and of the right of nations to self-determination', occasioning Godin to question France's hostility to a people struggling for emancipation. After his depiction of this inferno, only a few lines later, his journal whimsically juxtaposed nature's serenity: 'The mist dissipated, we set sail for Odessa. The sky is clear and the sea is beautiful.'[19]

Sight offered a medium of symbolic communication and, for that matter, of iconographical contestation. Occasional references appear in the testimonies of communication between the ships via semaphore flags and other forms of visual communication. So it was that the mutineers of the battleship *Jean Bart* requested delegates from the battleship *France*.[20] On Tuesday 22 April, the mutineers of the *Jean Bart* stuck up posters in the gun batteries calling for the crew to support the movement to the very last. The officers tore these down.[21] Visual communication might take an informal and spontaneous form. Sight allowed participants to read their emotional environment. At Marty's ceremonial loss of rank after his court martial, he saw sympathy in the eyes of the sailors present and several subtle friendly gestures.[22] Moreover, sight might be used to terrorise. To illustrate the counter-revolutionary terror of White Russians during the Civil War, Marty reproduced a photograph of two rail workers being publicly hanged in Odessa alongside the sign reading: 'A warning to the Bolsheviks'.[23]

Equally, the mutiny's visual dimension drew on established iconographical forms, most notably the red flag. Colour almost never appeared in testimony for its own sake, without a semiotic purpose. Being the most ubiquitous of these colour-defined visual icons, the red flag signified multiple meanings during the revolt. Raising this flag was a powerful act of transgression with the capacity to provoke both spatial contestation together with sensory, cognitive and emotional sequences. Ernest Duport recalled how applause accompanied the red flag being raised on 20 April aboard the battleship *France* and that the battleship *Jean Bart* responded in kind. This prompted Duport to ponder the revolutionary character of the mutiny.[24] For Notta too, the red flag signalled the diffusion of the mutiny, rendering the crowded decks of other warships comprehensible. Reaching as far as the eye could see, this act also initiated further dialogue between the ships, both widening the horizon of revolt and increasing the scope of strategic discussion.[25]

In mutineer reconstructions, sight instigated a cognitive response. For Nouveau of the battlecruiser *Waldeck-Rousseau*, the sight of 'the vermillion colours' of an immense flag over the principal monument in Odessa allowed the crew to 'guess without difficulty' what had puzzled them since the armistice: why they were still in military service and what their mission was. It was this, he observed, that encouraged their decision to refuse orders.[26] Jean Le Ramey envisioned the 'unforgettable spectacle' of Easter Sunday when the crew ignored the *branlebas* (bugle call to action), saluted the red flag (instead of the tricolour) and sang the *Internationale*.[27] For Leva of the *république*-class battleship *Patrie* – which mutinied in June 1919 in the port of Istanbul – the replacement of the Admiral's flag with 'our emblem' was the 'most beautiful act'.[28] Jean Carrière, an engineer on Amet's flagship the *Jean Bart* recalled how they made their own flag by tearing the red from the tricolour.[29] This was also the case aboard the rowboat from the *France* as it approached

Sevastopol's quayside on 20 April. The skipper of the rowboat drenched the tricolour three times in the sea, before tearing it apart to make a red flag to the applause of civilian spectators.[30] If the significance of the red flag relied upon a visual property, it connected to the metaphoric use of colour in the political spectrum (in the Russian context of the struggle between the Reds and the Whites).[31] If such allusions were common in testimonies, references to skin colour were less frequent. The discussions of the mutinies from the perspective of the authorities fell into a Republican colour-blindness, even when it came to the mutiny of colonial regiments.[32] In mutineer testimony, it was with the use of colonial troops as a repressive force that blackness signified race (rather than anarchism) though instances of this are rare. However, self-identification as white (rather than 'French') was almost non-existent in the testimony.

That the officers saw the red flag differently underlines the contentiousness of the visual realm. Even in his official report of the mutiny, an officer of the battleship *Justice* could not conceal his contempt for the 'red rag' ('*torchon*').[33] Amet, the Commander of the Second Fleet, also described it as a rag ('*chiffon*').[34] The removal of the flag symbolised a shift in the balance of forces and its significance was lost on nobody. On Saturday 20 April, the second day of the mutiny aboard the *France*, Commander Robez-Pagillon restored some calm in the early afternoon and ran the red flag down.[35] On board the *Jean Bart*, the lieutenant ordered that the red flag (which had been raised on the first night of the revolt) be removed early the following morning. A 'small group' of mutineers raised it once again at 8.15 a.m. Eventually, after a couple of attempts, the officers managed to get it taken down once more half an hour later.[36] This back-and-forth plight demonstrated the investment of both sides in the visibility of power.

The red flag, then, both posed the question of politics and allowed visual communication, disseminating the mutiny, complementing the aural reception of the flag's mutinous partner: revolutionary song. As mutiny spread across the fleet, the red flag reappeared wherever the revolt emerged, crossing the Mediterranean and reaching the French ports of the Atlantic. In Toulon, when sailors and workers staged what one participant described as a revolutionary day of action (*journée révolutionnaire*), the crowd of 2,000 tore down the tricolour at the Grand Tavern and replaced it with the red flag.[37]

From the testimonies, the signing of the *Internationale* accompanied the ceremonial raising of the red flag. A newspaper account based upon the memories of Marius Fracchia and Marius Ricros of the *France* described the scene after the *Internationale* was sung:

> Suddenly, there was amongst the men a silence. Then, applause, a delirious ovation. Someone had just climbed the bowsprit mast and now, up there, flew the red flag. The revolutionary emblem flapped in the wind; the colours of revolt, brilliant like the blood of men, ablaze above the uncovered heads.[38]

Sight and sound combined in the sensory delights of revolutionary ritual. The comparison between the two provides an interesting insight into the multisensory experience of the mutiny and the differences between the senses. Each sense made a distinctive contribution to the revolt and combined with others to make collective action possible. While the red flag could be seen further than voices could carry and prompted in the viewer a set of associative meanings, song with its more participatory quality and textual complexity offered a much greater capacity for the transmission of meaning. In other words, song was more apt for 'frame alignment' (whereby actors share outlooks and identities that make collective action and repertoire choice possible) during the mutiny.[39]

The sensory contest also had a material aspect as well as a semiotic one. Naval discipline entailed systematic surveillance and its evasion depended on being invisible and inaudible to the officers and their 'snitches'. In turn, the mutineers had to 'keep an eye' on those who might betray them.[40] Hearing played its role in the mutiny.[41] Being attuned to the mutinous soundscape offers a richer understanding of the dynamics of the revolt, just as historians of aurality have reworked our understandings of revolutions.[42] Despite modernity apparently privileging sight over hearing, the process of mutiny shifted the balance back again. This is particularly clear in the case of song (but also rumour and hearsay), which fed into the cognitive dimension of the revolt.[43]

A mutinous soundscape

If a mutinous soundscape was to emerge, to do so it had to displace a normative sound culture. Viewed from the *longue durée*, capitalist modernity assailed the ears, constituting a revolution in sound: the factory and the railway transformed the relative peace of the workshop and horse-drawn travel.[44] If anthropologist Marshall McLuhan posited a desensitivisation that accompanied modernity in contrast to the 'kaleidoscopic sensorium' of our 'tribal' past, industrialised warfare constituted its most extreme expression.[45] Regarding the danger of technological determinism, as Susan Stewart observed, Marx and Engels asserted the historically conditioned nature of the senses and that capitalist property relations (rather than modern technology per se) alienated the senses. Thus, human emancipation would entail an emancipation of the senses.[46]

Modernity re-equipped the sounds of warfare, assaulting the aural sense with tumultuous intensity. With regard to the Great War, Gaetan Bruel exposed the ubiquity of auditory damage in the trenches, with partial or total deafness being the most widespread of all war traumas. She noted the widespread references to the exorbitant noise amongst the literary witnesses of the war: Junger, Genevoix, Barbusse and Bloch.[47] Modern artillery and the capacity for round-the-clock bombardment rendered the auditorium of the trench inescapable and insupportable. Indeed, one mutineer aboard the *Waldeck-Rousseau* had begun the war in the trenches, suffering shell shock from an explosion in the first weeks of the war and spending several spells in hospital as a consequence. Although doctors declared him unfit for military service, this was never officially confirmed so he continued to serve despite shell shock and endocarditis.[48] 'Industrial killing' (as Omer Bartov termed it)[49] therefore rendered obsolete old military soundscapes such as the terror-inducing drum or war cry, surpassing them a hundredfold through chemistry and manufacturing. Though the primary intention was no longer to induce fear, the cacophony of the machine gun and heavy artillery transcended the capacity of premodern warfare to bring about a physiological effect through sound.[50] Those from a bucolic background experienced modernity through war as overwhelming aural excess. For this reason, as with 'shell shock' in English, several languages connected the traumatic pathologies of the front and artillery.[51]

The coal-fired steel-hulled warship did the same for the Navy. Engine rooms and heavy canon revolutionised the sounds of naval warfare. The *Jean Bart* and the *France* that were both in the same class of battleship weighed 23,500 displacement tons and could boast 305 mm guns firing 432 kg shells.[52] The battleship played a vital role in maritime commercial empires to defend commerce and investments but also to project power, particularly when larger ships could bombard coastlines. Even when their guns were silent, these twenty-ton leviathans were a powerful presence in any port.[53]

If the acoustic field of military modernity and the Great War set a backdrop for that of the revolt, Duport's letter to his parents communicates the mutiny's soundscape. Recounting the incident when Vice-Admiral Amet boarded the *France*, intending to harangue the crew so as to quell the insubordination, Duport emphasised the aural dimension of the event. Individual cries, boos, taunts, chanted slogans, song and silence suggest that the mutiny was an auditory test of strength: a struggle to be heard, an effort to silence opponents, and a contest in sound with modalities of form, semantics and volume. Here Bakhtin's distinction between the monological authorities attempting to impose a singular voice from above and the unruly dialogue from below seems apt.[54] This was not simply a vertical contest of sound, but one in which a singular authority confronted a plural subaltern. For instance, an official report defined the mutiny of the torpedo boat *Dehorter* through the noisiness of the crew's demonstration and remarked upon the spread of the idea across the French torpedo boats in the Azov Sea that clamourous (*bruyantes*) demands get results.[55]

If the mutiny's non-linguistic soundscapes calibrate the pattern and intensity of contestation, they also have a semantic dimension, with the protagonists reading noise for its meaning. Thus, a witness recalled how machine-gun fire and the telephone ring augured the news of the Morskaia Road 'ambush'.[56] Given the thirst for information, many mutineers referred to the sound of naval canon as part of their sense-making process of the Allied intervention, deciphering the size of guns, how far off they were, where they were firing on, from which direction, by whom and against whom. Notta, a delegate aboard the *France*, identified the guns of the battlecruisers *Ernest Renan* and *Bruix* during Odessa's evacuation.[57] Duport wished that he had counted the salvos fired as a record of the same 'atrocity'. From their timbre, Lachurie of the battleship *Vergniaud* could detect the calibre of 75 mm and 240 mm canon as well as the ship from which they came.[58] Eugène Ribot evoked with lyrical inflection the six-hour sequence of noise as cannon 'growled', machine guns 'cackled' and grenades 'exploded everywhere'.[59]

Rather than simply a void, scholars have probed the culturally variable meanings of silence alongside audibility and volume in social contestation.[60] As Esteban Buch observed, the Great War invested silence with much more profound importance in symbol, metaphor and reality, especially with the silence of death and mourning.[61] Schafter remarked that several writers such as Erich Maria Remarque and William Faulkner noted the quieter but perhaps more terrible sounds of the dead and the dying in war.[62] Surveying the relationship between silence and modern war in collective memory, Jay Winter noted how silence was socially constructed, framing public understandings, foreclosing conflict and privileging certain voices.[63] The modes of mutineer silence show the deceptive complexity of sound's negation. The sea itself has a powerful aural cultural dimension, suggesting silences of different types. The sea transmitted the silence of contemplation or of resistance. The semantic association between silence, death and the sea also possesses a fertile cultural lineage.[64] Equally, the rhythmic quality of the sea has inspired the anonymous songwriters of seafaring oral traditions and the great composer, such as Vivaldi, Tchaikovsky, Wagner, Ravel and Debussy, alike.[65] Establishing the cultural multivalence of silence, Alain Corbin's *Histoire du Silence* (2014) illustrated it being more than the simple absence of sound: silence was a tactic, a means of contemplation, an attribute of nature, a signifier of emotion (love or hate), or, finally, a marker of tragedy.[66]

Mutineer silence had similar inflections. François Perrone of the *Waldeck-Rousseau* talked of the silence of suffering while doing one's military service.[67] Eugène Ribot recalled an incident that exposed the potent contentious silence between officers and the ranks. When a lieutenant called men to assemble for inspection, one soldier in Ribot's section did not move. The officer ordered him to get into uniform. Ribot remarked upon the calm of his comrade and the pregnant silence that accompanied the subversion of deferential norms.

> But, calmly, he raised his head coldly, his eyes met those of the officer, for a moment they looked at each other, in silence, then, he responded:
>
> 'I am darning my socks.'
>
> 'But.'
>
> 'I am darning my socks, I am not moving.'
>
> Embarrassed, the lieutenant leaves, mechanically.[68]

Similarly, when the landing party of the *France* refused to fight the Bolshevik advance in Sevastopol, Le Roux recalled all the sailors sitting down, refusing to move and being absolutely mute.[69]

Silence could also signify the efficiency and consensus among the ranks of plans for rebellion. Thus, mutineers aboard the *Waldeck-Rousseau* reassured waiverers that the revolt would 'work well without a sound'.[70] In the revolt's preliminary stages, being inaudible to the authorities and their informants was key to avoiding detection and therefore achieving success. Nouveau recalled the 'silent order' (that is unheard by the officers) circulating amongst the crew to assemble on the foredeck at the beginning of the mutiny.[71]

Underlining the sensory disruption that the mutiny on the warships entailed, the revolt broke the silence of the night, of the sea and of naval authority.[72] When Semichon, the Commander of the cruiser *Guichen*, appealed for the assembled crew to disperse, Tillon described the outbreak of the mutiny as a powerful silence broken: 'The awful test of rigid silence transformed into an explosive release of pride.'[73] With the mutinies, the officers repeatedly and unsuccessfully demanded silence or calm, the desired tranquillity having both auditory and emotional dimensions. On 19 April, Robin, the Captain of the *Justice*, noted the silence of the forty or so men assembling to listen to the protests on the *France* before joining in with their cries. Able to silence them with his intervention, they fled in panic under the cover of night.[74] The officers on the *Justice* thus restored silence more successfully than on the *France*. The Commander of the *France* asked that the crew's delegates demand silence where he had failed.[75] It was only when Notta directly addressed Amet that the sailors listened.[76] Equally, during the mutiny on the *Waldeck-Rousseau*, only their delegate François Perrone could silence the crew during the Admiral's harangue 'by a spell, by my energy'.[77] Peter Bailey stressed the connection between silence and authority in such settings as the courtroom and the Victorian family home, or its subversion in rough music and laughter.[78] This applied to naval authority in 1919 as well. Such was the case when the twenty-year-old mutineer Ricros of the *France* came back from Sevastopol with provisions for the return to home. He announced that the two pigs that he had bought were named Pichon (the French Foreign Minister) and Clemenceau (the Prime Minister) to the raucous laughter of the crew.[79]

Calm might also denote those moments in the protest cycle when the crew deliberated future action, for instance when the delegates outlined their demands, or with the arrival of the news that the officers were arming themselves.[80] Witnesses also remembered the silence of repose after the emotional and auditory intensity of protest. Thus, after the failure of Amet's harangue on the evening of 19 April due to their hubbub, the crew of the *France* relaxed and fell silent.[81] Silence could also portend grave intent. When an officer of the *Jean Bart* in a loud authoritarian voice forbade the delegates of the *France* from boarding on 21 April, they left without saying a word but reflected upon its serious consequences. Silence could signify intimidation as well. The assembled crew of the battlecruiser *Bruix* remained insolently and threateningly calm in the face of their commander during their revolt.[82] Equally, the silence that followed the second master's acclamation 'Vive La France!', during an inspection on board the battlecruiser *Ernest Renan* on 23 June, signalled a powerful act of defiance.[83] Silence, then, meant consent, contestation, surprise, confusion, emotional change and mourning; it could fall gradually or abruptly; it could be environmental, human or both.

Volume of speech carried its own significance. In circumstances where the crew controlled the ship, an officer used 'a pitiful voice', asking them to spare him because he had a wife and children and the Admiral addressed the crew in the 'softest voice possible'.[84] Murmuring occupied more than simply an intermediary position between silence and intelligible voices. Muttering was present at the beginning of the process of defiance. It contained the paradox of only being comprehensible to the immediate associate but also sufficiently audible to censure the authorities anonymously. Murmurs were a subtle response to events, literally showing disquiet to the authorities. Several witnesses remarked upon its significance. François Peronne of the *Waldeck-Rousseau* noted that murmurings began in the fleet with rumours that the sailors would have to shoot those who refused to fight the Bolsheviks. 'Very strong murmuring' also occurred when the *Waldeck-Rousseau's* guns were trained on Odessa on 2 or 3 April.[85] Pierre Vottero's account of the mutiny's beginning on the battleship *Voltaire* in Bizerte harbour on 15 June 1919 identified the sequence of silence-murmurs-boos-shouts after Rear-Admiral de Margerie's speech.[86] Historian of hearing R. Murray Schafer deemed the 'keynote sound' to be the defining sound embedded deep into consciousness and articulating key values. Murmuring played this sonic function in the mutiny's emergence, just as song performed this role for the mutiny itself.[87]

A vernacular mutiny

The Bakhtin circle provides a perspective that integrates language into sound's social setting and into a nuanced understanding of human consciousness. Three scholars within the circle furnish insights into these relationships. All three insist on the social quality of consciousness and language. First, Volosinov mounted a powerful critique of Saussure's 'abstract universalism', proposing that language was not only socially situated, but located in conflictual social relations. For Volosinov, utterances possess a multi-accentality (that is they can articulate more than one meaning for more than one addressee simultaneously) and are inflected with social contestation.[88] Second, through his consideration of pedagogy and child psychology, Vygotsky examined consciousness as an emergent phenomenon and its relationship via inner speech to language. According to him, language acquisition occurs through a process whereby mature thought joins two processes: an externalised egocentric speech becomes internalised aligning with an inner semantic flux.[89] This situates language (and thought) in the social world and proposes a realist theory of reference that is not one of simple correspondence. Finally, in his study of the novel, Bakhtin in effect scaled up from Volosinov, elaborating the complex multiple character of national languages and of individual 'heteroglot' utterances. For Bakhtin, language is fundamentally about dialogue – always having an addressee – and needs to be understood in its specific temporal and social specificity. Although a national language may appear to be unitary, history and social life render it 'a social heteroglossia' that Bakhtin defined as:

> A multitude of concrete worlds, a multitude of bounded verbal-ideological and social belief systems; within these various systems (identical in the abstract) are elements of language filled with various semantic and axiological content and each with its own different sound.[90]

This approach helps to situate the language of the mutineers. In their accounts, the argot of the sailors and soldiers expresses a vernacular voice distinctive from the officers. The latter were known as '*fayots*' (officers or beans). This slang included: '*gradaille*' (senior student at officer school), '*saccos*' (military police), '*fortes têtes*' (tough nuts), '*bagne flottante*' ('floating prisons' or warships), '*salon flottante*' ('floating salon', that is the experience for the officers on warship), '*singe*' ('monkey' (tinned meat)), '*vaches*' or '*boeufs*' (cows or officers) and '*gros culs*' ('big arses' or battleships), etc.

Slang indicated several phenomena simultaneously: alien words learned by the uninitiated, a sense of emotional community and freedom, peer-defined group boundaries and subaltern identity, as well as signifying a claim to authenticity of experience. The mutineers' definition of the events illustrated this mixture of working-class, military and political terminologies and idioms: it was a 'revolt', a 'mutiny' and a 'movement'. Mutineers in the Army might be more likely to use the terms to refuse orders ('*ne pas marcher*'/'*ne pas monter en ligne*').[91]

The mutineers' register changed situationally with noticeable differences between letters, courts martial and memoirs. Language constituted a measure of contention with the use of slang in the face of officers being a strongly transgressive element of the revolt. The argot of the crews stands in marked contrast to the Admiralty's paternalistic language. As James C. Scott has observed, language offers a weapon to the weak in the shape of nicknames and offstage gossip.[92] Mutineers called Vice-Admiral Amet (the Commander of the Fleet in the Black Sea) the 'crocodile' for his duplicity.[93] Nicknames often possessed a gendered property such as *'quinze grammes'* (15 grams), which inferred a lack of manly physique, or *'boîte a clous'* (box of nails) and *'vrai brute à bord'* (real bully on board), which suggested an unthinking, even inhuman, thuggishness.[94] The crew of the *Jean Bart* knew the Captain-at-Arms as the 'cock' ('coq').[95] As well as an exaggerated masculinity, the crews attached a diminished manhood to some officers. Equating fear with a lack of manliness, Marcel Vergua of the 37th Colonial regiment described one of his superiors, Lieutenant Nougaro as *'un des plus grands froussards au grade de lieutenant'* (one of the biggest cowards at the rank of lieutenant). Conversely, for Vergua, Durand was a veritable madman, a decorated bully (*'brute galonnée'*), whose enthusiasm for surprise attacks managed to get a great number of *'prolos'* (proletarians) killed.[96] Similarly, for Ribot, officers were 'decorated villains' (*crapule galonée*).[97] Like the ubiquitous slang and nicknames for officers, the informant attracted a range of pejorative synonyms: *'casserole'*, *'cafard'* (bug, depression, snitch), *'punaise'* (cockroach, snitch), *'chique des fayots'* (chewing tobacco, flea) etc.[98] These words show the cross-fertilisation of working-class, criminal and military lexicons and their shared contentious quality.

The slang of the trenches and the naval crews also had distinctive features. The sailors spoke the residual language of seafaring with its discrete lexicon.[99] Etymology of terms such as *'fayot'*, *'Jean Le Gouin'* or *'gradaille'* discloses much about the mutiny's social heteroglossia. The word *'fayot'* evolved from the Provençal term for haricot beans (*'faïou'* or *'faïol'*). The word passed into military slang via naval slang, in the form of *'fayol'* with a silent 'l', from which came *'fayot'*. It entered the civilian slang of the nineteenth century because haricots often appeared in the food of prisoners. Especially, in the Navy, *'fayot'* refered to a sailor who remained in service after the regular term of enlistment, a re-enlisted naval officer. From that has come the civilian meaning (zealous pupil). In the Army, *'fayot'* designated a soldier who shows too much zeal vis-à-vis his superior, who seeks approval from the hierarchy. This generated a verb: '*fayotter*', meaning to do with zeal. The song *Chanson des Fayots* illustrated the scope for humorous double meanings of '*fayots*' (officers or beans), connecting superiors with indigestion and gastric or intestinal wind.

By the time of the Great War, '*Jean Le Gouin*' had come to mean an ordinary sailor in the Navy.[100] Originally, it derived from the Breton for white ('*gwen*'), referring to the white uniform. *Jean Le Gouin* emerged as a typical name used for sailors from Brittany, a region of heavy naval recruitment. At the beginning of the nineteenth century, *Gouin* was an insult for a poorly dressed sailor. Over the course of the century, losing its regional designation, it came to mean all sailors. For the mutineers, it became an anti-militarist identity in opposition to the officer, being adopted as a pseudonym or title for oppositional literature.[101] The term '*Gradaille*' initially emerged in the Army. It signified a pupil in the last year of the officer training at St Cyr, whose purpose was to train new arrivals. In the testimonies, it had the pejorative meaning of precocious presumption and haughty superiority on the part of officers.[102]

This cursory description of the etymologies of three common words ('*fayot*', '*Jean Le Gouin*' or '*gradaille*') in the mutineers' lexicon illustrates the complex processes at work in the emergence of a common language of mutinous naval ranks. Their vocabularies drew on dialect of regions with seafaring traditions, resulted from a vernacular expression of social antagonism in the Navy, transcended the naval milieu to become part of a composite, multiple or heteroglot national language. This last process inflected the social divisions within the Navy with wider associations of class antagonism in French society as a whole. Even at a level as basic as language, this illustrates the problem with attempting to understand the mutinies of 1919 exclusively within a military arena, within military norms, sealed off from the context of French class society or wider political discourses.

Hearing, improvising and singing: a mutinous songscape

Of vocal forms, song has a distinct quality. Unlike the individual shouted comment, song was a shared performance. Unlike booing, song possessed a semantic flexibility and the means of collective emotional self-exploration, allowing a fuller sense of group identification. Song straddled sound and language, possessing the capacity to move between oral and (via print) visual realms. Moreover, it combined all elements characteristic of 'social movement displays': worthiness, unity, numbers and commitment.[103] The unison of male voices also constituted a display of masculinity: of manly comradeship. Like the episode on the *France*, Amet boarded the *Justice*, hoping to silence the crew that had raised the red flag in response to the *France*. Once again, his harangue became an auditory battle. Indicating how the mutiny's sonic repertoire culminated in revolutionary song, François Mauence committed his memory to paper five years after the event:

> The Vice-Admiral Amet learning of our calm, believed it worth coming aboard to harangue us. With his cantankerous tone, the insulter of the Bolsheviks made us listen to a speech, during which he spoke of how campaign would continue. Within a few minutes he very quickly learnt that he was mistaken about our calm spirits. With a single outburst, the entire crew shouted in the face of this assassin of the workers, that they stood in solidarity with the comrades of the other ships and quickly accompanied it with the singing of the *Internationale*.[104]

Sympathisers and opponents alike pair the mutiny and song. In the play about the Odessa mutiny, revolutionary song provided a metonym of mutiny. In a note passed to Russian allies, the sailors observed that there were delegates on all the ships so 'fix the date soon, for we are delaying dancing the *Carmagnole* for the Admiral and his priest.'[105] Equally, the military authorities seized printed versions of revolutionary songs.[106] All historians of the mutiny, irrespective of their perspective, make reference to song but they largely fail to understand how song as an evidentiary form can nuance our understanding of events.[107] Song had a profound and revealing relationship to Marty's *Révolte de la Mer Noire*. A mutineer and communist, Marty reproduced two songs *Pour Liberté* and *Gloire aux Marins de la Mer Noire* in his text as appendices, fitting its celebratory and romanticising mode.[108] He incorporated other songs, notably *Fayots* and the *Odessa Waltz*, into the narrative of the revolt.[109] In his analysis, song constituted an index of the dissemination of the rebellion: the 'whole fleet sang the *Internationale*'. He noted the great joy that accompanied the song. This confirmed for Marty the revolutionary quality of the movement. Marty mentioned the moments when songs began and listed them: the *Internationale*, the *Chanson des fayots*, the *Salut du 17e*, *Chanson de Odessa* and *La Grève des Mères*.[110] These had a deeper meaning for Marty who explained the significance of both the *Salut du 17e* and *Fayots* in his footnotes. Endowing the former song with the ultimate communist honour, he remarked that Krupskaya's memoirs mentioned that Lenin loved to sing the *Salut du 17e* during his Parisian exile. Indeed, indicative of Marty's regional roots and personal connection to the song, Marty published a book about *Salut du 17e* after the Second World War.[111] As for the *Fayots*, Marty observed that sailors had been singing it for sixty years. Song, for Marty then, highlighted both the transnational quality of revolutionary sentiments and the popular tradition of opposition to the officers within the French Navy.[112] He emphasised song yet further in the pamphlet *Les Heures Glorieuses de la Mer Noire*, describing it as an arm of the struggle, briefly explaining improvised practices of oral transmission.[113] Although Marty identified the ubiquity of song, he missed its deeper relationship to the mutiny, preferring the aura of authenticity that it bestowed.

The fullest memoir of the naval mutinies of 1919 was that of Charles Tillon who served on the cruiser *Guichen* that revolted at the Greek port of Itea in the summer of 1919. *La Révolte Vient de Loin* (1969) was written six decades after the event. If uncertain about its representativeness, *La Révolte Vient* is clearly a suggestive example of how song insinuated itself into the development of political and class self-awareness for the mutineer generation. His account divulges a rich entanglement between song and every stage of his political maturation. Indeed, the former resistance leader and communist minister entitled his companion autobiography *On Chantait Rouge* (we sang red).

Tillon opened his chapter on his formative influences with Pédron's song about the massacre of nine workers at Fourmies on 1 May 1891.[114] Then, reminiscing about his school days, Tillon recalled Brizon's history textbook that introduced him to France's revolutionary past and *La Carmagnole*. Song suffused his memories of political coming of age.[115] He associated song with the *Confédération Générale du Travail*'s (CGT) campaign against pensions in April 1910 and the national rail strike in October of the same year.[116] His writing suggests that song anticipated his later more nuanced understandings of politics. He encountered in song a political differentiation that he was not at the time able to comprehend. Thus, on one occasion in 1913, he happened upon around one hundred shoemakers with younger workers at their head. They were singing Gaston Montéhus's *Jeune Garde*. Attracted by the music, he admitted that given his schoolmaster's influence, he would have decried the revolutionary violence that it advocated, though he certainly had no sympathy for 'the bourgeois, the well-fed ones (*les gavés*)' that it denounced.[117] Tillon's account of his youth hints that song was intrinsic to working-class socialisation. Many in the Navy did not come from such a background. Thus, the heterogeneous socio-geographical mix of naval recruitment set up a particular dynamic for the reception of song during the mutiny. So while Tillon hailed from industrial Rennes, the coastline of his native Britanny was both a bastion of naval recruitment and unfamiliar with working-class traditions. The obstinate persistence of song in Tillon's memory for half a century owed much to the social context of recall in which the songs were sung, allowing rehearsed associative reference points around which he could structure his past.

While Tillon's memoirs indicate how song persisted in the long-term memory of a mutineer with a long vintage of revolutionary activism, the shorter accounts closer in time to the events also refer to music. Indeed, music enters in the *majority* of mutineer testimonies. This raises the relationship between protest cycles and song, their cognitive frames and repertoires of action. From a methodological perspective then, exploring when song intersected the protest cycle in sufficiently significant ways to imprint itself onto the memory might offer new insights into the atmosphere of the mutiny and the part played by song in it.

The first consideration ought to be the role of song prior to the outbreak of protest. Testimonies noted song permeated clandestine oppositional networks. In a letter to Marty in 1926, Jean Camille of the *Du Chayla* told how rumours spread around the '*goguettes*' (workers' singing circles) in Istanbul during shore leave that their destination would be Odessa.[118] The revolutionary cell aboard Jean Le Ramey's battleship the *France* met under the cover of being a choir, singing love songs and hiding their literature if discovered.[119] Marius Jules Cyrille, a sailor helmsman on the battlecruiser *Ernest Renan*, sent extracts from his travel journal to Marty.[120] Cyrille met a group of sailors on 18 March in Odessa from battleships, including the *Jules Michelet* and the *Justice*. These sailors were singing *Jeune Garde*. Given that French and Greek troops were patrolling the city, the song manifested the militant intentions of the sailors, rendering possible the liaison and communication between revolutionaries from different ships.

Weeks before his ship joined the Black Sea Mutiny, Layarde, a helmsman of the *république*-class battleship *Justice*, recorded that after three days of fighting and eventual withdrawal from Kherson, he and his comrades were in flight from the Bolsheviks and barricaded themselves into some barracks, drinking all the wine and singing revolutionary songs.[121] Recalling discontent at the Anatolian port of Izmir (Smyrna) in March 1919, Hiarel, a sailor of the *république*-class battleship *Démocratie*, noted that those on shore leave roamed the town and the quayside, singing the *Internationale*. The crew assembled on the foredeck encouraged them, singing the *Internationale* warmly and forcing local notables to leave the ship. This revolt lasted from 6 p.m. until midnight when officers accompanied by fusiliers threatened the men. Those who had gone ashore continued to sing the *Internationale* as they returned to the ship.[122] Within mutineer narratives, then, isolated instances of revolutionary song anticipated the revolt, acting as a subtle indicator of what was to follow.

Much can be learnt from contentious performances as an emergent phenomenon.[123] According to three testimonies (those of Duport, Notta and Le Ramey), song facilitated the immediate initiation of protest on the *France*, each account offering a different perspective on precisely how this was so. First, Ernest Duport related his mutineer experiences in a letter to his parents shortly after the events on 1 May 1919 anchored in the Bay of Ponty, off Bizerte, Tunisia. He was on board the *France* as a stoker. He recorded that the crew sang the *Internationale* just as it assembled during the mutiny on 19 April. Shouting accompanied the singing and it appeared to coincide with the sailors becoming emboldened through numbers. This atmosphere led to the formulation of demands and strategic decision-making. To the sound of this *communard* anthem, the mutineers insisted 'by whatever means' for the Commander-in-Chief to speak to the delegates and for the right to board the *Jean Bart*.[124] This suggests that song was not only present at the emergence of protest, it also facilitated both collective confidence and 'frame alignment'. This was not simply a history of hearing, of passive sensory *reception*; through song, sailors orchestrated a new mutinous soundscape.

The second example of a testimony of a sailor aboard the *France*, the anarchist Notta, an ordinary sailor and a delegate of the crew, also referred more than once to song. When sailors were discussing whether to perform coal loading duties on Easter Sunday, they attracted the interest of the Captain-at-Arms. They sang in the hope that this would allay his suspicions, doing so for half an hour.[125] Thus, according to selection and context, song could display or dissimulate intentions. Notta recalled how the crew sang the *Internationale* when the mutiny over the coal duty was escalating. He had been to see the Commander-in-Second who had promised no punishment if order was restored. On Notta's return, he was taunted for trying to make peace with the officers. After their meal, the crew assembled on the foredeck once again singing the

Internationale and raising the red flag, as did the *Jean Bart*, the *Justice*, the *Mirabeau* and the *Vernigaud*.[126]

A third mutineer's testimony suggests that music had a yet deeper significance for the initiation of protest. According to Jean Le Ramey of the *France*, the revolt began after the evening meal of Easter Saturday, when 400 men assembled on the deck and began to sing together. Their songs initially disguised their intentions. Innocent love songs, all of a sudden ceded to the rebel lament the *Odessa Waltz*. When the Captain-at-Arms Louarn intervened to silence them, they sang the *Internationale*.[127] This sequence of song entailed an emotional sequence (from melancholic lament to combative anthem) that can also be found in Louis Barthas's account of the mutiny of 1917, wherein another lament, the *Chanson de Craonne* (upon which the *Odessa Waltz* was based) preceded the *Internationale*.[128]

The testimonies of the mutiny's overture divulge that it combined three reciprocating repertoires: of action, of song and of emotion. Our three mutineers had a different ear for musical memory. Their different lists of songs performed during the emergence of protest suggests that mutineers did not sing in perfect unison. First, it highlights a divergent significance or even familiarity of particular songs for mutineers. Only those with sufficient meaning merited mention in the testimony, thus none of the mutineers named the contemporary love songs that disguised the intentions of the mutineers, such as the *Costauds de la Lune* that lent the *Odessa Waltz* its tune. Sailors came from regions with political traditions as diverse as the Vendée and Paris, so the songs of the labour movement will have been much more familiar to some than others. Varying degrees of familiarity would have led to uneven participation, where the uninitiated learned through the repetition of songs or through initiation via the refrain. According to mutineer accounts, they sang for sufficient time for this to be the case.

Song was not only integral to the preparation or emergence of the revolt, but had an entangled relationship with the protest cycle as a whole. Illustrating this, song again played its part in an episode that amplified the movement: when Greek troops shot on a demonstration in Sevastopol, the news spread across the ships anchored in the port. Lachurie of the battleship *Vergniaud* heard revolutionary songs while he was on shore leave in Sevastopol that day. He had been discussing the intervention with Bolsheviks who gave him leaflets. He recalled the revolutionary anthem on a demonstration by the local population with a contingent of French mutineers participating. When Greek sailors fired, he claimed that the crowd of French sailors and citizens of Sevastopol continued bravely to sing the *Internationale* and the *Fayots*, despite the machine-gun fire.¹²⁹ For Lachurie, then, song transcended national borders, signalled revolutionary heroism and was associated with a pivotal moment of the mutiny. Even if it seems implausible that the demonstrators continued to sing, that Lachurie retrospectively connected song and the incident is significant. Repertoires of song thereby allowed a nuanced response to events and a medium of communication amongst the crews and with potential allies beyond their own ships, and even across the national boundaries.

If song held a multivalent significance in the memory of the sailors, so did it for the officers too. Amet reported that when the *Internationale* drowned out his attempt to address the crew of the *France* at 9 p.m. on Sunday 20 April, this amounted to the 'madness of the crowd'.¹³⁰ Captain Cazenau's report on the mutiny noted how after the Admiral's departure, irritation and edginess amongst the crew translated into conversation and song.¹³¹ So song indexed the intensity and character of discontent. For the officers, it also constituted the mutiny's transgressive substance. Cazenau and the Admiral heard of sailors ashore on leave whose offence was to be 'with the Red Flag at their head and shouting revolutionary songs'.¹³²

Conclusion

Using the insights of the history of the senses divulges a crucial component of the mutineer experience, helping comprehension of the social phenomenon of mutineer consciousness. Analysis of the senses as an object of investigation in their own right unlocks the visual and auditory dynamics of the mutiny: a subtle and significant realm of mutineer consciousness. Although their subjectivity was a mystery to the officers – who could only suspect a loss of morale – what mutineers saw and heard was both catalyst and substance of their revolt. Their eyes saw a multitude in revolt and their ears heard the shouts, cries, muttering, silences and songs of their peers. Judged from the perspective of the 'outside in', the very intensity of sensory experience allowed mutineers at crucial thresholds to engage in transgressive collective action. Their actions transformed the visual and auditory landscape, which was simultaneously a shared sense-making process and common cultural practices. This was truly a mutiny of senses. Mutineers engaged in a concerted effort to visually and aurally enrich and transform their sensual environment so as to make and spread a mutiny. This promised to free the senses from the alien experience of war and intervention on foreign soil or seas. Two years afterwards, though tempered by anxiety about its reversal, one mutineer articulated very clearly this sensory liberation of the day that the *France* set sail for home:

> On our way! 23 April! Unforgettable date, catastrophic date. Everywhere is radiant. And the sun, and the light, blue everywhere. The sky blue, pure blue, the blue of dreams ...[133]

Yet, at the same time, sensory analysis repeatedly uncovers its own limits, namely its connections to emotions, memory and reason. In this way, the prominence of the senses (or at least two of them) prompts new lines of enquiry. What happens from the 'outside in' begs the question how this stimulates a response from the 'inside out'. In other words, if sensory perception features in testimony, this requires an exploration of its relation to memory as well as how the senses interact with affective-cognitive aspects of mutineer consciousness. From the viewpoint of the latter problem, the senses drew in revolutionary sights and sounds (notably the *Internationale* and the red flag), which undermines an interpretation of the mutinies as a simple transposition of conventional industrial relations into the military sphere as with Guy Pedroncini's influential reading of the Chemin des Dames mutinies of 1917.[134] Moreover, mutineers did not just see and hear a mutiny, they were producers of the visual and sonic signs of mutiny through improvisation and mutineer agency.

Notes

1. Michel Serres, *The Five Senses: A Philosophy of Mingled Bodies* (London: Continuum, 2008).
2. David Howes (ed.), *Empire of the Senses: The Sensual Culture Reader* (Oxford: Berg, 2005), pp. 1–7.
3. Alain Corbin, *Le Miasme et la Jonquille: L'Odorat et L'Imaginaire Social xviiie-xixe* (Paris: Aubier Montaigne, 1982).
4. Mark M. Smith, 'Producing sense, consuming sense, making sense: perils and prospects for sensory history', *Journal of Social History*, 40, 4 (2007), pp. 841–58.
5. *La Vague*, 18 August 1919.
6. CHSP CT1 Tondut to Tillon, 7 March 1967.
7. Jean Norton Cru, *Du Témoinage* (Paris: Allia, 2008), p. 21. On the truthfulness of the trenches and the 'tyranny' of the witness, Henri Barbusse, *Le Feu:*

Journal d'une Escouade (Paris: Flammarion, 1965). Henri Barbusse, *Paroles d'un Combattant: Articles et Discours 1917-20* (Paris: Flammarion, 1920). Jean Norton Cru, *Témoins: Essai d'Analyse et de Critique des Souvenirs de Combattants Édités en Français de 1915 à 1928* (Paris: Les Étincelles, 1929). César Fauxbras, *Jean Le Gouin: Journal d'un Simple Matelot de la Grande Guerre* (Louviers: Éditions l'Ancre de Marine, 2004). Frédéric Rousseau, *Le Procès des Témoins de la Grande Guerre: l'Affaire Norton Cru* (Paris: Seuil, 2003). Stéphane Audoin-Rouzeau and Annette Becker, *14-18 Understanding the Great War* (New York: Hill and Wang, 2002).

8 On the history of the senses in general, David Howes and Constance Classen, *Ways of Sensing: Understanding the Senses in Society* (New York: Routledge, 2013), pp. 11-13. Constance Classen, *Worlds of Sense: Exploring the Senses in History and Across Cultures* (London: Routledge, 1993). Constance Classen, David Howes and Anthony Synnott, *Aroma: The Cultural History of Smell* (New York: Routledge, 2002). Mark Michael Smith, *Sensory History* (Oxford: Berg, 2007). George H. Roeder, 'Coming to our senses', *Journal of American History*, 81, 3 (1994), pp. 1112-22.

9 David Michael Levin (ed.), *Modernity and the Hegemony of Vision* (Berkeley: University of California Press, 1993). Martin Jay, *Downcast Eyes: The Denigration of Vision in Twentieth-Century French Thought* (Berkeley: University of California Press, 1993). Marshall McLuhan, *The Gutenburg Galaxy* (Toronto: University of Toronto Press, 1962), p. 42.

10 McLuhan, *Gutenburg*, p. 26. David Howes, "Culture tunes our neurones", in Howes (ed.), *Empire*, pp. 21-4, p. 23.

11 Howes (ed.), *Empire*, p. 129.

12 Steven Rose, *The Making of Memory: From Molecules to Mind* (London: Vintage, 2003), pp. 195-7.

13 Alain Corbin, 'Charting the cultural history of the senses', in Howes (ed.), *Empire*, pp. 128-40, p. 133.

14 ADSSD AM 281J V 3.16 Albert Cornier to Marty, May 1934.

15 Janice Carlisle, 'The smell of class: British novels of the 1860s', *Victorian Literature and Culture*, 29, 1 (2001), pp. 1-19. Pamela Fox, *Class Fictions: Shame and Resistance in the British Working-Class Novel, 1890-1945* (Durham, NC: Duke University Press, 1994). Dominique Memmi, Gilles Raveneau and Emmanuel Taïeb (eds), *Le Social à L'Épreuve du Dégoût* (Rennes: Presses Universitaires de Rennes, 2016).

16 ADSSD AM 281J I B1 André Marty, *Affaire du Protet (Marty-Badina) Galatz*, 12 August 1919, pp. 3-4.

17 Walter Benjamin, *Selected Writings, Volume 4: 1938-40* (Cambridge: Harvard University Press, 2003), p. 392.

18 SHD 20 N 770 Weekly report of events, 29 March 1919.

19 ADSSD AM 281J VI D2 91-2 Lucien Godin, *Carnet de route*.

20 SHD SS Ed 30 Commander of the *Jean Bart*, Secret report on the incidents on the *Jean Bart*, 19-23 April.

21 SHD SS Ed 30 Commander of the *Jean Bart*, Secret report on the incidents on the *Jean Bart*, 19–23 April.
22 ADSSD AM 281J I B1 André Marty, *Affaire du Protet (Marty-Badina) Galatz: 16 April 1919*, 12 August 1919, p. 37.
23 Marty, *Révolte* (1948), p. 51.
24 ADSSD AM 281J II D2.29–30 Duport.
25 ADSSD AM 281J VI D1.7 Notta.
26 ADSSD AM 281J VI D2.63–4 R. Nouveau, *De Toulon à Calvi par Odessa*.
27 Le Ramey and Vottero, *Mutins*, p. 51.
28 ADSSD AM 281J III D2.3 Leva, 29 November 1930.
29 ADSSD AM 281J IV D1.20 Jean Carrière to editor of *Ordre Communiste*, 27 September 1921.
30 SHD SS Ed 30 Admiral Lejay, Report on the demonstration of 20 April 1919, 27 April 1919.
31 Also not the black of anarchism.
32 SHD 7N 393 Noulens telegram from Archangel, 24 November 1918.
33 ADSSD AM 281J IV E2.7 Report from the *Justice*.
34 *L'Humanité*, 31 October 1922.
35 SHD SS Ed 30 Commander of the *France* to Vice-Admiral Amet, 23 April 1919.
36 SHD SS Ed 30 Commander of the *Jean Bart*, Secret report on the incidents on the *Jean Bart*, 19–23 April.
37 ADSSD AM 281J V A3.11–12 Anon. (with Marty's marginal note stating 'A.B.') Épisode révolutionnaire de 1919.
38 *L'Humanité*, 31 October 1922.
39 On frame alignment, a concept within social movement theory, David A. Snow, E. Burke Rochford Jr, Steven K. Worden and Robert D. Benford, 'Frame alignment processes, micromobilization, and movement participation', *American Sociological Review*, 51, 4 (1986), pp. 464–81.
40 ADSSD AM 281J AM I B1 Marty, *Affaire*, p. 10.
41 Mark Michael Smith (ed.), *Hearing History: A Reader* (Athens: University of Georgia Press, 2004).
42 Sophia Rosenfeld, 'On being heard: a case for paying attention to the historical ear', *American Historical Review*, 116, 2 (2011), pp. 316–34. Jacques Rancière, *The Politics of Aesthetics: Distribution of the Sensible* (London: Bloomsbury, 2013). Jean-Rémy Julien, 'Paris: cris, sons, bruits: l'environnement sonore des années pré-révolutionnaires d'après Le Tableau de Paris de Sébastien Mercier', in Jean-Rémy Julien et Jean-Claude Klein (eds), *Orphée Phyrgien: Les Musiques de la Révolution* (Paris: Éditions du May, 1989), pp. 39–60. Vincent Milliot, *Les Cris de Paris, ou, Le Peuple Travesti: les Représentations des Petits Métiers Parisiens (XVIe-XVIIIe siècles)* (Paris: Publications de la Sorbonne, 1995).

43 On the supposed irrational and untrustworthy status of hearsay, Bernard J. Hibbitts, 'Making sense of metaphors: visuality, aurality, and the reconfiguration of American legal discourse', *Cardozo Law Review*, 16 (1994), pp. 229–356. Marianne Constable, *Just Silences: The Limits and Possibilities of Modern Law* (Princeton: Princeton University Press, 2009).
44 Karin Bijsterveld, 'The diabolical symphony of the mechanical age: technology and symbolism of sound in European and North American Noise Abatement Campaigns, 1900–40', *Social Studies of Science*, 31, 1 (2001), pp. 37–70.
45 According to McLuhan in Howes, 'Culture tunes our neurones', in Howes (ed.), *Empire*, p. 23.
46 Susan Stewart, 'Remembering the senses', in Howes (ed.), *Empire*, pp. 59–69. Criticising later Marx for losing the insights of Fourier and Feuerbach into the sensory dimension of human emancipation, David Howes, *Sensual Relations: Engaging the Senses in Culture and Social Theory* (Ann Arbour, MI: University of Michigan Press, 2003), pp. 204–34.
47 Gaetan Bruel, 'L'oreille amputée', in Florence Gétreau (ed.), *Entendre la Guerre: Silence, Musiques et Sons en 14–18* (Paris: Gallimard, 2014), pp. 120–7.
48 ADSSD AM 281J VI D2.24 François Perrone, *Memoire de la Mer Noire: Bord du Waldeck-Rousseau*, 28 January 1920.
49 Omer Bartov, *Murder in Our Midst: The Holocaust, Industrial Killing, and Representation* (New York: Oxford University Press, 1996).
50 Steve Goodman, *Sonic Warfare: Sound, Affect and the Ecology of Fear* (Cambridge: MIT Press, 2010).
51 Special issue on shell shock: *Journal of Contemporary History*, 35, 1 (2000).
52 Jean-Marie Roche, *Dictionnaire des Bâtiments de la Flotte de Guerre Française de Colbert à nos Jours: Tome II: 1870–2006* (France: Cloître, 2013), n.p.
53 Victor Gordon Kiernan, *European Empires from Conquest to Collapse, 1815–1960* (Bungay: Fontana, 1982), p. 125.
54 Bakhtin, *Dialogic Imagination*, pp. 270–1.
55 SS Ed 30 Lieutenant Commander (*Captaine de Corvette*) Valat, *État d'ésprit des équipages*, 13 May 1919.
56 ADSSD AM 281J III D2.29 Duport letter to parents, 25 April–1 May 1919.
57 ADSSD AM 281J IV D1.3 Notta.
58 ADSSD AM 281J III D2.12 Lachurie, *Vergniaud: Souvenirs d'un ancien matelot du cuirassé Vergniaud*.
59 ADSSD AM 281J VI C1.29 Ribot.
60 Thus, in his study of the Suyá people from Brazil, Seeger highlighted the association between, on the one hand, silence or quiet noise and conflict, and on the other, loud music with conflict resolution. Anthony Seeger, *Why Suyá Sing: A Musical Anthropology of an Amazonian People* (Urbana: University of Illinois Press, 2004), pp. 67–9, 86. Maarten Walraven, 'History and its acoustic context: silence, resonance, echo and where to

find them in the archive', *Journal of Sonic Studies*, 4, 1 (2013), http://journal. sonicstudies.org/vol04/nr01/a07. Adam Jaworski, *Silence: Interdisciplinary Perspectives* (Berlin: Mouton de Gruyter, 1997).
61 Esteban Buch, 'Silences de la Grande Guerre', in Florence Gétreau (ed.), *Entendre la guerre. Sons, musiques et silence en 14-18* (Paris: Gallimard, 2014), pp. 128-33.
62 R. Murray Schafer, 'Soundscapes and earwitnesses', in Smith (ed.), *Hearing*, pp. 128-33, p. 7.
63 Jay Winter, 'Thinking about silence', in Efrat Ben-Ze'ev, Ruth Ginio and J. M. Winter (eds), *Shadows of War: A Social History of Silence in the Twentieth Century* (Cambridge: Cambridge University Press, 2010), pp. 3-31.
64 Alain Corbin, *Histoire du Silence: de la Renaissance à nos jours* (Paris: Albin Michel, 2014), pp. 50-2.
65 Jean Chatard, *Les Marins: Chants des Équipages* (La Rochelle: La Décourance, 2011), p. 7.
66 Corbin, *Histoire du Silence*.
67 ADSSD AM 281J VI D2.19 François Perrone, *Mémoire de la Mer Noire*, deposition at the Maison Centrale de Melun, 28 January 1920.
68 ADSSD AM 281J VI C1.18 Eugène Ribot.
69 CHSP CT1 *Contre-Courrant*, n.d., c. 1953.
70 ADSSD AM 281J VI D2.19 François Perrone, *Mémoire de la Mer Noire*, deposition at the Maison Centrale de Melun, 28 January 1920.
71 ADSSD AM 281J VI D2.63 R. Nouveau, *De Toulon à Calvi par Odessa*.
72 ADSSD AM 281J IV E2.5 Battleship *Justice* commanded by Robin Vessel Captain, n.d.
73 Charles Tillon, *La Révolte Vient de Loin* (Paris: Juillard, 1969), p. 251.
74 ADSSD AM 281J IV E2.5 Battleship *Justice* commanded by Robin Vessel Captain.
75 ADSSD AM 281J III D2.30 Duport letter to parents, 25 April-1 May 1919.
76 ADSSD AM 281J IV D1.5 Notta.
77 ADSSD AM 281J VI D2.19 François Perrone, *Mémoire de la Mer Noire*, deposition at the Maison Centrale de Melun, 28 January 1920.
78 Peter Bailey, *Leisure and Class in Victorian England: Rational Recreation and the Contest for Control, 1830-1885* (Oxford: Routledge, 1978).
79 *L'Humanité*, 12 December 1922. In a series of memories '*Les insurgés de la mer Noire*' that Victor Méric assembled from Badina, Vottero, Champale and Fracchia 'and other rebels' from 12 October 1922 until 1 January 1923.
80 ADSSD AM 281J III D2.34 Duport letter to parents, 25 April-1 May 1919. ADSSD AM 281J IV D1.5 Notta.
81 ADSSD AM 281J III D2.29 Duport letter to parents, 25 April-1 May 1919.
82 ADSSD AM 281J VI D2.96 Lucien Godin (Bruix), Extract of a travel diary (*carnet de route*), 30 March-22 May 1919.
83 ADSSD AM 281J III D2.8 Marius Jules Cyrille to Marty, 2 March 1931 (extracts of a notebook of the journey, cahier de route).

84 ADSSD AM 281J VI D2.65-6 R. Nouveau, *De Toulon à Calvi par Odessa*.
85 ADSSD AM 281J VI D2 19 François Peronne, *Memoire de la Mer Noire*, 28 August 1920.
86 Le Ramey and Vottero, *Mutins*, p. 90.
87 R. Murray Schafer, *The Soundscape: Our Sonic Environment and the Tuning of the World* (Rochester, VT: Destiny Books, 1993).
88 Volosinov, *Marxism*, p. 23.
89 Vygotsky, *Thought and Language*, pp. 217-19.
90 Bakhtin, *Dialogic Imagination*, p. 288. For the application of Bakhtin to music see Ken Hirschkop, 'The classical and the popular: musical form and social con-text', in Christopher Norris (ed.), *Music and the Politics of Culture* (London: Lawrence and Wishart, 1989), pp. 283-304.
91 François Dechlette, *L'Argot des Poilus: Dictionnaire Humoristique et Philologique* (Paris: Éditions de Paris, 2004).
92 James C. Scott, *Weapons of the Weak: Everyday Forms of Peasant Resistance* (Dehli: Oxford University Press, 1990).
93 *L'Humanité*, 13 December 1922.
94 Being one of the demands of the mutineers that this tyrant was disembarked immediately, ADSSD AM 281J VI D2.64 R. Nouveau, *De Toulon à Calvi par Odessa*.
95 ADSSD AM 281J IV E1.6 Eugène Lefort, *Souvenirs sur les événements de la Mer Noire*.
96 ADSSD AM 281J VI D4.59 Marceau Vergua, *L'armée française a l'oeuvre en orient, 1914-1919*, 14 January 1931.
97 ADSSD AM 281J VI C1.31 Ribot.
98 SHD SS Ed 30 Lieutenant Commander (*Du Chayle*) to Commander (*Captaine de Frégate*), 26 January 1919.
99 Chatard, *Marins*, p. 7.
100 Jean-Marie Cassagne, *Le Grand Dictionnaire de l'Argot Militaire* (Paris: Éditions LBM, 2007), p. 251.
101 Fauxbras, *Jean Le Gouin*. The Communist Party produced a periodical for sailors with this title.
102 Cassagne, *Grand Dictionnaire*, p. 233. It should also be noted that this slang included an ethnicised slang for nationalities and races, as well as sexualised heteronormative slang degrading women and homosexuals. References to such terms in mutineer testimony are relatively limited. For the police surveillance of bars frequented by homosexuals, sailors and communists in the ports of France, AN F7 13960.
103 Guigni, McAdam and Tilly, *How Social Movements Matter*, pp. 260-1.
104 ADSSD AM 281J IV E2.22 Mauence (*Justice*) to Marty, 31 August 1924.
105 P. Rolland, *Odessa: Les Mutins de la Mer Noire* (Paris: Bureau d'Éditions, 1927), p. 16.

106 On seizures of 'quite bolshevik' literature that included songs, SHD SS Ed 30 Enseigne de vaisseau Pirot to Rear Admiral Commander of the DNBO, 12 June 1919.
107 Masson, *Marine*, pp. 261, 268, 345–6. Raphael-Leygues and Barré, *Mutins*, pp. 26, 28, 30–1. Tico Jossifort, 'The Black Sea revolt', *Revolutionary History*, 8 (2002), pp. 99–114, p. 112. Le Ramey and Vottero, *Mutins*, p. 26.
108 Marty, *Révolte* (1949), pp. 20–1, 665–6.
109 Marty, *Révolte* (1949), p. 154.
110 Marty, *Révolte* (1949), p. 309.
111 André Marty and Raoul Calas, *A la Gloire des Lutteurs de 1907* (Montpellier: Impr. de Causse, Graille et Castelnau, 1947).
112 Marty, *Révolte*, p. 300.
113 André Marty, *Les Heures Glorieuses*, 1972 (a reprint of the 1949 edition), pp. 26–9. The songs that he lists are a little curious for, after the *Odessa Waltz* and *Fayots*, he cited three naval songs *La Complainte du Marin*, a song stretching back to the days of Colbert, *La Complainte des Compagnies de Discipline* and *Tu Leur Diras*, not apparently mentioned elsewhere. He catalogued the use of four political songs: *Hymn to the 17th*, *Marche Rouge*, *Grève des Mères* and *Jeune Garde*.
114 Tillon, *Révolte*, p. 48.
115 Tillon, *Révolte*, p. 81.
116 Tillon, *Révolte*, p. 84.
117 Tillon, *Révolte*, pp. 92–3.
118 ADSSD AM 281J III E 3.4–9 Jean Camille to Marty, 2 June 1926.
119 Le Ramey and Vottero, *Mutins*, p. 40.
120 ADSSD AM 281J III D2.5 Marius Jules Cyrille, Extracts of a notebook of the journey (cahier de route).
121 ADSSD AM 281J III E5. 3–8 J. Layarde statement.
122 ADSSD AM 281J III E 1.1 L. Hiarel, *Affaire de Smyrne*, March 1919, 5 February 1926. Smyrna is now Izmir.
123 Guigni, McAdam and Tilly, *How Social Movements Matter*.
124 ADSSD AM 281J III D2.26–35 Duport (of the *France*) to his parents, 25 April–1 May 1919.
125 ADSSD AM 281J VI C1.39 Notta, 5 November 1928.
126 ADSSD AM 281J VI C1.43 Notta, 5 November 1928.
127 Le Ramey and Vottero, *Mutins*, pp. 42–3.
128 Louis Barthas, *Poilu: The World War I Notebooks of Corporal Louis Barthas, Barrelmaker, 1914–1918* (New Haven, CT: Yale University Press, 2014), p. 326. Guy Marival, 'La chanson de Croanne. De la chanson palimpseste à la chanson manifeste', in Nicolas Offenstadt (ed.), *Le Chemin des Dames: de L'Événement à la Mémoire* (Paris: Stock, 2004), pp. 350–9.
129 ADSSD AM 281J III D2.12 Lachurie, *Vergniaud: Souvenirs d'un ancien matelot du cuirassé Vergniaud*, 7 May 1929.

130 SHD SS Ed 30 Amet report, p. 4, quoted in Masson, *Marine*, p. 260.
131 ADSSD AM 281J IV E2.3 Captain Cazenau, Report on the incidents that were produced on the 19–21 April 1919.
132 ADSSD AM 281J IV E2.8 Captain Cazenau, Report on the incidents that were produced on the 19–21 April 1919.
133 *L'Humanité*, 13 December 1922.
134 Pedroncini, *Les Mutineries de 1917*.

2

Mutinous emotion

The emotions of mutineers contributed to their subjectivity 'from the inside out', being their inner responses to the world around them, forming a circuit with their sensory experience and shaping the way that they interacted with their environment.[1] The passage of time and the selection of words mediated the raw emotion of the mutiny, rendering historical analysis a fragile business. The difficulties of reading emotions from their retrospective literary expression notwithstanding, certain emotions emerge during the process of revolt with witnesses particularly recalling anger, joy, hope, shame, fear and despair. Within this affective spectrum, these emotions hold specific relationships to the phases and dynamics of contentious politics. This offers a means of understanding the emotionality of protest rather than simply discounting it.[2]

Military and naval emotionologies

Reading the contemporary work of the Historical Service of the Navy, or the memoirs of admirals, divulges a stylised set of emotional rules.[3] Peter and Carol Stearns pioneered the scrutiny of such normative affective frames through the concept of emotionology.[4] The Navy's emotional code signalled a cultural hangover from the old regime, drawing on the honorific, martial and masculine rules of the nobility. Naval hierarchies were ones where status implied honorific emotional norms, resulting in an interdependent play of pride, respect, shame and humiliation.[5] This emotionology entailed extreme emotional repression: bravery as the suppression of fear, abnegation in service of France and a denial of the power of death. In this sense, it overlapped with the rest of the armed forces but with a particular intensity and some specifically maritime features. This persistence transcended a purely discursive association with an aristocratic past, given the sociology of the naval officer class, which had the greater proportion of those from noble families than the other services.[6] With biting hostility, mutineer Jean Carrière described officers as swordsmen (*'sabreurs'*) to denote their aristocratic mentality and background.[7]

The Navy also hoped to channel emotional release through the dutiful performance of sentimentalism before its institutional symbols and rituals. The emotional repression of the Navy manifested in the prison metaphors common in mutineer testimony. Leva of the *Patrie*, and Marius Cyrille of the *Vergniaud*, described their battleships as 'floating penal colonies' (*bagnes flottantes*).[8] A *Jean Le Gouin* (the nickname for an average sailor) wrote of the 'white terror' being exercised in the Navy with a repression of the freedom of opinion and arrests for defeatist talk. He described Toulon's maritime prison as 'the most sinister bastille that ever existed'.[9] In a poignant letter, Ernest Duport's declaration of love for his parents contrasts with his account of the naval authority's regime of 'terror' and of the contest of anger and fear between the officers and the ranks during the mutiny.[10] Helmsman Pierre Vottero described the failures of efforts of the mutineers to resist arrests on the *Voltaire* as 'others froze with fear'.[11]

The Navy expected comportment from its officers and its ranks that entailed considerable 'emotional management'.[12] For the ranks, this most obviously consisted of respect for higher authority, obedience, following orders, courage in the face of the enemy or danger and being willing to die heroically for country.[13] For the officers, it meant following such conventions as the captain remaining aboard his sinking ship and the value of an officer's word of honour.[14]

The honorific dimension of the emotional-cognitive relations between the officers and the crew appeared in testimony in a variety of ways. The Navy's honorific emotionology created an evident paradox for sailors who were also citizens.[15] According to the republican ideal, status hierarchies of such kinds should have dissolved in the free association of equal citizens. Albert Cornier wrote with bitter sarcasm about the 'bully' (*brute*) General Franchet d'Espèrey, the Commander of the Army of the Orient, as a 'worthy representative of the France of the Rights of Man and the Citizen' who occupied Istanbul and jailed the trade unionists.[16] This republican ideology intersected with class awareness, notions of the dignity of labour and the independence of the worker. Sailors thus felt the assertion of superior rank in the particular way that the officers did to be humiliating. Indeed, the entire apparatus of control and disciplinary routine earned the term '*brimades*' (humiliations) from the sailors, being designed to instil a sense of inferiority unworthy of a French citizen or worker. These were a profoundly felt 'hidden injury of class'.[17] Thus, Lucien Godin of the battlecruiser *Bruix* entered in his diary: '11 May. Still the same monotonous and absurd life of military service. Labour duty remains.'[18]

Emotional boundaries separated the officers and crews. Lefort of the *Jean Bart* recalled that when it became apparent that the officers, who were preparing for war against Soviet Russia, were joyous and tried to drill into their sceptical sailors that the Bolsheviks were their worst enemies.[19] Some mutineer testimony expressed a raw hatred towards the officers that was inflected with class consciousness. Thus, François Mauence of the battleship *Justice* fumed with contempt for the officers: 'the doddery Lejay, useless as an admiral, seconded by Ship's Captain Robin, a man of the church, […] these cretins of the cosmopolitan aristocracy.'[20] In unguarded moments, officers could reciprocate this hatred. Thus, the 'nervy and nasty' ('*énervé et méchant*') Lieutenant Commander Jean-Marie Gauthier de Kermoäl could not dissemble his 'terrible hatred' ('*haine terrible*') of the accused during the court martial of the mutineers of the *France*.[21] In Marty's memoir of his court martial, he recounted the hatred towards him of the officers of the *Protet*, his commander and those Non-Commissioned Officers (NCOs) close to the bridge.[22] In the mutiny's embarrassing aftermath (for conservative opinion), this hatred generalised across the right-wing press, which routinely designated him 'the traitor Marty'. Hostility to the industrial working class inflected official explanations of the mutiny. Vice-Admiral Henri Salaun perceived the lack of officers to be a catalyst of discontent and the boiler rooms with their proletarian recruitment to be the Achilles heel of naval authority.[23] In his report into the 'crisis of discipline' in the Navy written in July 1919, Rear-Admiral Charles Henri Dumesnil worried about the influence of 'too many young recruits from the centre of France, coming from industrial areas and most often to avoid the trenches'.[24]

More normally, the officers maintained a veneer of formality (as with the patrician language that infantilised the sailors), obscuring such feelings through a mannered emotional discourse. Dumesnil's report illustrates how the Navy understood discipline along an authoritarian-paternalistic axis from strictness to overindulgence. He believed that, in response to circumstances of war-weariness, officers had indulged the crews, blaming the overly paternalistic approach, which anti-militarist or anarchist propaganda had exploited.[25] Paternalism pervaded French society (represented as the fatherland '*patrie*'), reinforcing and legitimising its naval or military variants. While the military caste of mind drew on aristocratic ideals of honorific noble obligation, French industrial elites exercised paternalistic practices, often informed by social Catholicism.[26] Indeed, the French labour movement (or at least secular sections of it) challenged employer paternalism in efforts to develop class consciousness in the face of expectations of company loyalty. Moreover, French paternalism had a global reach, framing its colonial power relations.[27] Ultimately, paternalism's ideological persuasiveness rested upon the most apparently natural and taken-for-granted of all institutions and the one with the greatest claim to emotional intimacy: the family and the authority of the father within that.[28] Thus, under the affective mask of paternalism, military, gender, colonial and class oppression entangled.

Various mutineer testimonies objected to these habits of the officer class. Entering prison in Istanbul, alongside other mutineers of the battleship *Condorcet*, Albert Cornier registered their collective sensitivity to infantilisation when their new prison chief gave them a patronising speech ('*jeune père de famille*').[29] When an officer of the *Jean Bart* prevented a delegation of the *France* from boarding his ship, he called his interlocutor 'my boy'.[30] The commanders and the Admiral routinely addressed the crews as 'my children', failing to understand the extent to which this antagonised the sailors. The humiliations of class, rank and paternalism were so deeply engrained that when the officers tactically appealed to delegates as equals, efforts failed. Such was the case when the Chief Engineer shook Duport's hand and described him as 'an honest man'. Likewise, the Commander-in-Second Le Febvre appealed to Duport to 'speak to me as you would your older brother'. The delegate later bitterly recalled their earlier exchange, in which Duport had requested to see his brother on the *Justice*. Le Febvre had upbraided him for not standing to attention and had refused the request. When Jules-Aimé Robez-Pagillon, the Commander of the *France*, tried to placate Duport with a cigarette and a handshake, the former clumsily continued to address the delegate as 'my boy'.[31] Manhood was thus a contested terrain in the dual sense of gender and adulthood. Only when the mutineers felt that they had won did the symbolism and language of equality become meaningful for them. When the coal had been loaded without the supervision of the officers and the *France* was returning home, the delegates cordially shook the Commander's hand; and indicating the changed relationship, they did not salute him. Similarly, in Toulon, on 11 June, the sailors refused to form ranks and salute the Admiral, going into the town instead and 'royalist officers [previously] so swaggering and so hard towards the sailors became models of kindness'.[32]

Mutineer testimony also discloses the feeling of shame of having to perform demeaning tasks. For the sailors, these duties denoted servile status inappropriate for a citizen, a free man or in some cases a skilled worker. Scholars have noted the intrinsic nexus between shame or its absence and class relations.[33] Albert Cornier of the *Condorcet* refused to eat food that should not even be fed to pigs. Invoking his status as a citizen when a superior challenged him, he asked why his taxes were being spent on everything apart from adequate food for himself.[34] Shame shaped the way mutineers measured their own and their officers' behaviour against the latter's honorific pretention. The atrocities that the French military were committing undermined their moral authority. This resulting in the loss of 200 civilian lives according to Bolshevik sources, the French naval bombardment of Kherson of 16 March featured in several mutineer accounts. Indeed, Marty reproduced a touched-up photograph purporting to show victims of the atrocity. By the end of May 1919, letters from soldiers and sailors who participated in the intervention were appearing in *La Vague* detailing the atrocities. These letters articulated the deep indignation and antagonism to the officers deemed responsible for the atrocities conducted against Russian civilians, particularly reporting eye-witness accounts of brutality against women and children as well as summary executions.[35] The emotional language of the witnesses was not arbitrary, being framed in civilisational, aristocratic and republican terms.[36] For Roger Benoist, an encounter with a francophone Russian led him to understand the 'ignoble' role that the government was making his peers play.[37] Raymond Dufour observed that 'facing these horrors [...] I have retained such a profound disgust'.[38] Lucien Godin of the *Bruix* situated his feelings within France's official justification for the Great War and its imperial civilising mission:

> I am astonished now to belong to the same fatherland as these *depraved* individuals who by their actions have just *lowered* themselves to the same point as the vandals from across the Rhine. Here are a few words, the summary of the *shameful* work accomplished by men of a country which is represented in the world as being one of the champions of civilisation.

He returned to the theme: 'Oh how *shameful* for a country which bestows its *honour* into the hands of such *depraved* men (my italics).'³⁹ Hiarel of the *république*-class battleship *Démocratie* believed that the officers behaved 'outrageously' in an 'orgy' with Izmir's (Smyrna) high society.⁴⁰ In Marty's unpublished memoir of his court martial, he talked of the shameful lie that the Commander spread about Marty being a disciplinarian with his juniors.⁴¹

This dialectic of honour–shame insinuated itself into episodes about which many mutineers reminisced bitterly: the officers' words of honour. Such a focus for testimony is particularly pertinent to those, like Reddy or Bakhtin, who deployed speech act theory to understand emotion.⁴² The word of honour is an example of what John L. Austin called an illocutionary act, namely a category of word (promises, threats, denials, etc.) that changes the social circumstance.⁴³

Robez-Pagillon, the Commander of the *France*, promised that there would be no punishments if the coal was loaded on Easter Monday. Duport recalled and apparently quoted the Commander verbatim:

> My boy, we set sail tomorrow at 9am, we must set sail, I count on you for that ... Ah! If I can return to France with my command, if I can return to France with my ship, and nobody can see these things that have happened these four days, I will throw in the sponge on all that has happened and I promise you on my word of honour, that there will be no sanction taken against anyone.⁴⁴

Duport recommended compliance with this deal because of the Commander's honorific mentality, who Duport believed would use force against the crew if dishonoured and cornered. Writing before his arrest, Duport's letter to his parents concluded upon the point that they had the word of the Admiral and the General Staff and that therefore the matter should conclude without punishment for any crew member. Another delegate of the *France*, Notta also underlined the Commander's word of honour, which 'reassured them a little' despite sensing a trap when they were deciding whether to return to France without the other battleships.⁴⁵ In a letter to Marty, Émile Pleurot (another mutineer of the *France*) also confirmed that he had heard the Commander's and the Commander-in-Second's words of honour that there would be no punishment of the crew.⁴⁶ Mutineers attempted to use this guarantee in their defence at court martial. During Robez-Pagillon's court-martial deposition, Virgile Vuillemin intermittently requested the opportunity to challenge the Commander on this point. Eventually, Vuillemin asked the Commander if he remembered guaranteeing the crew that there would be no punishment. Vuillemin stated that he had said at the time: 'Commander, you do not have the right to give your word of honour. You have five stripes. But come one of your superiors, you will fall into line.' The Commander had promised that he would be the greatest defender of his crew. In response to Vuillemin's account, Robez-Pagillon denied giving his word but corroborated the rest.[47] Whether Captain Hippolyte Gauthier de Kermoäl had sworn that the delegates would not face punishment also arose at the court martial of the *France*. This was not just an issue regarding the *France*.

For François Mauence of the *Justice*, his faith in the Admiral's word of honour was the greatest mistake of his life.[48] With the revolt on the *Waldeck-Rousseau*, a week after that aboard the *France*, François Perrone recalled how the mutineers demanded (and duly received) the Admiral's word of honour on two counts: first, that they would return to France within the fortnight and, second, that there would be no punishments.[49] Nouveau, also of the *Waldeck-Rousseau*, noted that some mutineers disbelieved the Admiral, were reluctant to return to France and sarcastically later observed how the Admiral 'respected' his word of honour when the punishments came.[50] For Lucien Godin of the *Bruix*, the honorific guarantee carried such weight that he confided the exchange between the crew's delegate Leading Seaman fusilier Lombart and their Commander to his travel diary:

> *Commander:* Leading Seaman, you seem to have a lot of influence on the crew. Can you give me your word of honour that nothing will be tried as a general response?
> *Lombard:* Commander, give me your word of honour that all that has happened aboard will not be sent to the ministry.
> *C:* Yes. I give you my word.
> *L:* Commander, is it to the man that I speak or to the officer?
> *C:* To the officer.
> *L:* That's very good for if you had replied it is to the man, I would have asked to talk to the officer. Commander, I can guarantee you that nothing will be attempted for 8 days, after then I can no longer reply for the mentality of the crew.
> *C:* And if I promised […]
> *L:* I would not change my opinion, Commander and neither the English squadron nor the Japanese canons would make me back down. Then, as during the war, each will know how to die at his post, and you will see that

we will know how to die bravely and this will be an example for the whole of France, we are ready for anything.⁵¹

Eugène Lefort of the *Jean Bart* also emphasised his Commander's word of honour in response to the landing party's refusal to go on grenade exercises in Sevastopol. Captain Henri du Couëdic de Kerérant swore that there would be no punishments and, apparently unusually, stuck to this commitment. Lefort reflected, however, that du Couëdic was the only officer he had encountered who was honest in his four years of service.⁵²

The emotionology of the naval hierarchy thus set certain parameters for the emotional course of the mutiny. The subversion of these emotional conventions signalled how profoundly the mutiny transformed attitudes. If learnt rules were broken, or proved to be illusory, indeed ideological, then the Navy's emotionology became the open terrain of contentious politics and learning. Mutineers learnt to make their own emotional rules, or see through and rewrite those of their officers. Thus, former mutineer Mauence inverted the social hierarchy through the language of deference 'bowing before' the 'privileged' victims of the court martial: Marty and Badina.⁵³ Equally, Eugène Lefort recalled a 'little known accident' on the day that Admiral Amet received General Louis Franchet d'Espèrey on his flagship the *Jean Bart*. When the ship's Commander walked down the gangway to greet the General, the former was swept into the sea, which was particularly rough that day. Lefort observed that a sailor saved the Commander, diving into the waves despite the cold. Pointedly giving the Commander his full title and aristocratic surname 'Vessel Captain Du Couedic de Kerezan [sic]', contrasts both his humbling helplessness, having broken his arm in the fall, and the anonymous sailor's courage.⁵⁴

Body and mind in breaking emotional norms: fear and anger

Joanne Burke observed that '[h]istory is saturated with emotions, of which fear may be one of the most relentless. It is at the heart of historical struggle'.⁵⁵ Fear and its associated words (*peur, alarme, crainte, frousse, inquiétude, effroi, frayeur, lâchété, trouille, terreur, pétoche, épouvante*) reappear more frequently than any other word group in the emotional lexicons of mutineers. Within emotion scholarship, fear alongside anger occupies a special place.[56] For those who look to evolution to explain the emergence of human emotions, these are treated as primary emotions drawn from an animal fight-or-flight mechanism.[57] From the physiological standpoint, this mechanism consists of the adrenal glands, located at the top of the kidneys, pumping the hormones adrenaline and noradrenaline into the blood stream. The hormone acts as a stimulant increasing heart rate and blood flow. This results in several physiological effects noticeable and translated as the signs of fear (*avoir peur au ventre*) or anger. In both English and French languages, idioms emphasise the visuality of fear and anger: being 'red with rage' (*être vert de rage, écumer de rage, colère noire*) or 'white with fear' (*peur bleu*).[58] Given this cross-linguistic resonance, fear and anger pose the question of relationship of the body and emotion in an acute manner. These emotions provide a useful way to explore the influential psychological theory of emotion that William James pioneered that sees emotion as a somatic response to changes in the body, namely that the bereaved grieve because they cry.

A few mutineer accounts registered the bodily manifestations of emotions, notably with examples when weapons rendered a palpable threat to life. Such was the case when a Greek soldier drew a revolver on a Russian 'red' who was talking to some French mutineers in a café in Sevastopol. Eugène Lefort recalled how his blood chilled at the sight.[59] Likewise, when Robez-Pagillon, the Commander of the *France*, read the letter from the 175th Infantry regiment addressed to the 'soviet government aboard the *France*' in front of Vuillemin and the other delegates, the former displayed the bodily dimensions of fear, visibly trembling and turning pale.[60] After the coal was loaded on Tuesday 22 April, the Commander called for Vuillemin at 8 p.m. With revolver in hand and the Commander-adjoint and the Commander-in-Second by his side, Robez-Pagillon told Vuillemin that the delegates were no longer in charge and that he had retaken authority of his own ship. In the meeting that ensued with the crew at 6.30 a.m., it was Vuillemin who displayed corporeal signs of emotion, going pale and trembling with indignation.[61] According to Albert Cornier of the battleship *Condorcet*, many sailors had procured revolvers to stage an armed revolt but missed the moment because they 'chickened out'.[62] The term '*dégonfler*' suggested a lack of manliness via the image of animalistic display in unsuccessful competition between males for females, being the opposite of 'sticking one's chest out'. According to Nouveau, the chests of the crew filled as they confronted the Commander of the *Waldeck-Rousseau*.[63] Such evidence seems to support Charles Darwin's view that the continuities between animal display and human emotional expression indicated the evolutionary underpinning of human emotion.[64] Alex Barillon, another mutineer of the *Waldeck-Rousseau*, recalled his hairs stood on end at the thought of the conflict descending into bloodshed.[65] Describing a feeling of being overwhelmed during the mutiny on the *France*, Notta recalled his own reaction to fearful rumours, suffering a headache, blanching and going below deck to avoid the intolerable atmosphere.[66] When the Cheif Engineer unsuccessfully intervened with Duport, again aboard the *France*, with instructions for the crew to go below deck after their meal, he grew pale and withdrew.[67]

The physical manifestation of emotion allowed protagonists to read the emotions of others, both friend and foe. When the crew of the *Waldeck-Rousseau* revolted on 27 April, they approached the Commander, after having manhandled the Captain-at-Arms. Nouveau highlighted the bodily manifestation of emotional dynamics between mutineers and their superiors: the Commander with 'anger in his eyes' expressed his injured pride and arrogance. In turn, the crew's anger allowed them to pose him an ultimatum, with fear being inscribed on the officers' faces.[68]

Whether loss of composure or knowing performance, Robez-Pagillon, the Commander of the *France*, displayed bodily emotion both during the revolt and in the court martial. On the first occasion, tears rolled down his face as he begged for calm and the withdrawal of the red flag, with the effect that Duport had the flag taken down.[69] Later, during the military tribunal, Robez-Pagillon begged in lachrymose fashion for the court's indulgence towards the delegates but could never forgive the 'hooligans' who seized the rowboat or who raised the red flag.[70]

On occasion, mutineers sought to control physically their emotional reactions to events. Another radical veteran of the intervention, Salvarelli recalled squeezing his fists with rage during the naval bombardment of Novorossisk of 25–27 March 1921.[71] Similarly, repression of bodily manifestations of emotion featured also in Lefort's testimony. He noted that when his landing party was refusing orders and absent without leave in Sevastopol, they controlled their biliousness when they heard of patrols searching for them. Obviously, here as elsewhere, we encounter the difficultly of discriminating between bodily metaphors of emotion versus the genuine physiological responses that at some point may have underpinned the verbal construction, adding an element of provisionality to our assessments.

Most mutineer testimonies neglected emotion's bodily expression. Such manifestations occupy an interpretative dilemma concerning the study of emotions.[72] Privileging evidence of bodily manifestation of emotion (as the James-Lange organic theory of emotion would suggest) seriously limits the scope of the historical investigation. What is noticeable is not only the rarity of reflections upon the bodily manifestations of emotion but also that witnesses recall a much narrower range of emotions corporeally, notably fear (and to a lesser extent anger). If the 'body-first' or organic theory yields limited purchase upon the evidence of mutineer subjectivity, its opponents such as Reddy or the Bakhtin school, or social movement scholars, would point either in the direction of a somatic, mind-first, language-centred approach or as a dialectic of mind and body.

The relationship between fear and terror highlights the problematic translation between subjective emotional processes and language. Synonyms were not interchangeable in a straightforward way. 'Terror' featured repeatedly in mutineer vocabulary but less so than its synonym 'fear'. The influence of the language of the day infused terror with meaning. Indeed, one mutineer – a *'Jean le Gouin'* in a letter to *La Vague* – wrote of the 'white terror' being exercised in the Navy.[73] During the Russian Civil War, beginning in Finland with massacres of Social Democrats, white terror denoted the actions of the volunteer army of counter-revolutionaries in former Tsarist territories and beyond, notably in Hungary. This occurred against the red–white contest of terror and counter-terror and its propaganda representations, seeking to delegitimise opponents through the exposure or manufacture of atrocity. The use of the term 'terror' in a more general way might also prompt associations with the revolutionary episodes of the previous century such as the Chouan or Jacobin terrors or the repression of the Commune. Thus, the Commander of the *France* asserted in his report to the Vice-Admiral that three-quarters of the crew remained in their hammocks in terror throughout the events.[74] Conversely, Duport recorded the Navy's 'regime of terror' in his explanation of the revolt to his parents, wherein it was dangerous to be seen with a newspaper, even from the provincial press, given the fear on the part of the authorities of libertarian ideas.[75] This terror intensified in Odessa when his friend received thirty days' solitary confinement for leaving his post during watch duty.[76] Terror had a further connotation that would not escape those from a French revolutionary milieu: the use of political assassination, 'propaganda of the deed' and how this prompted the repression of 1894. Thus, the hidden meaning of the word terror derives from this contemporary connotation linking violence, terror and repression, thereby helping to explain the hesitations before the threshold of violence apparent in all the mutinies of 1919. More explicitly, Duport noted the fear of revolution amongst mutineers as their revolt spread from one battleship to another.

> The red flag is raised at the forward end of the ship. We applaud. The *Jean Bart* responds with a red flag. Would this be a revolution then? Everyone fears so.[77]

Such paradoxical reactions show the very complexity of emotions that escape Marty's *Révolte*. Fears mixed with other emotions and came from many different sources. On the day of the demonstration in Sevastopol, Duport feared for his brother Jean's life, who was a sailor aboard the battleship *Jean Bart*, believing that he may have been ashore and a victim of Greek machine guns.[78] Alex Barillon of the *Waldeck-Rousseau* wrote to Marty telling him of the joy when Perrone told him of plans to return to France but the latter's fear of confessing too much or being denounced.[79] Careful recall of lived experience offers a more dissonant mix of emotions less apt for didactic narrative than Marty's pure model of epic emotion.

Scholars of emotion face the dilemma of whether emotion is involuntary or performed (which is another way of expressing the distinction between body- or mind-first approaches to emotion). William James pioneered the organic theory of emotion, which suggested that emotions were mental responses to bodily perturbation (such as crying, the heart racing, etc.). Rendering this tradition more sophisticated, Antonio Damasio argues that such bodily changes register in the mind (as 'somatic markers') via evolutionary adaptation in a way to prompt sophisticated social reasoning and the exercise of decision-making.

Alternately, favouring emotion as utterance, William Reddy stressed the performative quality of emotional speech acts. In so doing, he adapted Austin's speech act theory – how words 'do things' – to emotions. Bakhtin in a 1975 essay makes a similar step from such utterances (oaths, promises, threats and the like) to their 'emotional-evaluative' character.[80] Despite the temptation to view all use of emotional words (or 'emotives') as a self-exploratory performance, as Reddy suggests, the mutiny provides a strong case for *instances* of this performative quality to such utterances. Emotional talk allowed rebels to perform fearlessness publicly and collectively conquer fear. Thus, Notta addressed the crew on hearing that the officers were arming themselves, saying that 'we are not afraid of a revolver', to hurrahs from his audience.[81] Other testimony suggests emotion was involuntary, even exercising control over actors. According to Jean Le Ramey, fear actually drove events, noting that fear impelled the officers to arm themselves when 700 sailors began to protest on deck on Saturday April 19 on the *France*.[82] A letter from Sevastopol to *La Vague* observed such was the fear of the Russian elites that they demeaned themselves, loading coal onto the French warships to speed their flight from the revolution. As they would otherwise never perform dirty manual work, the spectacle amused the correspondent greatly.[83] It would be speculative to read such references as evidence of emotions prompting behavioural reflexes and counter much of the testimony that insists on the intermediary of reason.

A third position might be found beyond Reddy's emotive as cultural performance and Damasio's evolutionary psychology. Indeed, mutineer testimony suggests such a solution. To use Arlie Hochschild's phrase, this 'emotional management' – rather than actual control – could be about disguising or simulating emotions.[84] Thus, according to Eugène Ribot, fear of the authorities discouraged mutineers from telling the truth and showing their emotions.[85] Equally, a contrast between Duport and Marty and their affective family bonds is instructive here. Duport engaged in an epistolary convention of sentimentalism when addressing his parents. In his parents' absence, he conjured an emotional literary performance, with expressions of love for his 'dearest' parents, begging for their sympathy and for them to believe him. He was concerned to justify his role in the mutiny to them.[86] Concluding that the Admiral's word of honour meant that there would be no punishment, Duport probably suspected otherwise at this stage, implying an emotional pretence intended to deceive his parents. Conversely, Marty suffered both the loss of his father and grandmother in September 1918 and February 1919 respectively. For Marty, his postponed affective response to family bereavement was a psychological denial, which was sufficiently powerful for his opponents to capitalise upon and suggest mental instability. So, unlike Duport's letter with its conventions of family intimacy, an unarticulated grief disrupted Marty's emotional self-control. Four months after the mutiny and after his two courts martial, Marty rehearsed his emotional state of mind prior to the mutiny in his notebook.[87] He wrestled to come to terms (in both senses of verbal expression and self-understanding) with the impact of grief upon him in these pages. He noted that his sense of duty and the situation on board had prevented him taking the necessary leave of absence to mourn his two losses. The juxtaposition of Duport and Marty indicates the inadequacy of explanations of emotion based on the dichotomies of speech act theory or evolutionary legacy. These alternatives of performed or involuntary emotion do not capture the dialectical quality of emotion, namely the more or less 'managed' axis of and tension between performative control to loss of self-control, between mind and body, or between evolution and culture.[88]

Anger has been at the centre of the dispute between anthropologists and evolutionary psychologists over emotions.[89] The latter connect anger, like fear, to the fight-or-flight mechanism and designate this amongst the 'primary', 'universal' emotions. Conversely, the anthropologist Jean Briggs, working amongst the Utku people, proposed that anger was a social construct and entirely absent from this culture. Further underlining its pertinence, anger has been a staple of the historiography of emotions.[90]

Anger certainly featured recurrently in mutineer testimony and in the historiography of the mutiny, therefore being of critical heuristic significance. Le Ramey noted several instances in the protest cycle. He remembered the fury ('*fureur*') of those who had served the entire war without significant leave and remained without a date for demobilisation. Furthermore, when a rumour spread in Istanbul on 29 March that the ship was sailing to the Black Sea, a 'great anger' spread on board.[91] Through his choice of words, he implied that the mutineers' passionate fury to be a force of nature, rather than being performed or voluntary: a 'wind of anger that shook the sailors' with the announcement of coal loading on Easter Sunday.[92] With the realisation that the authorities were dividing the crews in order to restore control when in Bizerte harbour, Le Ramey recalled another final wave of anger on board the *France*.[93] According to Duport, also of the *France*, the news of the Morskaïa Road shooting generated anger right across the battleships with demands for justice, the seizure of arms and retaliation.[94] In the exchanges between the mutinous assembly of sailors aboard the *France* and Vice-Admiral Amet, his anger was clearly visible.[95] In Émile Buffet's narrative, growing anger motivated the decision to refuse to 'march against brothers of same class'. Buffet, a veteran of the mutinies of 1917 and the Army of the Orient situated this anger within the Army's trope of 'morale', which might be best understood as an institutional cipher for the emotional self-management of the ranks. As far as Buffet was concerned, the general staff were responsible for the low morale that made even the most fanatical patriot ('*fanatique patriotard*') suddenly change his outlook.⁹⁶ He recalled the 'deaf anger' ('*colère sourde*') of troops stationed in camps near Salonika when rumours suggested that they were to join counter-revolutionary forces in Russia.⁹⁷ Mutineers, then, stressed the importance of anger and fear within the events, but did not provide a uniform interpretation of these emotions as either performed or involuntary.

Anger was more than an immediate reaction to unfolding events. The anger of officers was an emotional norm when sailors or soldiers did not behave as required. There was a performative quality to the response of officers to ill-discipline, this being part of the military's emotionology. Mutineer testimony recalled several examples. Army of the Orient veteran Émile Douchy heard on the day after the notorious event how a French officer, alongside a group of White Russian officers, had killed Jeanne Labourbe in a fit of rage.⁹⁸ Given the uncertainty of the claim of French involvement in her death, Douchy no doubt believed that the detail added plausibility to indirect testimony. Recalling Christmas Day 1918, Jean Camille of *Du Chayla* vividly remembered an officer's fury, screaming like a 'madman' when the crew refused inspection.⁹⁹ Lucien Godin, of the *Bruix*, registered the Commander's anger when informers told him that the crew had learnt of the Sevastopol revolt and were planning to emulate it.¹⁰⁰ Leva, who was by then a gardener, wrote to Marty in November 1930. He recalled the 'fury' of the 'instructing officers' ('*gradaille*') aboard his battleship *Patrie* as its crew and that of the *Jean Bart* refused orders to light the engine room furnaces.¹⁰¹ Those who courted such responses from the officers and possessed sufficient emotional management to withstand their behaviour were known as '*forte tête*' ('hard-headed').

Viewing the references to anger and fear within mutineer testimony as a whole, emotion manifestly suffused the mutiny at two levels. First, it signalled 'activation' or emotional attention and mobilisation of energies necessary to challenge authority. Indeed, the mutineers' anger or fear elicited an emotional response against which to measure opponents. Anger and fear, then, appeared to be necessary to break the emotionology of the French military, allowing the mutiny to emerge from within the mutineers themselves. Beyond that, the multiple iterations of these powerful emotions facilitated the extension or renewal of protest cycles. Second, emotion assisted in the communication and diffusion of the mutiny. Latent anger was clearly embedded in social relations and associated with meanings distinct to social groups within the Navy. If we are to concede to evolutionary psychology that anger did indeed possess a universal character, it was certainly culturally mediated, and if as cultural anthropologists insist, cultural difference constructs anger, this was a product of a long history whose common roots in an evolutionary past are now easily overlooked. Anger brought with it a host of cultural mediations and associations learnt in social conflict, political traditions and long-standing everyday grievances.

Hope, via joy to despair: the emotional patterns of contentious politics

If anger signalled an immediate response to opponents or events, a cluster of emotions – hope, happiness and joy – registered the emotional experience of actual or anticipated liberation.[102] Hope also featured in testimony and the cultural record of the mutiny. As those ashore disseminated the news of the mutiny on the *France*, an 'immense hope' spread amongst the sailors and soldiers in Sevastopol. A correspondent from Perpignan spoke of the infectious hope that the mutiny prompted:

> At the moment of the revolt of the sailors of the Black Sea, a formidable hope ran through the companies and the conversations followed at the same rhythm; the sentries of the German school at Pera watched to see if sailors would come to train us, we waited for Marty, the enthusiasm was high, one heard all the time: 'But, good, what are they waiting for to come to find us?'[103]

The trace of hope lingered in the mutiny's afterlife. Former engineer on the battleship *Voltaire*, Georges Wallet wrote a letter requesting to join the PCF still hoping that the day would come to join his comrades in the breech.[104] The song *Glory to the Sailors of the Black Sea* (1921) deemed revolutionary hope to be sacred.[105] This sacralisation served to reify and render timeless an ephemeral emotion that promised emancipation, thereby signalling its loss. The song recalled, ritualised and performed hope, whereas, during the mutiny, this emotion emerged from the affective flux of the protest cycle.

Some evidence pertained not so much to the quality but the intensity of emotion during the mutiny. Several French military personnel specifically remarked upon the emotional turbulence of the Revolution and Civil War. Historians of the American Revolution have recently pursued the heightened emotionality of events, believing that such revolutionary passion facilitated rather than precluded conscious agency and the exercise of reason.[106] Here Bakhtin's formulation of the 'emotional-volitional tone' within social dialogues links emotion to determination or willpower, proposing the motivational circuits between emotion, reason and action.[107] Aboard the *Condorcet*, Albert Cornier observed the 'overexcited' ('*surexcité*') mood at mealtimes when the detestable mussels served to trigger the revolt.[108] François Perrone recalled how, with Marty's incarceration aboard the *Waldeck-Rousseau* on 19 April, the ship was in an 'excited' and 'heightened' state.[109] Marty used the phrase 'general effervescence' for the same moment.[110] Eugène Ribot indicated a general mood of overexcitement (*surexcité*) amongst soldiers in late November 1918.[111] Pierre Vottero remarked on the great emotion of the reception amongst his colleagues aboard the *Voltaire* of the stories that the mutineers of the *France* had confined the officers to their cabins on the journey between the Black Sea and Bizerte.[112]

Viewed from above, explanations of this intensity of mutineer emotion drew on contemporary gendered notions of emotionality, irrationality and the femininity of the crowd.[113] Captain Robin's report into the events in Sevastopol of 19–21 April alluded to the affective state of the crews on several occasions. He infantilised them for their 'excitability', 'overexcitement' and 'state of emotion', which he tried to calm.[114] Throughout Robez-Pagillon's report, he underplayed the scale of the mutiny, identifying specific breeches of discipline that might be subject to court-martial proceedings. He dismissively attributed the events to overexcitement and nervousness.[115] He observed that in the aftermath of the Morskaïa Road incident, an emotional intensity seized the entire town.[116] Indicative of the emotional management that was expected from officers, the investigation into the events of 20 April praised Ensign Pommier for giving the order to shoot on the crowd on the grounds that he had followed procedure and displayed the appropriate emotion: the *sang-froid* of the officer.[117] This commendation went to the Supreme War Council of the Allies.

An emotional intensity spread with the wave of rebellion that reached French ports in the summer months. As the squadron revolted in the streets of Toulon on 11 June 'effervescence reigned'.[118] Indeed, testimonies suggest that the keyword 'calm' acts as a cipher, not so much for a tranquil acceptance of naval discipline amongst the crew, but for emotional repression and management. This illustrates how the shared bond of experience allowed sailors to listen for the mood, even when they could only hear silence, and how officers were oblivious to this emotional soundscape. Here Bakhtin's 'emotional-volitional tone' seems particularly apt. Emotion acts as an motivational catalyst for transcending individual capacities through collective action, opening possibilities considered hitherto impossible. Virgile Vuillemin, who was one of the three delegates aboard the *France*, provides a striking illustration. Following Marty's encouragement to address public meetings across France in 1921, Vuillemin replied that such things were against his nature. Only when emotion animated him (*'sous le coup d'une émotion'*) could Vuillemin harangue a crowd, as he had during the mutiny.[119] This is all the more remarkable given Huret and Ricros's depiction of Vuillemin as the uncowed hero of the court martial, whom the provincial newspaper *Petit Var* dubbed the 'orator of the accused'.[120]

Some testimony allows a diachronic scrutiny of emotion during the mutiny, through consideration of emotional sequences. These strings of emotions help to reconstruct the conscious process of revolt, showing the complex interaction of emotion and reason. Not all the testimonies are sufficiently rich to allow an insight into these sequences. Some note only one or two emotions. Nevertheless, several witnesses recalled the succession of two contrasting emotions, highlighting the intense juxtaposition of contradictory emotions. The most frequent instance of this emotional reversal was the way that the news of peace did not lead to demobilisation but to a new campaign of undefined nature in the East. Le Ramey opened his reminiscences with the 'great joy' that welcomed the Armistice. This enthusiasm cooled when he learnt on 8 December that they were sailing away from France. Lucien Godin noticed too the emotional reversal after the initial hope of the Armistice.[121] Likewise, Pierre Vottero of the *Voltaire* recalled how 'immense joy' became 'bitter disappointment' after 11 November.[122]

The idea of emotional sequence should not lead to the assumption of simple linearity. Sequential emotional exchanges took place between actors. Thus, when Duport reacted to the Commander of the *France*, whom the former believed to be insinuating bribery, the officer cautioned Duport not to get angry, which in turn saddened the delegate.[123] In another emotional dialogue, the sound of gunfire from the shore on Sunday 20 April and the news that troops had fired on protesters elicited anger from the crew but fear from the officers. As the Commander of the *Jean Bart* observed in his report: 'This incident causes a new overexcitation of spirits making it possible to fear acts of revenge.'[124]

Other mutineers paid more attention to these matters. Emotions were not binary but formed longer sequences. Ribot's account of mutiny in the Army followed a fluid emotional sequence of hope, anxiety, fear, anger, terror, rage, joy and delight.[125] These fuller sequences challenge the emotional oversimplification of the historiography of the mutiny, be that Masson's sailors responding to the external stimuli of harsh conditions and agitators, or Marty's mutineers who possess the appropriate palette of emotions for 'immortal heroes'.

Within a shorter timeframe, Duport provided the most complex emotional sequence of the eyewitnesses for the situation aboard the *France* around the time of the 'ambush' of Morskaïa Road. Before the event, the sailors experienced the joy of the unity of the ships in revolt. This turned fear at the sound of machine-gun fire to anger as the news arrived via telephone.[126] This anger deepened to immense fury, as sailors in panic returned to the ship from the scene. The emotional flux of this micro-sequence highlights the limits of most emotional accounts of the mutiny; even those of mutineers themselves. Duport's temporal proximity to the events allowed this rich description, writing only weeks after the events, rather than years, or decades, as with other witnesses. This suggests that memory filters and reifies emotion, privileging an emotion or two at the expense of the affective process within contentious politics.

The words joy or happiness appeared repeatedly in mutineer accounts.[127] Joy accompanied the realisation of collective strength. According to Le Ramey, the liberation of Eugène Delarue, Léon Coette and Virgile Vuillemin from arrest on Easter Saturday resulted in a 'delirious enthusiasm' among demonstrators on the *France*.[128] Joy punctuated the revolt at moments of apparent victory. An ex-Leading Seaman gunner recalled the joy of forcing the general staff to renounce their criminal acts and withdraw from the Russian Civil War.[129] Likewise, in his report on the events in Sevastopol, Captain Robin observed the crew's long joyful cheers at the news that the *Justice* was going to return to France.[130] When, on 26 April, aboard the *Jean Bart*, the Admiral committed in writing that the evacuation of Sevastopol would take place by 26 April, the crew's delegates experienced sheer delight.[131]

Sometimes, officers and crews shared the same emotions. Happiness on both sides denoted the apparent resolution of conflict. At a meeting of the crew on Tuesday 22 April, Notta argued for the return home with the coal loaded, despite the ship losing contact with other rebel battleships. With the apparent guarantee of no punishments, the final decision on the part of the crew of the *France* to return home, elicited applause and expressions of happiness from crew and officers alike. The lieutenants present shook the hands of the sailors and when Duport notified the Commander-in-Second, the latter thanked him warmly. Duport recalled that 'Everyone was happy'.[132] He underlined with a sense of irony that this emotional resolution of the conflict contrasted with the dishonourable reversal of this guarantee.

The idea of being master of the situation was one that appeared in the mutineer narratives. Joyous liberation thus entailed a collective sense of inverted hierarchies, servants becoming masters. So, on 20 April, when the Admiral addressed the crew, Duport recalled interjections overturning power relations: 'He's boring us, don't listen to him, throw him overboard' and most significantly 'Who is in charge here? It's us!'[133] Mauence reminisced to Marty of the time when his comrades aboard the *Justice* were 'masters of the ship'.[134] Equally, a witness to the turbulent protests of 11 June in Toulon used the same phrase to express the momentary sense of liberation:

> It was the world upside down. The *fayots* themselves became polite and soft. In the streets of Toulon, we sang *'C'est la faute aux fayots!'* without our hats and in all liberty. The sailors were the masters![135]

Joy was not only associated with the liberating sensation of empowerment that the revolt brought, but also the emotional liberty that accompanied the suspension of hierarchical control over the military labour. The emotional emancipation of self-managed work contrasted with the alienating and demeaning associations of labour under conditions of military service. Several mutineers on the *France* pointed to their feelings on Tuesday 22 April. Knowing that they were to return to France, refusing any orders from the officers, Duport recorded his joy that the coal loaded under the crew's control was done so in record time.[136] Ironically, this was the very duty that was despised as being a humiliating servile exercise and that had provoked the revolt. On the same day, as those on the *France* heard singing from the *Jean Bart*, the entire crew filled with joy. When Duport persuaded the engineers to fire up the engines to leave Sevastopol because he had secured the Commander's word of honour that there would be no punishment, he evoked the universal happiness. As Duport invited the engineers to descend 'to your machines wholeheartedly for liberty'; the applause would not dry up.[137]

Reddy's concept 'emotional liberty' does not adequately capture the transformative, emergent or even revolutionary quality of this feeling. This was far from being a general condition of an emotional regime. It was not a consequence of constitutional change but a process of self-emancipatory elation. It was one that the authorities closed down as soon as they could, but one that some mutineers apparently never forgot. Viewing matters as an outsider, Robez-Pagillon, the Commander of the *France*, was completely at odds with the crew about the meaning of the coal duty of Easter Tuesday; for him, this restoration of calm was the return of discipline: 'The crew worked well during the day and remain calm. Spirits seem to have become wiser but we still feel an anxiety pervade.'[138] Revealingly, the *Jean Bart's* Commander also closed his secret report into the mutiny with the notion of the return to normal, the end of an exceptional moment: 'From this day, service on board takes on little by little its normal course.'[139] This underlines the incommensurable nature of emotion across the divide between officers and crews that ran from beginning to end of the mutiny and why the categories of the Navy are incapable of *capturing the nature of mutineer subjectivity, of their 'truth'*.

Common patterns did not stop with the mutiny's conclusion. The despair in the aftermath of the mutiny's defeat signified the most significant emotional reversal. This surfaced in many mutineer testimonies and coloured the act of memory.

Conclusion

The challenge of applying the history of the emotions to social contestation poses serious problems of both empirical and interpretative orders. From the viewpoint of formal evidence, this enquiry was at a great disadvantage. Four dozen or so accounts of mutineers provided a reasonable – if not entirely unproblematic – sample, from which to base generalisations. Nevertheless, despite the restricted quantity of the sources, the testimonies were of a richly subjective quality not found in the much greater volume of official documents (which were also consulted). Though the sample is small, there are sufficient areas of confirmation, of connection, of coherence to suggest that this offers a deeper insight into the mutiny than when perceived from the outside through hostile eyes, ears and words.

This approach yields the following insights. The degree of overlap in the accounts is such as to confirm a shared subjectivity of the mutineers, and that this stretches beyond the events in the Black Sea to other mutinies in this protest cycle. As Nicole Eustace observes in relation to the American Revolution, once revolutionaries had decoupled passion from sin, emotion acted not against reason but as a motivational force in conjunction with it: borrowing from Alexander Pope, reason was their compass and passion their gale.[140] However, where hope, fear or anger acted as motivation, despair demotivated and closed the cycle of contestation, irreparably separating many mutineers from the sense of possibility that they had once known.

This is not to say that the mutinies all followed the same course. They did not. If a shared subjectivity existed, it also had a kaleidoscopic individuation, being dialogical and dynamic. Marty's sample of witnesses went beyond those in the epicentre of the mutinies. Eugène Ribot's experience was very different from those aboard the *France*. Being in Odessa at the time of Labourbe's murder, he admitted: 'What prevents me from telling you about it most is that I always acted alone down there.'[141] Part of the difficulty is that the authorities sought to prevent, punish and fragment their subjectivity; or as the mutineers saw it, the military authorities wanted *revenge*. It is instructive that the Ministry of War 'note' on the mutiny of the 58th Infantry Regiment saw their crime as all the greater because they came to an agreement in advance of the act and persisted in their collective decision in the face of threats.[142] The character of this shared subjectivity requires a major revision of current understandings of the French naval mutinies, be that of the traditionalist Vincennes school or of that crafted by Marty. The existing conceptual and interpretative toolkit of morale, propaganda, madness and heroes requires critical distance and supplementary frameworks. Anger and fear, shame and disgust, hope and despair, questioning and insight, managed emotion and emotional self-emancipation, sights and sounds all thread their way through accounts of the mutiny. Their own conceptual repertoire suggests that a history of the emotions is a necessary but insufficient condition of a reconstruction of mutineer subjectivity. To achieve this requires a holistic understanding of consciousness. It is to the sense of place and the memory of the revolt that we now turn in the remaining chapters.

Notes

1 Susan J. Matt, 'Current emotion research in history: or, doing the history from the inside out', *Emotion Review*, 3, 1 (2011), pp. 117–24. Susan J. Matt and Peter N. Stearns (eds), *Doing Emotions History* (Champaign, IL: University of Illnois Press, 2013).

2 Aristide R. Zolberg, 'Moments of madness', *Politics and Society*, 2 (1972), pp. 183–207.

3 A notable example is Paul Chack, head of the Historical Service of the Navy for much of the interwar years, who produced dozens of popular histories of the Navy. Paul Chack, *Branlebas de Combat* (Paris: Éditions de France, 1932). Paul Chack, *Deux Batailles Navales: Lépante-Trafalgar* (Paris: Éditions de France, 1935). Paul Chack, *Marins à la Bataille: Méditerranée 1914-1918* (Paris: Gerfaut, 2001), 3 Volumes. Paul Chack, *Pavillon Haut* (Paris: Éditions de France, 1929). As an example of the genre of memoirs produced by admirals, Vice-amiral Louis Dartige de Fourchet, *Souvenirs de Guerre d'un Amiral, 1914-16* (Paris: Plon, 1920).
4 Stearns and Stearns, 'Emotionology', pp. 813-36.
5 William M. Reddy, *The Invisible Code: Honor and Sentiment in Postrevolutionary France, 1814-1848* (Berkeley: University of California Press, 1997).
6 Hood, 'The French Navy and parliament between the wars', pp. 386-403. Hood, *Royal Republicans*.
7 ADSSD AM 281J IV D 1 20 Jean Carrière to editor of *Ordre Communiste*, 27 September 1921.
8 ADSSD AM 281J III D2-3 Leva to Marty, 29 November 1930. ADSSD AM 281J III D2.6 Marius Jules Cyrille to Marty, 2 March 1931 (extracts of a notebook of the journey, cahier de route). AN F7 13164 *Honneur aux marins rouges*: paroles de Georges Drouard, Section du Havre de l'Union Fraternelle des Anciens Marins.
9 ADSSD AM 281J VI A4.27 *La Vague*, 7 August 1919.
10 ADSSD AM 281J III D2.26 Duport letter to parents, 25 April-1 May 1919.
11 Le Ramey and Vottero, *Mutins*, p. 102.
12 Arlie Russell Hochschild, *The Managed Heart: Commercialization of Human Feeling* (Berkeley: University of California Press, 2012).
13 Paul Chack, *Tu Seras Marin* (Paris: Éditions de France, 1939).
14 Matt Perry, 'Vive la France! Death at sea, the French navy and the Great War', *French History*, 26, 3 (2012), pp. 344-66.
15 On the paradox of soldier-citizens, Smith, *Between Mutiny and Obedience*.
16 ADSSD AM 281J V A3.24 Albert Cornier to Marty, May 1934.
17 To borrow a phrase denoting the depth of the experience of class among US workers supposedly with no sense of class consciousness, Richard Sennett and Jonathan Cobb, *The Hidden Injuries of Class* (New York: Vintage, 1972).
18 ADSSD AM 281J VI D2.98 Lucien Godin (*Bruix*), Extract of a travel diary (*carnet de route*), 30 March-22 May 1919.
19 ADSSD AM 281J IV E1.4 Eugène Lefort, *Souvenirs sur les événements de la Mer Noire*.
20 ADSSD AM 281J IV E2.22 Mauence (*Justice*) to Marty, 31 August 1924.
21 ADSSD AM 281J IV D5.7-9 Huret and Ricros, *Court Martial of the France*, 18 July 1920.

22 ADSSD AM 281J I B1 Marty, *Affaire*, pp. 5–6.
23 SHD SS Ed 119 Vice Admiral Salaun's secret report to the Minister of the Navy, 12 May 1919.
24 SHD SS Ed 30 Rear Admiral Dumesnil, Note on the Present Situation of our Crew from the Viewpoint of Discipline, 12 July 1919.
25 SHD SS Ed 30 Rear Admiral Dumesnil, Note on the Present Situation of our Crew from the Viewpoint of Discipline, 12 July 1919.
26 Sarah C. Maza, *Servants and Masters in Eighteenth-Century France* (Princeton: Princeton University Press, 1983), p. 7.
27 Robin Bidwell, *Morocco under Colonial Rule: French Administration of Tribal Areas 1912–1956* (London: Routledge, 2012). Elizabeth Thompson, *Colonial Citizens: Republican Rights, Paternal Privilege and Gender in Syria and Lebanon* (New York: Columbia University Press, 2000).
28 Donald Reid, 'In the name of the father: a language of labour relations in nineteenth-century France', *History Workshop Journal*, 38, 1 (1994), pp. 1–22. Donald Reid, 'Industrial paternalism: discourse and practice in nineteenth-century French mining and metallurgy', *Comparative Studies in Society and History*, 27, 4 (1985), pp. 579–607. Robert S. Stuart, '"A 'de profundis' for Christian Socialism": French Marxists and the critique of Political Catholicism, 1882–1905', *French Historical Studies*, 22, 2 (1999), pp. 241–61. Colin Heywood, 'The Catholic Church and the formation of the industrial labour force in nineteenth-century France: an interpretative essay', *European History Quarterly*, 19, 4 (1989), pp. 509–33.
29 ADSSD AM 281J V A3.16 Albert Cornier to Marty, May 1934. They were also annoyed that he suggested that he was more socialist than they were.
30 ADSSD AM 281J III D2.35 Duport letter to parents, 25 April–1 May 1919.
31 ADSSD AM 281J III D2.35 Duport letter to parents, 25 April–1 May 1919. On the handshake of Wat Tyler and King Richard III, J. A. Burrow, *Gestures and Looks in Medieval Narrative* (Cambridge: Cambridge University Press, 2002), pp. 87–8.
32 ADSSD AM 281J V A3.11–12 Anon. (A.B. in Marty's marginal note), Episode révolutionnaire de 1919.
33 Diane Reay, 'Beyond consciousness? The psychic landscape of social class', *Sociology*, 39, 5 (2005), pp. 911–28. Fox, *Class Fictions*. Of course, arguing that shame played a vital role in social solidarities, see E. P. Thompson, *Customs in Common: Studies in Traditional Popular Culture* (New York: New Press, 1991).
34 ADSSD AM 281J V A3.15–16 Albert Cornier to Marty, May 1934.
35 *La Vague*, 17 July 1919 and 18 August 1919.
36 On the force and contradictions of Republicanism in commemorative practice since 1870, Sudhir Hazareesingh, 'Conflicts of memory: republicanism and the commemoration of the past in modern France', *French History*, 23, 2 (2009), pp. 193–215.

37 ADSSD AM 281J III E12.2–6 Roger Benoist to Marty, 4 April 1928.
38 ADSSD AM 281J III E12.7–8 Raymond Dufour to Marty, n.d.
39 ADSSD AM 281J VI D2.93–94 Lucien Godin (*Bruix*), *Carnet de route*.
40 ADSSD AM 281J III E1.1 L. Hiarel, *Affaire de Smyrne*, 5 February 1926.
41 ADSSD AM 281J I B1 Marty, *Affaire*, p. 29.
42 Mikhail Mikhailovich Bakhtin, *Speech Genres and Other Late Essays* (Austin: Texas University Press, 1986), pp. 164–7. Walter Benjamin praises Vygotsky for his understanding of the emotional-gestural character of the origins of language in the transition from Ape to human, Walter Benjamin, *Selected Writings, Volume 3: 1935–1938* (Cambridge: Harvard University Press, 2002), p. 81.
43 John L. Austin, *How to Do Things With Words* (London: Clarendon, 1962). John R. Searle, 'Austin on locutionary and Illocutionary acts', *The Philosophical Review*, 77, 4 (1968), pp. 405–24.
44 ADSSD AM 281J III D2.34 Duport letter to parents, 25 April–1 May 1919.
45 ADSSD AM 281J IV D1.7 Notta.
46 ADSSD AM 281J IV D2.7 Pleurol to Marty, 7 November 1923.
47 ADSSD AM 281J IV D5.7–9 Huret and Ricros, *Court Martial of the France*, 18 July 1920.
48 ADSSD AM 281J IV E2.22 François Mauence (*Justice*), 31 August 1924.
49 ADSSD AM 281J VI D2.18–23 François Perrone, *Memoire de la Mer Noire: Bord du Waldeck-Rousseau*, 28 January 1920.
50 ADSSD AM 281J VI D2.66 R. Nouveau, *De Toulon à Calvi par Odessa*.
51 ADSSD AM 281J VI D2.96–97 Lucien Godin (*Bruix*), Extract of a travel diary (*carnet de route*), 30 March–22 May 1919.
52 ADSSD AM 281J IV E1.13 Eugène Lefort, *Souvenirs sur les événements de la Mer Noire*.
53 ADSSD AM 281J IV E2.22 François Mauence to André Marty, 31 August 1924.
54 ADSSD AM 281J IV E1.3 Eugène Lefort, *Souvenirs sur les événements de la Mer Noire*.
55 Bourke, 'Fear and anxiety', pp. 111–33. For the role of fear and other negative emotions in the making of Empire see Harald Fischer-Tiné (ed.), *Anxieties, Fear and Panic in Colonial Settings: Empires on the Verge of a Nervous Breakdown* (Cham, Switzerland: Palgrave Macmillan, 2017).
56 Joanna Bourke, *Fear: A Cultural History* (Emeryville, CA: Shoemaker & Hoard, 2006). Peter N. Stearns, *American Fear: The Causes and Consequences of High Anxiety* (New York: Routledge, 2006). Jean Delumeau, *Sin and Fear: The Emergence of a Western Guilt Culture 13th–18th Centuries* (New York: St. Martin's Press, 1991). D. Keetley, 'From anger to jealousy: explaining domestic homicide in antebellum America', *Journal of Social History*, 42 (2008), pp. 269–97. William V. Harris, *Restraining Rage: The Ideology of Anger Control in Classical Antiquity*

(Cambridge: Harvard University Press, 2002). Stearns and Stearns, *Anger*.
57 Joseph LeDoux, *The Emotional Brain* (London: Phoenix, 1998), pp. 45–6.
58 Anna Wierzbicka, *Emotions across Languages and Cultures: Diversity and Universals* (Cambridge: Cambridge University Press, 1999).
59 ADSSD AM 281J IV E1.8 Eugène Lefort, *Souvenirs sur les événements de la Mer Noire*.
60 ADSSD AM 281J IV D5.7–9 Huret and Ricros, *Court Martial of the France*, 18 July 1920.
61 Le Ramey and Vottero, *Mutins*, p. 74.
62 ADSSD AM 281J V A3.16 Albert Cornier, May 1934.
63 ADSSD AM 281J VI D2.65 R. Nouveau, *De Toulon à Calvi via Odessa*.
64 Charles Darwin, *The Expression of the Emotions in Man and Animals* (London: John Murray, 1872).
65 ADSSD AM 281J VI D2.59 Alex Barillon to Marty, 15 March 1926.
66 ADSSD AM 281J VI C1.36–46 Notta, 5 November 1928 (Using the term *Monder*).
67 ADSSD AM 281J III D2.29 Duport letter to parents, 25 April–1 May 1919.
68 ADSSD AM 281J VI D2.63–74 R. Nouveau, *De Toulon à Calvi par Odessa*.
69 ADSSD AM 281J III D2.30 Duport letter to parents, 25 April–1 May 1919.
70 ADSSD AM 281J IV D5.8 Huret and Ricros, *Court Martial of the France*, 18 July 1920.
71 ADSSD AM 281J VI D4.39 Salvarelli in *La Provençe*, 27 April 1929.
72 For emotion as an evolutionary inheritance, Darwin, *Expression*. For the James-Lange theory of organic (body-to-mind) emotions, William James, *Principles of Psychology* (Bristol: Thoemmes, 1998). For a sophisticated and renewal of the organic theory, Antonio R. Damasio, *The Feeling of What Happens: Body and Emotion in the Making of Consciousness* (New York: Harcourt, 1999).
73 *La Vague*, 7 August 1919.
74 SHD SS Ed 30 Commander of the *France* to Vice-Admiral Amet, 23 April 1919.
75 ADSSD AM 281J III D2.27 Duport letter to parents, 25 April–1 May 1919.
76 ADSSD AM 281J III D2.27 Duport letter to parents, 25 April–1 May 1919.
77 ADSSD AM 281J III D2.29 Duport letter to parents, 25 April–1 May 1919.
78 ADSSD AM 281J III D2.30 Duport letter to parents, 25 April–1 May 1919.
79 ADSSD AM 281J VI D2.57 Barillon to Marty, 15 March 1926.
80 Bakhtin, *Speech Genres and Other Late Essays*, pp. 164–7. Benjamin, *Selected Writings, Volume 3*, p. 81.
81 VI C6.41 Notta to Marty, 5 November 1928.
82 Le Ramey and Vottero, *Mutins*, p. 43.

83 ADSSD AM 281J VI A4.27 *La Vague*, letter dated 12 April 1919, published 1 May 1919.
84 Hochschild, *The Managed Heart*.
85 ADSSD AM 281J VI C1.11 Eugène Ribot to Marty, n.d. (November 1928).
86 ADSSD AM 281J III D2.26-35 Duport (of the *France*) to his parents, 25 April-1 May 1919.
87 ADSSD AM 281J I B1 Marty, *Affaire*, p. 1.
88 L. S. Vygotsky, *The Collected Works of L.S. Vygotsky, Volume 6: The Scientific Legacy* (New York: Springer, 1999), pp. 71-235 for a posthumously published essay on emotion. Perhaps Vygotsky comes closest to a solution in his understanding of conscious thought as inner speech operating in parallel planes of pre-verbal semantic-affective and verbalised thought.
89 Jean L. Briggs, *Never in Anger: Portrait of an Eskimo Family* (Cambridge: Harvard University Press, 1970).
90 Carol Z. Stearns, '"Lord help me walk humbly": anger and sadness in England and America, 1570-1750', in Carol Z. Stearns and Peter N. Stearns (eds), *Emotion and Social Change: Toward a New Psychohistory* (New York: Holmes & Meier, 1988), pp. 39-68. Stearns and Stearns, *Anger*. Barbara H. Rosenwein (ed.), *Anger's Past: The Social Uses of an Emotion in the Middle Ages* (Ithaca, NY: Cornell University Press, 1998).
91 Le Ramey and Vottero, *Mutins*, p. 39.
92 Le Ramey and Vottero, *Mutins*, p. 42.
93 Le Ramey and Vottero, *Mutins*, p. 75.
94 ADSSD AM 281J III D2.31 Duport letter to parents, 25 April-1 May 1919.
95 ADSSD AM 281J III D2.28 Duport letter to parents, 25 April-1 May 1919.
96 ADSSD AM 281J VI C1.9 Émile Buffet to Marty, 1 December 1928.
97 ADSSD AM 281J VI C1.9 Émile Buffet to Marty, 1 December 1928.
98 ADSSD AM 281J VI C1.8-9 Émile Buffet to Marty, 1 December 1928.
99 ADSSD AM 281J III E2.8 Jean Camille (*Du Chayla*) to Marty, 2 June 1926.
100 ADSSD AM 281J VI D2.95 Lucien Godin, *Carnet de route*, 28 April 1919.
101 ADSSD AM 281J III D2-3 Leva to Marty, 29 November 1930.
102 On hope in contemporary movements, Manuel Castells, *Networks of Outrage and Hope: Social Movements in the Internet Age* (Cambridge: Polity, 2012).
103 ADSSD AM 281J IV E3.8 Pseudonym 'Voyageur Marseille' (Perpignan) to Marty, 27 October 1927.
104 ADSSD AM 281J V A3.4 *L'Humanité*, 28 February 1924. See Marty's tribute to Wallet, including refusing to replace Tunisian electricians on military service, *L'Humanité*, 1 March 1924.

105 Robert Brécy, *Florilège de la Chanson Révolutionnaire de 1789 au Front Populaire* (Paris: Editions de l'Atelier, 1990), p. 247. Marty, *Révolte*, pp. 665-6.
106 Nicole Eustace, *Passion is the Gale: Emotion, Power, and the Coming of the American Revolution* (Chapel Hill, NC: University of North Carolina Press, 2008). Andrew Burstein, *Sentimental Democracy: The Evolution of America's Romantic Self-Image* (New York: Hill & Wang, 1999). Sarah Knott, *Sensibility and the American Revolution* (Chapel Hill, NC: Omohundro Institute of Early American History and Culture, 2008).
107 Mikhail Mikhailovich Bakhtin, *Towards a Philosophy of the Act* (Austin: University of Texas Press, 1992), pp. 32-37. Articulating something similar when deploying cognitive psychology's category 'activation', see William M. Reddy, 'Emotional liberty: politics and history in the anthropology of emotions', *Cultural Anthropology*, 14, 2 (1999), pp. 256-88. Also registering the dialectic of effect and action in revolutionary subjectivity, Antonio Gramsci advocated a 'pessimism of the intellect, optimism of the will.', see W. John Morgan, 'The pedagogical politics of Antonio Gramsci: "pessimism of the intellect, optimism of the will"', *International Journal of Lifelong Education*, 6, 4 (1987), pp. 295-308.
108 ADSSD AM 281J V A3.16 Albert Cornier, May 1934.
109 VI D2.18-23 François Perrone, *Memoire de la Mer Noire: Bord du Waldeck-Rousseau*, detained at the Maison Centrale de Melun, 28 January 1920.
110 Tillon, *Révolte*, p. 350.
111 ADSSD AM 281J VI C1.14 Eugène Ribot to Marty, n.d. (November 1928).
112 Le Ramey and Vottero, *Mutins*, p. 87.
113 Originally published in 1895, Gustave Le Bon, *The Crowd: A Study of the Popular Mind* (New York: Penguin, 1977).
114 ADSSD AM 281J IV E2.5 Battleship *Justice* commanded by M Robin, Vessel Captain.
115 SHD SS Ed 30 Captain of Vessel Robez-Pagillon report, 23 April 1919.
116 Le Ramey and Vottero, *Mutins*, p. 64.
117 SHD 20 N 273 Colonel Trousson's report on the occupation of Sevastopol, appendix 17: Major de Villepin's report on the events of 20 April 1919.
118 ADSSD AM 281J V A3.11-12 Anon. (A.B. in Marty's marginal note), Episode révolutionnaire de 1919.
119 ADSSD AM 281J VI D4.33 Vuillemin to Marty, 3 October 1921.
120 ADSSD AM 281J IV D5.7-9 Huret and Ricros, *Court Martial of the France*, 18 July 1920. Articles from *Petit Var*, 29 September-10 October 1919 are reproduced in Le Ramey and Vottero, *Mutins*, pp. 142-210.
121 ADSSD AM 281J VI D2.95 Lucien Godin, *Carnet de route*, 28 April 1919.
122 Le Ramey and Vottero, *Mutins*, p. 84.
123 ADSSD AM 281J III D2.33 Duport letter to parents, 25 April-1 May 1919.

124 SHD SS Ed 30 Commander of the *Jean Bart*, Secret report on the incidents on the *Jean Bart*, 19–23 April.
125 ADSSD AM 281J VI C1.11 Eugène Ribot to Marty, n.d. (November 1928).
126 ADSSD AM 281J III D2.31 Duport letter to parents, 25 April–1 May 1919.
127 Antonio Damasio, *Looking for Spinoza: Joy, Sorrow, and the Feeling Brain* (Orlando: Harcourt, 2003); Darrin M. MacMahon, 'Finding joy in the history of emotions', in Matt and Stearns (eds), *Doing Emotions History*, pp. 103–19. Jeff Goodwin, James M. Jasper and Francesca Polletta (eds), *Passionate Politics: Emotions and Social Movements* (Chicago: University of Chicago Press, 2001).
128 Le Ramey and Vottero, *Mutins*, p. 44.
129 ADSSD AM 281J III D2.9–10 'An ex-Leading Seaman gunner' to Marty, 25 August 1932.
130 ADSSD AM 281J IV E2.11 Battleship *Justice* commanded by M Robin, Vessel Captain.
131 Le Ramey and Vottero, *Mutins*, p. 70.
132 ADSSD AM 281J III D2.35 Duport letter to parents, 25 April–1 May 1919.
133 ADSSD AM 281J III D2.29 Duport letter to parents, 25 April–1 May 1919.
134 ADSSD AM 281J IV E2.22 Mauence to Marty, 31 August 1924.
135 ADSSD AM 281J V A3.11–12 Anon. (A.B. in Marty's marginal note), Episode révolutionnaire de 1919.
136 ADSSD AM 281J III D2.33–4. Duport letter to parents, 25 April–1 May 1919.
137 ADSSD AM 281J III D2.34–5 Duport letter to parents, 25 April–1 May 1919.
138 SHD SS Ed 30 Commander of the *France* to Vice-Admiral Amet, 23 April 1919.
139 SHD SS Ed 30 Commander of the *Jean Bart*, Secret report on the incidents on the *Jean Bart*, 19–23 April.
140 Nicole Eustace, 'Emotion and political change', in Matt and Stearns (eds), *Doing Emotions History*, pp. 163–83.
141 ADSSD AM 281J VI C1.12 Eugène Ribot.
142 SHD 7 N 800 Note on the affair of the 58th Infantry in southern Russia, n.d.

3

A mutineers' world: transnationalism and the sense of place

The spatial dimension of subjectivity and transnational approaches are recent innovations of historical enquiry. Their application to the mutinies of 1919 demonstrates that protest does not take place in a neutral container of space.[1] For Henri Lefebvre, space is socially produced and thus the mutineers constructed their 'lived, perceived and conceived' space. Moreover, that the naval authorities view matters through the national lens provides a compelling reason for adopting a transnational approach (though this is not to say that the mutineers did not do so themselves). The critique of methodological nationalism suggests alternate points of reference.[2] First, this perspective frames the mutiny within a global conjuncture of networks, circulating information, a *zeitgeist*, structural processes (imperialism, war, capital accumulation, nation-state formation) and their teleconnections. Second, scholars should look for transnational dimensions to events previously deemed to be 'local' or 'national'. For instance, the temptation to read the evidence of homesickness and desire to return to France as an uncritical nationalism on the part of mutineers would be a profound error.[3] Third, this critique can be applied to the existing literature of the mutinies to understand the blind spots that a naturalised nationalism or nation-state formation creates in relation to sources, institutions, archives and agents. Finally, the critics of methodological nationalism have proposed a transnational, non-Eurocentric and global approach with its own conceptual toolbox, from which this chapter borrows (circulations, encounters and travel as a transformative experience).[4]

More concretely, without the nation state as the exclusive frame of analysis, transnational approaches open new ways of perceiving the mutinies of 1919. First, transnationalism suggests an emphasis upon fraternisation prior to and during the mutiny. Fraternisation requires careful theoretical and methodological consideration of the complications resulting from linguistic and cultural difference. Rejecting the definition in the French military code of justice, fraternisation should be considered a word with contested and shifting meanings as well as (though not exclusively) a *transnational* practice. Second, the spatial orientation of transnationalism has encouraged greater scholarly scrutiny of travel and the maritime itinerant occupation of the sailors.[5] The political or transformative significance of travel has become a staple theme of transnational history.[6] The mobilisation of the conscript armies of the Great War contributed to great movements of people, expectations of change and the yearning for home. This connected with the circulation of mutineer ideas and practices so crucial to the dissemination of the wave of mutiny. At this time, transnational activism recovered from wartime disruption with conferences of the Women's International League for Peace and Freedom in Zurich, the founding conference of the Comintern in March 1919, as well as other initiatives such as Barbusse's efforts to organise veterans and intellectuals into international movements.[7] Third, transnationalism spurs considerations of the global patterns of military, colonial and capitalist competition as structural processes shaping the conjuncture of mutiny, providing potential explanations of the mutineer moment (1917–19). This helped to make the revolt what it was. Thinking about space at a wider level of generalisation, David Harvey has described how moments of global crisis in capitalist modernity constitute a time-space compression: 1919 was such a moment. In this regard, the transnational interpretation of the mutiny zooms between micro and panoramic viewpoints. This multiplicity of scales ensures that this account of the mutiny does not become a pictorialist portrait of mutineers against an out-of-focus background. To complement the mutineer subjectivity, the perspective of the authorities adds depth of field.

Circulation and the spread of mutiny

Precisely how the mutinies spread is unclear. If we begin at the microlevel, when mutineers seek to explain the reason for their act of rebellion, they underline the cognitive dimension of their voyages. A principal theme that emerges within mutineers' accounts was their efforts to recover truth from official evasion. They sought to achieve through the test of their itinerant experience, through observable reality, trusting their own senses above information from the official channels. They used what scraps of information that circulated amongst troops to dispel the '*bourrage*' (brainwashing) of the officers. One aspect of the officers' discourse that came to infuriate many mutineer witnesses was the demonisation by the Bolsheviks. Thus, Duport observed that the landing company of the *France* returned unscathed, despite the Red Army's entry into Odessa as the French troops withdrew and evacuated.[8] Sailors and soldiers were sharing experiences that contradicted the official perspective. Duport recounted to his parents examples of the Bolsheviks acting in good faith, as told to him by sailors of the *Bruix* and the *Justice*.

This reasoning entailed a trust of plebeian insiders (irrespective of nationality) and a profound scepticism of official sources. When the news arrived on board the *Waldeck-Rousseau* of the mutiny in Sevastopol, according to Nouveau, the crew had already figured out the counter-revolutionary nature of their mission and had resolved to refuse to participate in it.[9]

One feature of this informational pattern was the proliferation of rumour, which was viewed very differently either side of the officer-ranks divide. Hearsay was a crucial counter-hegemonic circuit of information. The circulation of news of atrocities connected second- and (apparent) first-hand witnesses amongst the naval ranks, many passing from latter to the former (or claiming to be). Notta heard from others on coal duty in the port of Sevastopol that a French sailor had killed an old woman for taking firewood and a second master had cut three fingers off a local civilian for trying to rescue a box of jam from being destroyed.[10] Several mutineers recalled their outrage as they witnessed specific events of this character. The evacuation of Odessa also outraged sailors who had witnessed these events. Georges Decorps aboard the *république*-class battleship *Justice* described the pillage of goods, the arson of the tobacco factory and cars being pushed into the sea, all while the battlecruiser *Ernest Renan* bombarded other parts of the city.[11] If the weight of rumour and hearsay pressed in a counter-hegemonic direction, this is not to say the officers did not use rumour against the mutineers. As a means to set the crews against Marty during his court martial, he recorded that rumours spread that he had planned to sell the *Protet* for 100,000 francs or seize the ship to torpedo the French battlecruisers *Waldeck-Rousseau* and the *Ernest Renan*.[12] Moreover, the officers of the *Voltaire* circulated rumours in Bizerte that the mutinous crew had hanged three officers and sabotaged the engines.

Mobilisation scholar James Jasper's concept of 'moral shock' seems appropriate in these cases, encompassing as it does both a cognitive or learning dimension as well as a sudden emotionally charged dénouement as the catalyst for a protest frame. For Mauence of the *Justice*, the precedents of the killing of women and children at Kherson and the murder of Jeanne Labourbe legitimised the revolt.[13] Eugène Lefort of the landing party of the *Jean Bart* recounted the refusal of his comrades to go out on exercises in Sevastopol with grenades as it was simply not 'logical'.[14] Intellectually grappling with the conflictual dynamics of the revolt, Notta remembered how everyone believed that the offer of shore leave for anyone who wanted it and the shooting on Morskaïa Road were no mere coincidence but an ambush. Likewise, Notta recalled that when the *France* left for home without the other mutinous ships, the mutineers sensed a trap, as well they might.[15] For the mutineers, then, their itineraries were a learning process. They drew unofficial knowledge from others undergoing their own journey in order to construct a spatial understanding of their situation.

Individual rebels, their reputations and their movements contributed significantly to the dissemination of unrest. Military authorities were anxious about such 'dangerous elements', describing their influence in pathological terms (contagion, unhealthy, epidemic, infection and virus) or binary morality (good, evil). Thus, Ensign Laguardière warned of the 'contagion of evil' that the sailor Louis Jacquet spread. The latter had been removed from the *Ledorez* to the *Hedwig*, upon which he exhorted his comrades to refuse to set sail and was, at the time of writing, corrupting 'good elements' from his cell at the base of Galați and would have to be escorted to Istanbul along with other troublesome characters.[16] Though this should not be overstated, there is evidence that such individuals networked on a clandestine micro-level. Revolutionary cells formed on some of the ships such as the *France*.[17] However, to see the mutinies in terms of individuals carries methodological dangers. Such assumptions might suggest that external elements introduced mutiny from without, rendering further analysis redundant. Indeed, the authorities made such claims, seeking to discredit mutiny as the work of outsiders, troublemakers or ringleaders.

When the authorities transported mutineers, this risked spreading unrest. On 27 April, Rear Admiral Louis Alfred Marie Caubet, the Commander of the *Waldeck-Rousseau*, telegrammed Rear Admiral Baron Louis Rémy Antoine Exelmans the 'very secret' information that the present state of mind of the *Waldeck-Rousseau's* crew meant that it was not possible to keep Marty on board much longer.[18] If the contagion model – to which the authorities subscribed – required isolation, then transportation for punishment, or for court martial, entailed significant dangers. Thus, the *France* left the Black Sea without the other mutinous crews so as to isolate the ship identified as the epicentre of the revolt. While its arrival in the Tunisian port of Bizerte offered the opportunity to arrest the mutineers, it also brought the famed vessel into close proximity with other French warships. Within six weeks, the crew of the *Voltaire* staged a mutiny there. The correlation between the presence of ships that had witnessed the Black Sea Mutiny and the wave of protest also occurred in Toulon. In early July, the arrival of *Du Chalya* and *Bruix* coincided with four days of unrest in the naval port.[19] Beyond these instances of direct contact, the wave of protest also required forms of transmission that went beyond direct face-to-face interaction.

In addition to the activity of individual rebels, the mutinies circulated as information, as unofficial knowledge, inspiring emulation. The authorities feared as much and sought to limit or suppress this knowledge. News of the mutiny spread via three major sources: first, letters; second, verbal communication between crews, mixing during shore leave or due to reassignment; and finally, the revolutionary press and reports from the Chamber of Deputies that debated the mutinies in the Army in March and in the Navy in June.[20] Indicating the circulation of revolutionary moods between France and the sites of mutiny – which by this time had spread from the Black Sea to the Baltic through the Mediterranean and into France's ports – Rear Admiral Charles Henri Dumesnil complained about the influence of letters from family members that 'in no small way' contributed to the 'state of discontent' amongst the crews.[21]

The revolutionary and pacifist press did circulate in clandestine manner amongst troops, despite attempts to prevent this happening, with *La Vague* in particular receiving correspondence from troops about the intervention. As one correspondent to *La Vague* noted, the circulation of revolutionary ideas would not respect borders. Of his return from the intervention into the Russian Civil War, he observed:

> [...] but if we do not bring back luggage on our return, we will pass all the same through customs with overexcited spirits and Bolshevik ideas in our heads. They have brainwashed us in France; the newspapers have supported the reactionaries; they have shown us caricatures of Bolshevik criminals; well, it was nothing of the sort...[22]

While Marty and Tillon recalled the newspaper's popularity amongst troops, its distribution was quite limited. The authorities had another advantage in the informational battle: the way in which technology that they controlled seemingly shortened distances and accelerated time. The Ministry of War could rely upon circuits of encrypted information via radio, with which all ships and regiments were equipped. In contrast, mutineers needed weeks for their letters to appear in the pages of the French revolutionary press. *La Vague* published news of the death of a sailor on the Sevastopol demonstration on 22 May; it had been sent on 22 April.[23] By the summer, news of the mutiny in the Black Sea had spread throughout the fleet resulting in widespread dissent. As one sailor in Toulon recalled:

> Since April the events of the Black Sea are known on the boats. We knew of the arrest of Marty and Badina. We were told of the exploits of the sailors of the *France*, who having locked up their officers, had led their ship to Bizerte, the red flag had flown on the fleet: we had contempt for the crew of the *Algol* which was the only French ship that had bombarded the Russian workers.[24]

Given that the news of the act of mutiny influenced others to refuse orders, it would be a mistake to think in purely French terms regarding mutinies. Within the camp of those fighting the Soviet regime, mutinies circulated amongst White Russian, US and British troops, crossfertilising with the mutinies amongst French troops. It might be better to consider the wave of mutinies as a transnational process negotiating national, ethnic and language barriers, in a set of complex interactions. For instance, after two mutinies of French troops in the region, American troops refused orders to fight in Archangel on 30 March, threatening a general mutiny if there was no news of a date of return coming from Washington.[25] Indeed, Lieutenant-Colonel Donop noted the influence of mutinies of British troops upon the rebellious 21st Colonial Infantry there.[26]

If a macro-scale is considered, the French Navy were transporting large numbers of troops between fronts, returning some to France, carrying some to the East to intervene against the Soviet regime. The cruiser *Guichen*, for instance, ferried troops from Tarento across the Adriatic and Ionian Seas to Itea to move on from there to Romania and the Ukraine. Port cities played a nodal function in these maritime circulations, contributing to the complex pattern of unrest during 1919.

They concentrated labour, ethnic, military and national conflict, configuring these elements in a variety of ways. Thus, port cities witnessed the following: general strikes in Glasgow and Seattle; race riots in Cardiff, Bristol, Glasgow and Liverpool; irredentist occupation in Fiume; fights between Italian and Yugoslav sailors at Cattaro; clashes between Entente troops and the local population in Bremen; and revolutionary dual power with workers' councils in several German ports.[27] Where the Black Sea Mutiny was concerned, interactions with local populations as well as between sailors and soldiers of different nationalities occurred in the ports of Odessa and Sevastopol. Considerable labour unrest also occurred in French metropolitan and colonial ports in May 1919 among dock and arsenal workers in Lorient, Rochefort and Cherbourg, among transport workers in Bordeaux. In Oran, in the same month, strikes affected the docks and fishing fleet. In July, arsenal workers in Rochefort, shipyard workers in La Seyne as well as dockers in Bizerte and Brest all took strike action and employers locked out dockworkers in Le Havre. While the barracks in port cities were also a site of unrest, the ease of communication across civilian-military or ethnic-racial-national or corporate lines should not be exaggerated. So the wave of mutinies and unrest in the French armed forces and then France's maritime ports forms part of a wider transnational pattern of complex systemic relations, rather than a simple domino-style causal sequence.

Amongst these global circulatory processes was the epidemiological distinctiveness of 1919. The authorities routinely made recourse to metaphors of contagion, virus, or epidemic with regard to indiscipline or Bolshevism. A note on intervention from the General Staff provides a revealing instance:

> We must extirpate this cancer to restore health and prosperity to Russia to which we are so directly interested, and to prevent this unfortunate contagion to spread externally.[28]

Such metaphors had an ironic poignancy given the effects of the '*grippe espanol*' (Spanish flu).[29] The year 1919 was one of exceptional mortality.[30] According to recent estimates, the influenza pandemic (1918–20) may have claimed fifty million lives globally. Indeed, the mutiny coincided with one of the waves of the pandemic in Europe, February to April 1919. With time, this was one of the forgotten elements of the mutiny. Like military records of the mutiny, mutineers' testimonies rarely mention the influenza pandemic and on no occasion render it a meaningful part of the mutiny's context, neither as a cause of the revolt nor a symptom of a general crisis of 1919. Although Marty, in his prison notebooks written in the summer of 1919, recalled that in late 1918, of thirty-three engineers on the *Protet*, twenty-four were hospitalised with Spanish flu, including Marty himself who spat blood. Later mutineer accounts overlooked this question.[31] Only on rare, but nonetheless significant, occasions did evidence about the flu and mutiny entwine. Thus, 120 on board the battlecruiser *Jules Michelet* were exempted from coal duty in early January 1919 for this reason. Already worried about discontent, Rear Admiral Gustave Lejay noted how this and dock strikes in Odessa intensified the unpopular burdens on other sailors.[32] An official report on the causes of the mutiny on the *Justice* noted the poor hygiene aboard and that the daily rate of those exempt from duties because of the flu in Odessa was seventy to one hundred.[33] The mutiny thus spread alongside transnational circuits of people, germs, information and contentious politics. Historians might do more to gauge the relationship between the contentious politics and the epidemiology of 1919.

Sense of place

Mutineers framed their memory of the mutiny within the semantics of place. Nouveau of the battlecruiser *Waldeck-Rousseau* titled the account 'from Toulon, to Calvi, by Odessa'. He began with France's premier site of French naval power in a journey to the redoubtable naval prison colony, via the notorious location of mutiny.[34] The mutiny had an important spatial dynamic. The division between the crew above and below deck showed the complex spatial sociology of the battleship. The deck separated the engineers from the rest of the crew. Those below deck worked in the engine rooms and were most likely to be recruited from the industrial regions of France, notably the Parisian region and the north. Accordingly, the Chief Engineer of the *Du Chalya* believed that the ill-disciplined sought refuge in the 'depths' of the ship so as to avoid surveillance.[35]

Space had a strategic weight in the revolt. Thus when the protest movement emerged on the battlecruiser *Waldeck-Rousseau*, the Admiral unsuccessfully attempted to manoeuvre the crew onto the middle deck so as to calm and contain them.[36] Places that allowed ease of communication and mass visible presence were central to the events, so the physical occupation of the deck by the mutineers was a feature of all of the mutinies. There were also spaces that defined the limits of the power of protagonists: the radio room, the punishment cells, the arms store and the engine rooms. There was a territorial aspect to the ships, with certain locations being the preserve of different groups. The officers had their own quarters and their own wardroom. Where the *Waldeck-Rousseau* was concerned, the occupation of the deck and the officers' remaining away from the crew made the rebels feel 'masters of the ship'.[37]

Place attachment and identity featured in mutineer testimony. Recruitment to the Navy was not a geographically uniform phenomenon with concentrations of recruitment along the Atlantic and Mediterranean coast as well as recruitment of those in the engine rooms from the industrial heartlands of France, notably the Paris region. These areas of recruitment carried with them their own regional identities, stereotypes, dialects, religious and political traditions. At Marty's second court martial on the *Condorcet*, his defence counsel astonished Marty in his summation when he argued as mitigation the influence of Marty's birthplace on his actions, known as it was for its 'violent political passions'.[38] Likewise, Marius Fracchia of the *France* explained that he had the 'hot blood' of the peasants of the Var in his veins and did not easily accept discipline.[39] Fellow *Guichen* mutineer Denis Dupuit, who was living in Toulon, was not alone in wondering why Charles Tillon had abandoned his native Brittany for Aix-en-Provence after the Second World War: 'Here you are, an Aixois now, is this to help the education of your young ones? Have you left St Justin [a Breton saint] definitively?'[40] Learning that he had holidayed in Brittany with its 'drinkable' weather, Tondut also probed Tillon about his Breton identity, saying that he knew Bretons and Brittany, as he too had Breton blood flowing in his veins from his mother.[41] When Eugène Lefort from St Quentin and his comrade took their bayonets to make a Greek NCO with a revolver back down, the former described his colleague as 'a sailor from Marseille', signalling the regional difference between them and the strength of memory of this attribute even above his comrade's name. It might also connect with stereotypes of Marseille as a place of routine violence.[42] For all the evidence of regional identity, mutineers yearned to return to France, signalling a shared demand underpinned by a sentiment of homesickness and war-weariness irrespective of birthplace. Mutineer sources constructed France in specific ways. In his prison notebook, Marty articulated homesickness that time and distance exacerbated and fed a sense of grievance against the authorities: 'and me after four and a half years away from France of which three and a half were spent on torpedo boats at Brindisi, was sent to the Black Sea!⁴³ Others evoked this sense of aggravating distance. Ribot recounted the mood in his infantry regiment in December 1918 was one of great lassitude and a vague bad will in the continued obedience, expecting to return to France but '[finding] ourselves pushed further away still'.⁴⁴

For several mutineers, France was an ethical, moral and political ideal that the intervention was undermining.⁴⁵ Emotion saturated their constructions of France, with news of return being greeted with joy.⁴⁶ From the sensory perspective, it was the sight of France that mutineers longed for, freeing vision from the unfamiliar. As Lucien Godin confided in his travel journal: 'Today all the hearts are joyful and on every mouth escaped these words "At last we will see France again."'⁴⁷ Equally, mutineers saw no inconsistency between the desire to return and rejection of the chauvinism of the officers or their fellows. Marius Cyrille, a helmsman of the *Ernest Renan*, noted in his travel journal returning from shore leave in Sevastopol with his peers provocatively singing the *Internationale* and shouting the demand of return to 'France, France'.⁴⁸ He also recorded how weeks later, on 23 June, during an inspection from the Admiral, when the Second Master shouted 'Long live France!', the officer was alone in doing so. In their memoir, two mutineers ridiculed the Commander of the *France* Robez-Pagillon's exaggerated sentimentalism regarding the 'dear land of France' during their court martial.⁴⁹ The demand for a return to France, then, needs to be understood through the mutineers' subjective constructions of France. Once this is done, the equation between the desire to return and a simple loyalty to the French state fails to capture the contested ideal of France that emerged during the mutiny.

Fraternisation as a transnational encounter, practice and its (racial) limits

Although US historian Orr has dismissed fraternisation during the mutiny as the product of hindsight and exaggeration for party purposes, fraternisation featured prominently in the testimony of several mutineers. Fraternisation is both a contested word and has a range of practices.⁵⁰ From the perspective of the French code of military justice, fraternisation constituted collusion with the enemy, an act of treason, and even espionage. Many soldiers and sailors did not understand fraternisation according to this military and evaluative definition. One reason for this could well be that from the perspective of the French republican imagination, fraternisation had a connotation that stretched back to the revolutionary tradition of the nineteenth century. The 'fraternisation of the people' entailed the exercise of revolutionary fraternity (sometimes between troops and the crowd) and unity in popular insurgency and revolutionary festival.[51] From the military standpoint, the practice of fraternisation had featured in the trenches during the First World War.[52] From the perspective of participants, this fraternisation between soldiers suggests a universalist ethic recognising in opponents a shared humanity. In this spirit, the song *Silent Night* famously acted as a catalyst for the Christmas truce of 1914. The truces might be situated within the 'live-and-let-live' practices, whereby informal truces along the front pragmatically ensured mutual survival.[53] These practices formed part of the unofficial knowledge of the *poilu* (Great War slang for an infantryman, literally the 'hairy man' as those who spent time in the trenches neglected to shave). *Poilu* meanings of fraternisation ranged from mundane pragmatism to ethical humanism, and were not equivalent to the treacherous fraternisation of the turncoat. Moreover, the Armistice rendered the meaning of fraternisation fluid. With the emergence of the Communist International, fraternisation shifted from ethics and pacifist sentiment to a revolutionary strategy. Fraternisation therefore encompassed a range of practices and meanings, entailing tensions between political, ethical and pragmatic dimensions. From the methodological perspective, this book is interested in fraternisation as a transnational encounter and practice, with the potential to change attitudes to nationalism and national institutions.

Several mutineer witnesses recall fraternisation occurring between the ranks of Allied nationalities. This, of course, does not conform to the definition of French military justice (at least prior to intervention in Russia). However, it established a transnational practice and mutineer witnesses saw it as such. National-chauvinist (or later anti-Bolshevik) propaganda did not prevent such cordiality. With so many soldiers of different nationalities serving in France and the mixture of sailors in ports, French military personnel had developed the habit of fraternisation with troops of other nationalities prior to the intervention in Russia. Indeed, this included Franco-Russian fraternisation, either with Russian units serving in France or with the French Army of the Orient. Georges Decorps of the battleship *Justice* had fraternised with Russian soldiers in Brest before the war ended and took this up again in Sevastopol.[54] Reflecting upon his indirect encounter with the Russian Revolution ten years after the event, Henry, serving in the Army of the

Orient, revealed the linguistic dynamics of Franco-Russian fraternisation.[55] The civil labour duties expected of those on military service provided one opportunity for fraternisation. In 1917, Henry was stationed in Koritza (Albania), working to maintain the roads. Alongside him were local Albanian, Romanian and Macedonian workers. One day, disarmed Russian soldiers passed by, returning from the frontlines, under the watch of colonial troops with bayonets in their rifles. They joyfully used pidgin French to relay their news: '*Franchousky, finich la guerre*' (Frenchy, the war is finished). Henry recalled that the French reaction was one of resentment, that the Russians had abandoned them, allowing the German Army to concentrate resources on the western front. Wanting repatriation, the soldiers were kept in a camp nearby. On one occasion, Henry had orders to cut down trees to make bridges on a work detail with twelve Russians. Amongst them, an ex-adjutant spoke a few words of French. Henry complained to the Russian that the Bolsheviks had mistreated the French. The Russian (whom Henry realised was a revolutionary) asserted proudly that it was not Russian soldiers, but their own masters, who were the traitors and that, on the Russian front, they were sent to their death without a single cartridge in their rifles. The prisoner argued that the Bolsheviks were working for the freedom and welfare of workers and that the French and Russian peoples should unite against the bourgeoisie who lived off their hardship.

Several possibilities existed for communication across the boundary between national languages.[56] A pidgin tongue allowed the most basic understanding followed then by exchanges of gifts and non-verbal communication. This was the case with Raymond Dufour of the *Phénix*, which was patrolling the Azov Sea. While French sailors were on duty protecting French officers – as they negotiated with the Bolsheviks on 31 March – the sailors fraternised with Russian workers via shared cigarettes and handshakes.[57] An engineer from the battleship *Jean Bart* also illustrated this process. After desertions and shore leave had allowed some interaction, Lefort reported on the exchanges between sailors and the working-class population of Sevastopol. Often they hailed him in the street, 'You Bolshevik' ('*Vous Bolchévik*') and, if he replied 'da', they would formulate the pidgin phrase '*Matros Franki-Karacho*' (Frenchy sailors good) and managed to communicate that he should not kill the Bolsheviks.[58] In these exchanges, male and female workers in the streets of Sevastopol implored Lefort that the arriving Bolsheviks could be their own brothers or husbands.[59]

Sometimes, despite amicable intentions, language proved an insurmountable barrier to fraternisation. When a veteran of the intervention encountered 'some Russian comrades' who were imprisoned on the Prinkipo Islands, he states that: 'unhappily we could not understand each other'.[60] Marty recorded his difficulty conversing with sympathetic Romanian Social Democrats in Galați. None of them spoke French, having to resort to English, and they struggled to understand each other.[61] In another scenario, an intermediary with basic language skills could facilitate communication between groups or allow the flow of news and rumour to circulate more widely. Moreover, Henry's testimony suggests that the dynamics of Franco-Russian fraternisation suffered (temporarily) as a consequence of the Russian exit from the war, despite previously being allies. It does seem apparent that the presence of large numbers of German troops in the Crimea countervailed this Franco-Russian hostility and by then the memory of the alliance prevailed. The paradox in the Ukraine was that the intervention seemed to reverse ally for foe. This was not lost on French service personnel. In a letter to Marty in 1926, Jean Camille, formerly of the battlecruiser *Du Chayla*, was indignant that they had been expected to fraternise with German officers and kill Russians.[62]

The Russian Revolution introduced what Bakhtin and Volosinov termed 'alien words', namely unfamiliar words expressing unfamiliar conceptions of the world, encountered in a 'living tension-filled interaction' with the familiar, thereby offering a route to new ideas and truths.[63] The soldiers and sailors translated these alien words into quotidian words embedded in their own political culture. One such alien word was 'Bolshevik'. The officers' repeated efforts to demonise the Bolsheviks only made Eugène Lefort and his comrades sceptical:

> For many of us, this word Bolshevik, the meaning was unknown; our first priority in going ashore was to discover what it meant. We got the response that the Bolsheviks meant the workers and that the Bolsheviks or rather the Russian workers were being prevented from making their revolution to bring down Tsarism in Russia.[64]

Despite strictures to the contrary, civilian-military fraternisation occurred when soldiers and sailors were on leave, especially in port cities. The scale is difficult to assess but episodes of such fraternisation were quite common in testimonies. Leave would afford such opportunities to all sailors and soldiers. In a letter to *L'Humanité*, Lefebvre of the 176th

Infantry regiment recalled fraternising with 'Russian' workers and peasants during his time in Odessa. He nursed fond memories of them and reflected that fraternisation transformed the attitude of the troops to their mission. From that point, they refused orders, demanding a return to France.[65] What he recalled most of all was the enthusiasm of the Ukrainian and Bessarabian peasants for Bolshevism. Unfortunately, he did not outline precisely what kinds of interaction occurred or how cultural or linguistic barriers were negotiated. It is noteworthy just how vivid and emotionally charged passages about fraternisation were in the testimonies of mutineers.

Detailed to a landing party from the *Jean Bart*, Eugène Lefort recounted an episode of fraternisation on 19 April in Sevastopol. He and some comrades were drinking in a café. A Russian bought them wine. The Bolshevik sympathiser began to converse with them in a basic French. The sailors reassured him that French troops were 'good' but that Greek ones would fire on Russians. Venting his anger, he declared that he would kill all the Greeks. At that moment, a Greek NCO appeared, having overheard the entire conversation. He drew his revolver, seized the Russian by the collar and said that he would kill him. Lefort and a comrade with their bayonets in their hands overpowered the Greek officer. The latter then upbraided the sailors for being unworthy of the French Navy and left. Lefort and his friends encouraged the Russian to leave as they expected the Greek officer to return with a patrol. Writing almost a decade after the event, Lefort recalled vividly how the Bolshevik embraced each of them with tears in his eyes before his departure.[66] Lefort's *Souvenirs* recounted a lingering hostility towards the Greek nationality as a consequence of the actions of Greek troops on 20 April. During their return from the Black Sea, sailors of Lefort's ship the *Jean Bart* refused to perform their labour duty on Greek cargo ships, as they would not help those who had fired on them in Sevastopol.[67]

French soldiers and sailors also interacted with Russian and Ukrainian civilians who were hostile to the Bolsheviks. They responded in an unsympathetic way to their plight, measuring their social status against their own and calculating that they were not natural allies. Thus, a widow of a Russian naval officer warned engineer Lefort of the Bolsheviks and the need to defend Sevastopol against them. He was unmoved by her account of her husband's death at the hands of mutinying Russian sailors 'and [she] never again came to bother us with her stories'.[68] Mutineers' accounts blurred ethical and political understandings of fraternisation. Thus, for mutineers, fraternisation was not a general humanitarian or cosmopolitan sympathy but discriminated transnational friend and foe.

With the mutinies, civilian-military fraternisation politicised, leading from civilian-military encounter to collaborative political action. The French military authorities worried about this.[69] According to François Peronne of the *Waldeck-Rousseau*, while they were anchored at Odessa, sailors would smuggle Bolshevik leaflets, pamphlets and newspapers aboard the ship from the tugs that would approach the ship on a daily basis.[70] Mauence of the *Justice* recalled being sent ashore in Odessa to root out Bolsheviks and denounce French sailors who were in communication with them.[71] Frédéric Daucros and his fellow sailor Tubiana were working in the naval base performing coaling duty on 26 February when two Russians who spoke French approached them, asking if they wanted to meet a French woman. That evening, they met Jeanne Labourbe who was accompanied by an old woman. Labourbe explained why they were in Russia, spoke of Jacques Sadoul and René Marchand, and gave them leaflets that they distributed at the base. They were due to meet again but learned that she had been shot on 2 March by French officers and White Russians. Having previously been on the *Condorcet* in Fiume and been disciplined, Daucros arrived in Odessa in January on the Greek ship *Armopolis*. On 3 April, he joined the *France* allowing him to spread the news of Labourbe's death on the battleship at the centre of the mutiny.[72] A French artillery lieutenant arrested Louis Espagnet and a sailor from the battlecruiser *Jules Michelet* in a restaurant in Odessa on the day of Labourbe's abduction. The lieutenant told Espagnet and his friend that General Borius had ordered their execution and that they should confess to fraternisation with Labourbe and Michel, a Parisian taxi driver.[73]

This form of fraternisation appears to be rarer and would only develop in specific circumstances. Jeanne Labourbe personified political fraternisation in the Black Sea revolt. Mutineer testimony related both instances of encounters with the celebrated revolutionary and reflected upon the significance of news of her death for French troops and sailors. Jean Camille, an engineer of the battlecruiser *Du Chayla* recounted his fraternisation with Russian Bolsheviks to Marty in 1926. He and two other sailors (Richard and Portevain) went ashore for a meeting in Mykolaiv (Nikolaev) with a Russian propagandist. Two stokers who knew the Russian brokered the liaison. At the meeting, the Bolshevik supplied them with French language newspapers that they distributed on board. During a second meeting the following Sunday, Richard and

Portevain met the Mykolaiv Bolshevik committee, amongst whom one spoke very good French. The latter told them of the Bolshevik advance and the deaths (fifteen or so including women and children) caused by their gunboat's shelling of the town.[74] Layarde, a helmsman of the battleship *Justice*, also learned from political fraternisation about the human cost of French intervention. On shore leave in Odessa, he came across Bolsheviks who secretly gave him newspapers in French concerning 'the awful task that we had come to do here'.[75]

Fraternisation's extraordinary quality of transforming the idea of internationalism into a personal experience had a powerful effect on several mutineers. To bridge obstacles of language in the circumstances of momentous events left its emotional mark. Jean Camille sent Marty a photograph of the Bolshevik propagandist that he had met seven years previously.[76] The encounter obviously moved the sailor as he asked Marty to try to discover anything he could about the Russian and imploring him to return the photo as it was his only souvenir of the events. Eugène Ribot passed on a similar keepsake to the revolutionary press that a Bolshevik in Odessa in 1919 had given to him. Under the headline 'A Moving Souvenir', it reproduced a brochure with a translated Russian song *The Red Flag* used as part of the efforts to fraternise with French troops.[77] The song itself deployed the universal rhetoric and symbolism of socialism: the red flag, brotherhood, liberty, slavery, oppressed peoples and liberation. It therefore mixed the affective connotations of kinship bonds and the language of contested hierarchies. Emotional suffering ('tears' and 'suffering') counterpointed emotional liberty and refuge ('love' and 'joy'). Moreover, the third verse refers to the power of song itself, through which 'an entire people call us' summoning liberty and the 'dawn of new and bright days'.[78] Walter Benjamin noted the paradox of song in translation: while music needed no translation, lyric poetry which was closest to song was the least amenable to translation.[79] For Ribot, fraternisation had a stronger impact than the revolutionary politics that it conveyed. Though he regretted distancing himself from the communist cause, he still dreamed of returning to the Soviet Union to once again meet the comrades with whom he had fraternised.[80]

With or without material mementos of fraternisation, fond memories persisted. In a letter to Marty in 1928, Roger Benoist depicted his first act of fraternisation on the quay of Mariupol, while guarding two French cargo ships. Two 'red Cossacks' approached and spontaneously shook the French sailors' hands. One French sailor knew some Russian. The French sailors were asked why Russians were treated as enemies when they were fighting for freedom. For Benoist, this illuminated what the French mission was about. The French sailors undertook to do everything that they could not to prevent their liberation. They parted good friends.[81] Similarly, Cabasset talked of his pleasure of fraternising with Bolsheviks, who held the French soldiers and sailors in high esteem and sardonically remarked that they did not have a knife between their teeth (as the anti-Bolshevik propaganda portrayed them).

Fraternisation played its part at a critical moment in the cycle of protest: the participation of French sailors in the Sevastopol demonstration that ended in bloodshed on Morskaïa Road. On 20 April, Lachurie of the *Vergniaud* and two of his comrades went on shore leave in Sevastopol. They came across a group of Bolsheviks handing out leaflets prior to the demonstration. A French-speaking Bolshevik showed the sailors around the town, taking them to a great garden, to the naval museum, then to the great museum. They spoke a lot about life under the old regime. On their return to the port, they saw a cortege of Russian civilians with great red banners. The Bolshevik invited them to fraternise, which they did straightaway.[82]

Beyond its diversity of form, the relative invisibility of fraternisation plays into difficulties of understanding its proportions. According to testimonies in Marty's papers, both fraternisation and refusals of duty were more widespread than the trials of mutineers or official documents or press would indicate. Action on smaller ships was more likely to be quietly forgotten. A baker aboard the torpedo boat *Mameluck* Albert Clouzeau had both fraternised with the Bolsheviks and had been a leader of the mutiny aboard. Though he had been detained in anticipation of a court martial, his charges were dropped due to the solidarity of the crew.[83] Fraternisation also transformed attitudes to the deaths of those Bolsheviks who organised the practice. In his preface to the script of the play *Odessa*, Marty reflected:

> Those who knew these tragic hours will not relive without emotion the memories that the first act recalls. The hanging of the two railway workers on 18 February 1919, the almost daily summary executions, the snitches, the terrible HQ of the French security force, Catherine Square, the meeting under the threat of the firing squad for the slightest suspicion.[84]

Mutineer testimony adopted the political language of class fraternisation, identifying Russians as 'workers', 'our comrades' or 'our brothers'.[85] Fraternisation allowed French sailors and soldiers to see beyond the demonisation and homogenisation of the enemy. Thus, Albert Cornier learned in prison in Istanbul from an Austrian inmate that, in the Austrian Army, there was no enthusiasm for the slaughter of 1914–18.[86] Jailed for his part in the mutiny, Cornier registered the transformative quality of fraternisation with imprisoned trade unionists of Austrian and Greek nationalities:

> From this moment, our life changed and the hours passed quickly. What charming people and what good memories I have of them! Very educated (the least clever only spoke French, English and Arabic, the others added Spanish, Greek, German and Russian!) their conversation was most interesting. Their president Demetre Kanakaris was very schooled in revolutionary and trade union matters, he knew very well about French politics and society. He said that he participated in 1905 in the revolutionary movement in Russia where he was at the time! Two other of these friends remained strongly in my memory.[87]

Fraternisation featured as a motif in Marty's *Révolte*.[88] He highlighted such interactions between French armed forces personnel and non-French citizens. Indicating the noblest spirit of internationalism, these rendezvous were 'beautiful', 'great', a 'miracle'. He adduced evidence of fraternisation in the form of leaflets, mutineer testimony and photographic images, celebrating the martyrs of fraternisation, notably Jeanne Labourbe. He wove fraternisation into his chapter structure and it acted as a dramatic denouement in his narrative. For Marty, the lofty significance of such gestures culminated in Lenin's tribute to French troops for their part in the miracle of the defeat of the imperial powers.[89] It is perhaps significant that Lenin was addressing the Pan-Russian Conference of Cossacks, signalling the communist commitment to cross-ethnic solidarity.[90] In *La Révolte*, Marty reproduced several Bolshevik leaflets that were written in French in order to encourage French soldiers to fraternise with Russian workers (the same leaflets found their way into the Ministry of the Navy's files).[91] They used the language of tyranny, liberty and equality familiar within French republican traditions.

If the fraternisation of French troops did not explicitly and apparently extend to colonial troops within their own ranks, neither did Bolshevik propaganda appeal to these troops specifically. Indeed, in Bessarabia, the Bolshevik leaflet that Marty reproduced incited French troops to liberate three million Bessarabian inhabitants from Romanian oppression, namely 'the yoke of Hungarian Gypsy [*Tzigane*] slaveholders'.[92]

Colonial troops and the mutinies: silence and visibility

The relationship between colonial troops and the mutinies was complex.[93] As the Allies formulated their strategy for Russia after Brest-Litovsk, colonial troops became a significant feature of the occupation forces sent to Siberia. As Colonel Trousson observed in his assessment of the withdrawal from Sevastopol, General d'Espèrey had envisaged an expeditionary force comprising White Russian troops and experienced Algerian riflemen, though this did not materialise.[94]

French military doctrine applied racial schema to their own troops. From Mangin's advocacy of the 'black force' to post-war evaluations of the efficacy and future use of colonial troops, the French military categorised the aptitudes of battalions according to supposed racial characteristics. Thus, an internal report produced in April 1919 attempted to distil the experience of the Great War regarding colonial troops. It argued that 'Senegalese', 'Malgache' (Malagasy/Madagascans) and 'Annamite' (Vietnamese/Indochinese) possessed innate military abilities (comparable to the British imperial notion of the martial races).[95] The document used Senegalese interchangeably with 'black', thereby generalising from ethnicity or nationality to race identified by skin colour.[96] The Senegalese made for excellent riflemen suitable for deployment in both the colonies and Europe, though only in the European summer (as another report observed 'the only inconvenience is their lack of resistance to the cold').[97] Their supposed racial inferiority rendered them unsuitable for engineering regiments or motorised services being apt for infantry, artillery, cavalry and trains. Malagasy, in contrast, could be deployed in all seasons. Consequent upon assumptions linking race and intelligence, they could work across all the specialisations, even in medicine. 'Annamites' could provide infantry, specialising in mountain terrain, auxiliary engineers and, given their artisanal aptitude, they might be used in different services not requiring great physical strength. The report, however, worried about the political repercussions of training Annamites for radio communications and artillery range finders. If the French military created a racially segmented armed forces, it also sought to integrate these racial groups together vertically with French or European troops. In a regiment of Senegalese riflemen composed of 3,099 men, 389 were European (a proportion that was roughly equivalent to the officers, NCOs, together with those who were responsible for motor vehicles) and 2,710 'indigenous' ('*indigène*').[98] In a battalion, the proportions were nineteen (European) officers, 105 European troops and 1,020 '*indigènes*'.[99]

Despite the military hierarchy instrumentalising division, colonial regiments participated in the sequence of mutinies. In the Siberian zone of French intervention a group of troops of the 21st Colonial regiment mutinied in November 1918 and again in early March 1919. The government papers say relatively little about this revolt but do provide a fair amount of context. These were amongst the few mutinies for which no testimony remained in Marty papers, though his notes include two names: Roy of Puymiclan (Lot-et-Garonne) and Bieulant of St-Ouen.[100] However, several of Marty's witnesses came from other colonial regiments: four from the 4th Colonial, two from the 37th Colonial, one who had been in both the latter, one from the 4th *Chasseurs d'Afrique* and two from the 1st *Regiment de Marche d'Afrique*. Judging by their addresses and names, all these witnesses appear to be white Frenchmen.[101] Thus, Gaston Moquet of the 37th Colonial was the secretary of the *unitaire* rail workers of Nice.[102]

Marceau Vergua who sent Marty a memoir of his time in the Army of the East had been sent from the 117th Infantry into the 37th Colonial regiment as a punishment in March 1918. He reveals the contradictions of a rebellious soldier, repeatedly falling foul of the military authorities with spells in jail, who sympathised with the Russians, but viewed the Senegalese as situational opponents and Balkan Muslims with a degrading nonchalance.[103] Marty's sample of witnesses failed to include or seriously reflect upon the experience of mutineers of colour, though he did record a single rebel with a non-French name, Omar B'Ahmed, a soldier of the 117th Heavy Artillery, who faced court martial after the unrest in the Toulouse events of 31 May–1 June.[104]

Marty made fleeting mention of troops of colour within the French armed intervention. At the time of the mutiny, he held racialised assumptions about the impossibility of engaging colonial troops in mutiny.[105] His *Révolte* traded on the myths of the ferocity of the *force noir*, noting how the deployment from the 30 March of two divisions of 'black' troops from the 'army of General Mangin' would certainly announce the 'return of pitiless war'.[106]

A counter-revolutionary *force noire*? Mutinies aboard the *Guichen* and the *Austria*

Charles S. Maier observed that 'stabilisation is as challenging a historical problem as revolution'.[107] As victors in a war that destroyed four Empires, French military elites in 1919 were faced with the difficult task of diffusing the revolutionary threat across not only their own empire but well beyond. In such a circumstance, French military planners saw clear advantages to the continued use of colonial troops after the Great War. A study that advocated the post-war use of a black reserve force to respond to 'unforeseen needs' revealed the anxieties about potential challenges to white superiority and racial hierarchies. It asserted the need to balance the formation of a black reserve force against the 'prestige of white troops' in the colonies to 'affirm our sovereignty', especially through European officers. The author positively worried about putting into contact 'races so dissimilar'.[108] The study also gratifyingly noted the 'irrational terror' that the black troops instilled in the enemy. Consequently, it envisaged the possibility of deployment in the following terms:

> However numerous problems could present themselves for a long time still, needing the use of reliable and battle-hardened troops (occupation of enemy countries, and certain points of the Mediterranean basin, security and police functions in France and in Algeria, reinforcement of troops in Morocco, colonial expeditions, etc...).[109]

Such policing operations in France and Algeria clearly stood as code for the revolutionary threat that labour and colonial revolt posed to the French Empire. Moreover, the report anticipated the black reserve force acting as a conduit of expanded imperial ambitions. The study proposed four regiments, namely 12,000 black reservists, to be stationed in France for these eventualities. Such cases materialised during the occupation of the Rhineland and the Ruhr, the revolt of Abd el-Krim in the Rif War, the Great Syrian Revolt and even during the Marseilles dock strike of 1938.[110] Indeed, Senegalese troops had already been used to repress agitation against conscription in South Constantine from November 1916 to January 1917. For local Algerians, 1916–17 became known as the 'years of the blacks'.[111]

The French authorities felt more confident using colonial troops in the repression of mutinies, exploiting ethnic divisions between French and colonial troops. The Commander of the *France* sent a message to the Admiral to ready a company of Senegalese riflemen to come aboard to halt the mutiny.[112] The reputation of the '*force noir*' was certainly present in the imagination of mutineers. Eugène Lefort remarked that when sailors were reading the signs of the preparations for war against Soviet Russia, they accorded special significance to the 'news' of the arrival of the 'Mangin division'.[113]

In his prison notebook, Marty saw colonial troops in a negative light. His notes recalled after his initial arrest his incarceration at the depot of the 8th Colonial regiment at Galaţi that Madagascan sentries threatened to kill him.[114] The authorities clearly used the Madagascan guards in order to insulate Marty from French troops, about whom the authorities were already worried in relation to Bolshevik propaganda. Such a policy of divide and rule developed into mutual distrust and animosity. Thus, in his notes about the affair, Marty made a passing remark, stereotyping Madagascan troops as being easily bribed.[115] In Marty's last statement before his verdict at the court martial on the *Condorcet*, he claimed that the authorities knew that they could not find a firing squad among French soldiers or sailors. He foresaw one composed of black troops in Taksim Square, Istanbul, preferring that his execution would allow the donation of his body for medical purposes (presumably meaning the guillotine).[116] His comments indicate the belief that black troops would be routinely used in repression, that they were not amenable to appeals of solidarity, and even may suggest that to die at their hands would be a shameful indignity.[117]

Marty's prison notebook of 1919 contrasts sharply with his later attitudes. During the thirtieth anniversary commemorations of 1919, Marty underlined the mutinies of colonial troops: the 21st Colonial regiment on 7 April in Archangel, the 4th and 37th Colonial regiment on 27 May at Bender, in addition to the battalion of Algerian *tirailleurs*, who refused to embark for Russia at Constanza in early April 1919.[118]

In Itea, Greece, the authorities used Senegalese riflemen to suppress the revolt aboard the cruiser *Guichen*. Charles Tillon's memoir highlights how, even in retrospection, ideas of race shaped attitudes and showed the limits of fraternisation. With the mutineers having taken the vessel, Tillon recalled how two barges of Senegalese riflemen arrived alongside the *Guichen*. The sailors tried to prevent the riflemen from boarding by pulling up the ladders. They also dropped the cruiser's whaling boat onto the tug that brought the barges, badly injuring two riflemen in the process. The sailors armed themselves with a variety of weapons that came to hand to attempt to repel their opponents. The Senegalese troops fixed bayonets and had their machetes ('*coupe-coupe*') at their sides. With their superior weapons, the Senegalese were able to retake the ship step-by-step and seized one mutineer after another. Placing blame with power structures, Tillon explicitly condemned the French officer who commanded the 124th battalion of Senegalese riflemen Captain Fauchen, who brutally beat imprisoned mutineers in the military jail of Itea.[119] However, while he did not use racist terms for the Senegalese troops, Tillon's focus upon the bayonet and the machete played upon the Senegalese troops' very reputation for brutality that the French military attempted to construct for them. In a letter from Charles's wife Raymonde Tillon, this stereotype continued to define Henri Lecaze's participation in the *Guichen* mutiny, she writes about his 'nearly receiving a machete blow from a black soldier'.[120] Théo Le Coze provided another eyewitness account of the *Guichen* mutiny for *L'Ouest Journal* (Reims) on the thirtieth anniversary of the event. He too highlighted the role of the Senegalese troops in suppressing the revolt but noted their initial reaction before they could board the ship. They observed the fist fight between officers and crew to prevent the ladders being lowered to allow the troops aboard. Le Coze recalled 'The Senegalese leaning on their rifles were staggered, never having seen anything like that.'[121] Their status as bemused observers did not last long, with other Senegalese riflemen on a second barge being able to board at the rear of the *Guichen* and suppress the mutiny.

An eyewitness report of the mutiny aboard the *Austria* during March 1919 further revealed the contradictions of ethnic difference in the wave of protest at war's end. The *Austria* was a cargo vessel that was being used for transporting troops back to France. The basic amenities were totally ill-suited for the number of troops aboard, who were crammed into a vast hold without proper washing and toilet facilities. In such circumstances, dysentery broke out and the ship was quarantined outside the port of Marseilles. This news provoked a mutiny. Two Senegalese sentries were overpowered and manhandled as part of the revolt. The sailors seized the ship, docked and the troops dispersed. The account written some years later and published in *L'Humanité* regretted the violence used to overpower the Senegalese sentries, who were innocent victims of the mutiny. For the author, the violence against the sentries resulted from the absence of revolutionary propaganda amongst the Senegalese troops, which was the consequence of the lack of communist leadership of the mutiny. The article's conclusion sought to draw out the lessons that could be learned from 1919 within the communist movement.[122]

The French military authorities not only used colonial troops to repress mutinies, they deployed these regiments to substitute for French soldiers who were refusing orders. Reproachfully, Jean Carrière, of the *Jean Bart*, recalled that Algerian and Senegalese troops obeyed orders to fight in Sevastopol against the Red Army advance after the refusal of 175th Infantry.[123]

An account, apparently from a mutineer, about the French Antilles reveals some of the ambiguities of the mutineers' position over the colonial question and the recruitment of colonial troops. He described a scene of children swimming in the sea while he was at anchor in Fort-de-France as a 'dozen little blacks (*'negrillons'*), veritable amphibians' but went on to criticise the imperialist exploitation of the island. Here he witnessed the training of *'tirailleurs'* (riflemen) and the toil of women. He mused about the hollowness of the word equality for these women. He contrasted the island's idyllic state of nature with French extraction of its most precious resources.

> I returned aboard, disillusioned. This is how this marvellous island, dispensing incalculable riches, received hardship and capitalist exploitation. And its women, doubly enslaved, the mother country took her child to make him to a soldier – civilisation.

The reflections, thus, combined the internalisation of discourses going back to the enlightenment of the noble savage and the attendant racist clichés awkwardly juxtaposed with a critique of imperialist exploitation and apparent sympathy for the oppressed.[124]

Conclusion

The history of the mutinies of 1919 has been framed almost exclusively within French history, even on the part of those with an internationalist political orientation. One important consequence of this is that the transnational dimension of the mutiny has largely been lost. The travel and discovery were intrinsic to how soldiers and sailors became mutineers. Great circulatory processes shaped the distinctive conjuncture that produced the wave of protest. Subsequent to the rebellion, however, the mutiny's afterlife was drawn into national institutions: the press, political parties, parliament, courts and amnesty campaigns. This meant that the transnational experiences and practices were deemed illegitimate, distorted into narrow communist readings of Franco-Soviet friendship, or forgotten.

The mutinies of the French armed forces of 1918–19 became a heroic myth at the moment of the remaking of the French labour movement. Like the wider account of the formation of the French Communist Party, the mutinies require disentangling from their legend. For communists, the mutinies signalled the point of direct connection between the Russian Revolution and the French people. Producing spaces of free association between nationalities, the mutineers apparently exhibited the noblest spirit of internationalism, anti-imperialism and fraternisation of the peoples. Yet at the same time, for all the greatest sentiment associated with contacts with Russian workers, any effort to fraternise with colonial subjects was apparently absent. Skin colour therefore complicated the transnational practice of fraternisation. If whiteness signalled a weakness or inconsistency on the mutineers' part, it was one that the authorities skilfully exploited.

The military authorities instrumentalised racial division. Several mutineers associated colonial troops with repression. The historians of the mutiny have thus far been largely colour blind, not considering the mutinies as part of a moment in which working-class identities were remade along the lines of colour and gender. In France, 1919 was a year in which labour militancy peaked, even having a revolutionary dimension, but one also in which both people of colour and women were expelled from the workplaces. With regard to the mutinies, the revolutionaries who initiated the mutiny did not consider the possibility that colonial troops might play a part in the revolt. They viewed them as a counter-revolutionary force, assimilating General Mangin's construction of a terrifying black force. It showed a strategic weakness of the French left and the contradictions of its internationalism. So a hidden vulnerability marked the apparently heroic moment of the PCF's birth: a blind spot over the question of colonialism and race. The limits of fraternisation showed the distance between the French left and the 'Twenty-one Conditions' of entry into the Communist International formulated that year, upon which it insisted. The year 1919 then formed a threshold after which – at least formally – the French far left adopted anti-colonialism and solidarity with the victims of colonial oppression.

Marty's retrospective shift in interpretation of the role of colonial troops and this belated emphasis upon colonial mutineers requires scrutiny. In part, the Twenty-one Conditions that required an anti-imperialist position from a party member, which Marty only became upon his release from prison in 1923. Also, the colonial question created hidden divisions within the party that became telling at moments like the Rif War (1924–26) or the Indochina War (1946–54). At the time of his expulsion from the PCF in 1952, Marty explained the rift between himself and the rest of the Central Committee on the grounds of their inconsistency regarding anti-colonialism. Both in commemoration and personal memory, Marty and other mutineers had to navigate the colonial dimension of the mutiny, doing so through oblivion, through regret at political shortcomings or through the persistence of assumptions about people of colour.

As a transnational practice, fraternisation was thus significant in mutineer memory but was conditioned by racial and linguistic limits. Reaching beyond the nation-state was one feature of the way in which mutineers reconceptualised their world, producing mutinous spaces that they believed would allow them to meet immediate demands, but also perceive a new post-war world, a future in which revolution in Russia formed part of France's new horizon. For some mutineers, then, the revolt should be thought of as a new world imagined. The conditions for this new subjectivity were the particularly fluid global conjuncture of war's end. It was a moment that stayed with them in personal memory and through the continued association of mutineers.

Notes

1 Lefebvre, *The Production of Space*. Charles W. J. Withers, 'Place and the "spatial turn" in geography and in history', *Journal of the History of Ideas*, 70, 4 (2009), pp. 637–58.
2 Andreas Wimmer and Nina Glick Schiller, 'Methodological nationalism and beyond: nation-state building, migration and the social sciences', *Global Networks: A Journal of Transnational Affairs*, 2, 4 (2002), pp. 301–34.
3 Svetlana Boym, *The Future of Nostalgia* (New York: Basic Books, 2001).
4 Marcel van der Linden, *Workers of the World: Essays Towards a Global Labor History* (Amsterdam: Brill, 2008), p. 7.
5 Leon Fink, *Sweatshops at Sea: Merchant Seamen in the World's First Globalized Industry from 1812 to the Present* (Chapel Hill, NC: University of North Carolina Press, 2011). Peter Linebaugh and Marcus Rediker, *The Many-Headed Hydra: Sailors, Slaves, Commoners, and the Hidden History of the Revolutionary Atlantic* (Boston: Beacon Press, 2013). On unrest in Royal Navy 1919–23, Anthony Carew, *The Lower Deck of the Royal Navy, 1900–39: The Invergordon Mutiny in Perspective* (Manchester: Manchester University Press, 1981), pp. 110–13. George Robertson, Melinda Mash, Lisa Tickner, Jon Bird, Barry Curtis and Tim Punam (eds), *Travellers' Tales: Narratives of Home and Displacement* (London: Routledge, 1994).
6 Robertson, Mash, Tickner, Bird, Curtis and Punam (eds), *Travellers' Tales*. Pernilla Jonsson, Silke Neunsinger and Joan Sangster (eds), *Crossing Boundaries: Women's Organizing in Europe and the Americas, 1880s–1940s* (Uppsala: Uppsala University, 2007).

7 Nicole Racine, 'The Clarté movement in France, 1919-21', *Journal of Contemporary History*, 2, 2 (1967), pp. 195-208.
8 ADSSD AM 281J III D2.28 Duport letter to parents, 25 April-1 May 1919.
9 ADSSD AM 281J VI D2.63 R. Nouveau, *De Toulon à Calvi par Odessa*.
10 ADSSD AM 281J IV D1.2 Notta. Amongst others identifying the role of rumour, ADSSD AM 281J III D2.27 Duport letter to parents, 25 April-1 May 1919. ADSSD AM 281J VI C1.14 Eugène Ribot to Marty, n.d. (November 1928). ADSSD AM 281J VI D2.18-23 François Perrone, *Memoire de la Mer Noire: Bord du Waldeck-Rousseau*, 28 January 1920.
11 ADSSD AM 281J IV E2.21 Georges Decorps.
12 ADSSD AM 281J I B1 Marty, *Affaire*, pp. 5-6.
13 ADSSD AM 281J IV E2.22 Mauence (*Justice*) to Marty, 31 August 1924.
14 ADSSD AM 281J IV E1.5 Eugène Lefort, *Souvenirs sur les événements de la Mer Noire*.
15 ADSSD AM 281J IV D1.7-8 Notta.
16 SHD SS Ed 30 Enseigne de vaisseau Laguardière to Pirot, Commandant, Base Navale de Galatz, 24 May 1919.
17 CHSP CT1 *Contre-Courant*, n.d., 1953, p. 7.
18 ADSSD AM 281J I B5.76 Caubet to Exelmans, 27 April 1919. ADSSD AM 281J VI D2.63-74 R. Nouveau, *De Toulon à Calvi par Odessa*.
19 SHD 6N 287 report, 10 June 1919 & report, 21 June 1919.
20 *Journal Officiel* (Chambre des Députés), 24, 26 & 29 March 1919; 11, 12, 13 & 17 June 1919. A letter dated 12 April 1919 from a 'Bolshevik sailor of the *Ernest Renan*' was published five weeks later, *La Vague*, 22 May 1919. ADSSD AM 281J III A2.23.
21 SHD SS Ed 30 Rear Admiral Dumesnil, Note on the Present Situation of our Crew from the Viewpoint of Discipline, 12 July 1919.
22 *La Vague*, 22 May 1919.
23 VI A4.27 *La Vague*, letter dated 12 April 1919, published 1 May 1919. VI A4.23 *La Vague*, 'Lettre de Russie', Sevastopol 22 April, published 22 May 1919, reporting death of a sailor of the *Vergniaud*. VI A4.21 *La Vague*, 'Lettre sur les Bolchéviks', Le Marin bolchévik de l'Ernest Renan', 12 April 1919, published 22 May.
24 ADSSD AM 281J V A3.11-12 Anon. (with Marty's marginal note stating 'A.B.') Episode révolutionnaire de 1919.
25 SHD 6N 233 Army General Staff to Ministry of War, 1 May 1919.
26 SHD 7N 817 Analysis of Lieutenant-Colonel Donop report, incidents in the 21 BMIC in Archangel, 2 April 1919. Steven Balbirnie, '"A bad business": British responses to mutinies among local forces in Northern Russia', *Revolutionary Russia*, 29, 2 (2016), pp. 129-48. Benjamin Isitt, 'Mutiny from Victoria to Vladivostok, December 1918', *Canadian Historical Review* 87, 2 (2006), pp. 223-64. Andrew Rothstein, *The Soldiers' Strikes of 1919*

(Basingstoke: Palgrave MacMillan, 1980). Edmund Ironside, *Archangel, 1918–19* (London: Constable, 1953), pp. 112–15.
27 SHD SS Ed 98 EMG 4e section: Adriatique correspondance réçu: April–December 1919–20. SHD 6 N 287 Synthesis of telegrams from the Navy.
28 SHD 6 N 233 General Staff to President of the Council, Note on the Allied Intervention in Russia, 8 December 1918.
29 For example 'contagion of evil', 'epidemic', 'quarantine' (isolement) in SHD SS Ed 30 Vice-amiral Moreau to Ministre de la Marine, 13 January 1919.
30 Niall P. A. S. Johnson and Juergen Mueller, 'Updating the accounts: global mortality of the 1918–1920 "Spanish" influenza pandemic', *Bulletin of the History of Medicine*, 76, 1 (2002), pp. 105–15.
31 ADSSD AM 281J I B1 André Marty, *Affaire du Protet (Marty-Badina) Galatz: 16 April 1919, Conseil de guerre du Paris: 11 June 1919 and Condorcet: 4–5 July 1919 at Constantinople*, 12 August 1919.
32 SHD SS Ed 30 Lejay to Amet, 9 January 1919.
33 ADSSD AM 281J IV E2.5–17 Report on battleship *Justice* commanded by M Robin, Vessel Captain.
34 ADSSD AM 281J VI D2.63 R. Nouveau, *De Toulon à Calvi par Odessa*.
35 SS Ed 30 Baudoin, Note sur le personnel chauffeur, 15 January 1919.
36 ADSSD AM 281J VI D2.64 R. Nouveau, *De Toulon à Calvi par Odessa*.
37 ADSSD AM 281J VI D2.65 R. Nouveau, *De Toulon à Calvi par Odessa*.
38 AM I B1 Marty, *Affaire*, pp. 33–4.
39 *L'Humanité*, 28 October 1922.
40 CHSP CT1 Dupuit to Tillon, 20 April 1966.
41 CHSP CT1 Tondut to Tillon, 6 October 1966.
42 ADSSD AM 281J IV E1.8 Eugène Lefort, *Souvenirs sur les événements de la Mer Noire*. ADSSD AM 281J VI D2.19 François Peronne, *Mémoire de la Mer Noire*, 28 August 1920. ADSSD AM 281J IV D1.8 Léon Hurel, *La Mutinerie de la Mer*.
43 ADSSD AM 281J I B1 André Marty, *Affaire du Protet (Marty-Badina) Galatz*, 12 August 1919, p. 3.
44 ADSSD AM 281J VI C1.15 Eugene Ribot to Marty, n.d.
45 ADSSD AM 281J V A3.27 Albert Cornier to Marty, May 1934. ADSSD AM 281J VI D2.91–2 Lucien Godin, *Carnet de route*. ADSSD AM 281J IV D1.20 Jean Carrière to editor of *L'Ordre Communiste*, 27 September 1921. ADSSD AM 281J V A3.12 *Dans les Antilles*.
46 ADSSD AM 281J VI D2 98 Lucien Godin, *Carnet de route*.
47 ADSSD AM 281J VI D2 98 Lucien Godin, *Carnet de route*.
48 ADSSD AM 281J III D2.8 Marius Cyrille, Extraits from cahier de route.
49 ADSSD AM 281J IV D5.7–9 Huret and Ricros, *Court Martial of the France*, c.18 July 1920.
50 Orr, 'The myth'.

51 Eric Fournier, '"Crosse en l'air": l'insaisissable motif d'une histoire effilochée (France, 1789–1871)', *Romantisme*, 4 (2016), pp. 121–31.
52 Johannes Großmann, '1914, un lieu de mémoire européen? de la commémoration nationale à l'émergence d'un consensus mémoriel', *Guerres Mondiales et Conflits Contemporains*, 1 (2017), pp. 119–32. Anne Geslin-Ferron, 'Des fluctuations du consentement patriotique à travers les trêves et les fraternisations (1914–1918)', *Cahiers d'histoire. Revue d'Histoire Critique*, 127 (2015), pp. 95–114.
53 Tony Ashworth, *Trench Warfare, 1914–1918: The Live and Let Live System* (London: Palgrave Macmillan, 1980).
54 ADSSD AM 281J IV E2.21 Georges Decorps's statement.
55 ADSSD AM 281J VI D1.16-7 Henry, *Il y a dix ans? Et comment j'ai connu un peu la révolution Russe.*
56 Showing the importance of languages in the context, SHD 7 N 800 Becker, president of the council of War Ministry, Note: object: measures relative to the study of foreign languages in the Army, 30 June 1919.
57 ADSSD AM 281J III E12.10-18 Raymond Dufour to Marty, n.d.
58 ADSSD AM 281J IV E1.4 Eugène Lefort, *Souvenirs sur les événements de la Mer Noire.*
59 ADSSD AM 281J IV E1.3 Eugène Lefort, *Souvenirs sur les événements de la Mer Noire.*
60 ADSSD AM 281J IV E3.8 Voyeur Marseille, Perpignan 27 October 1927.
61 ADSSD AM 281J I B1 Marty, *Affaire*, pp. 9–10.
62 ADSSD AM 281J III E3.4-9 Jean Camille to Marty, 2 June 1926.
63 Bakhtin, *Dialogic Imagination*, p. 279. Volosinov, *Marxism*, p. 75.
64 ADSSD AM 281J IV E1.4 Eugène Lefort, *Souvenirs sur les événements de la Mer Noire.*
65 ADSSD AM 281J III E2.8 Lefebvre letter to *L'Humanité*, press cutting, n.d.
66 ADSSD AM 281J IV E1.13 Eugène Lefort, *Souvenirs sur les événements de la Mer Noire.*
67 ADSSD AM 281J IV E1.13 Eugène Lefort, *Souvenirs sur les événements de la Mer Noire.*
68 ADSSD AM 281J IV E1.8 Eugène Lefort, *Souvenirs sur les événements de la Mer Noire.*
69 SHD 7 N 802 Diverse information from a former agent of the SR in Russia arrived recently from southern Russia, 15 January 1919.
70 ADSSD AM 281J VI D2 18-23 François Peronne, *Mémoire de la Mer Noire*, 28 August 1920.
71 ADSSD AM 281J IV E2.22 François Mauence to Marty, 31 August 1924.
72 Frédéric Daucros, 'Comment les marins français d'Odessa ont connu Jeanne Labourbe [dated 26 October 1970]', *Cahiers de L'Institut Maurice Thorez*, 5, 21 (1971), p. 86

73 ADSSD AM 281J I 2.3 Louis Espagnet, 1927.
74 ADSSD AM 281J III E3.4-9 Jean Camille to Marty, 2 June 1926.
75 ADSSD AM 281J III E5.3-8 J. Layarde, *Matelot timonier: cuirassé Justice*.
76 ADSSD AM 281J III E3.4-9 Jean Camille (*Du Chayla*) to Marty, n.d.
77 ADSSD AM 281J VI B2.9 'A moving memory' (newspaper cutting, no publication details).
78 ADSSD AM 281J VI B2.9 newspaper cutting.
79 Benjamin, *Selected Writings*, Volume 3, p. 250.
80 ADSSD AM 281J VI C1.33 Eugene Ribot to Marty, n.d.
81 ADSSD AM 281J III E12.2-6 Roger Benoist to Marty, 4 April 1928.
82 ADSSD AM 281J III D2.12 Lachurie, *Vergniaud: Souvenirs d'un ancien matelot du cuirassé Vergniaud*.
83 ADSSD AM 281J IV D2.84-5 Eugène Lefort to Marty, 1 June 1927,
84 Rolland, *Odessa*, p. 8.
85 ADSSD AM 281J IV E3.8 Voyeur Marseille, Perpignan 27 October 1927.
86 ADSSD AM 281J V A3.24 Albert Cornier to Marty, May 1934.
87 ADSSD AM 281J V A3.24 Albert Cornier to Marty, May 1934.
88 Marty, *Révolte*, pp. 78, 219-25, 241, 311, 372-8, 425, 599-607.
89 Marty, *Révolte*, p. 509.
90 Lenin's Speech on 1 March 1920 at the First All-Russia Congress of Working Cossacks. www.marxists.org/archive/lenin/works/1920/mar/01.htm (last accessed 7 November 2017).
91 Marty, *Révolte*, pp. 372-8. Also to be found in SHD SS Ed 30.
92 Marty, *Révolte*, p. 374.
93 Jacques Frémeaux, *Colonies dans la Grande Guerre: Combats et Épreuves des Peoples d'Outre-mer* (Cahors: 14-18 Éditions, 2006). Dick Van Galen Last, *Des Soldats Noirs dans une Guerre des Blancs (1914-22): Une Histoire Mondiale* (Brussels: Éditions Université de Bruxelles, 2015), pp. 23-4.
94 SHD 20N 273 Colonel Trousson's report on Sevastopol.
95 Joe Lunn, '"Les races guerrières": racial preconceptions in the French military about West African soldiers during the First World War', *Journal of Contemporary History*, 34, 4 (1999), pp. 517-36. Heather Streets, *Martial Races: The Military, Race and Masculinity in British Imperial Culture, 1857-1914* (Manchester: Manchester University Press, 2004).
96 SHD 7N 441 Note pour la direction des Troupes Coloniales, 7 April 1919.
97 SHD 7N 441 Etude sur l'organisation d'une reserve d'armée noire après la guerre.
98 SDH 7N 441 Tableau 1: Regiment de Tirailleurs Sénégalais (Type Réserve Noire).
99 SDH 7N 441 Tableau d'effectif d'un battalion Sénégalais de renfort.
100 ADSSD AM 281J VI D4.8 Marty's list: 'Souvenirs de la mer Noire'.

101 Marceau Vergua, Dubus, Reverdan, Vergat, Marcel Lapp, Elie Guillemont, Gaston Mocquet, Jean Baliran, Eugène Ribot, AM VI D4.6–12 Marty's list: 'Souvenirs de la mer noire'.
102 ADSSD AM 281J III E11.1–10 Moquet to Marty, 19 May 1928.
103 ADSSD AM 281J VI D4.56–64 Marceau Vergua (37–38 and 4e colonial): VI D4.56 An accompanying letter to Marty, 14 January 1931. VI D4.57 L'Armée Française à l'Oeuvre en Orient, 1914–1919.
104 Marty, Révolte (1949), p. 646.
105 ADSSD AM 281J I B1 Marty, Affaire, p. 34.
106 Marty, Révolte (1949), p. 210.
107 Charles S. Maier, 'The two postwar eras and the conditions for stability in twentieth-century Western Europe', *American Historical Review*, 86, 2 (1981), pp. 327–52.
108 SHD 7N 441 Lt-col. Chef du Section d'Afrique, Etude sur l'organisation d'une reserve d'armée noire après la guerre, n.d. late 1918.
109 SHD 7N 441 Etude sur l'organisation d'une reserve d'armée noire après la guerre.
110 Gregory Mann, *Native Sons: West African Veterans and France in the Twentieth Century* (Durham, NC: Duke University Press, 2006), p. 18. Jacques Cremadeills, 'Le mot d'ordre de fraternisation pendant la guerre du Rif (1924–1926)', *Cahiers de la Méditerranée*, 14, 1 (1977), pp. 53–64. Nicole Le Guennec, 'Le Parti communiste français et la guerre du Rif', *Le Mouvement social*, 78 (1972), pp. 39–64. David Drake, 'The PCF, the Surrealists, Clarté and the Rif War', *French Cultural Studies*, 17, 2 (2006), pp. 173–88. Charles-Robert Ageron, 'La presse parisienne devant la guerre du Rif (avril 1925-mai 1926)', *Revue de l'Occident musulman et de la Méditerranée*, 24, 1 (1977), pp. 7–28. Danièle Joly, *The French Communist Party and the Algerian War* (London: Palgrave Macmillan, 1991), pp. 20–41. David H. Slavin, 'The French Left and the Rif War, 1924–25: racism and the limits of internationalism', *Journal of Contemporary History*, 26, 1 (1991), pp. 5–32.
111 Charles-Robert Ageron, *"L'Algérie Algérienne": de Napoléon III à de Gaulle* (Paris: Sindbad, 1980), p. 101.
112 SHD SS Ed 30 Captain Robez-Pagillon report, 23 April 1919.
113 ADSSD AM 281J IV E1.3 Eugène Lefort, *Souvenirs sur les événements de la Mer Noire*. Similarly describing 'the indigenous mercenaries' who surrounded mutineers in Odessa, ADSSD Am 281J IV D1.20 Press cutting *L'Éveil Communiste*, c.1920–1.
114 ADSSD AM 281J I B1 Marty, *Affaire*.
115 ADSSD AM 281J I B1 Marty, *Affaire*, pp. 13–14.
116 ADSSD AM 281J I B1 Marty, *Affaire*, p. 34.
117 ADSSD AM 281J I B1 Marty, *Affaire*, pp. 33–4.
118 *La Vie du XIIIe*, 1 May 1949. Marty had not mentioned the 21st Colonial mutinies in his book.

119 CHSP CT2 Témoignage de Charles Tillon sur la mutinerie: la révolte du Guichen, 1957.
120 CHSP CT1 Raymonde Tillon to Roger Vollet, 11 June 1971.
121 CHSP CT1, press cutting *L'Ouest Journal* (Reims), 1949.
122 ADSSD AM 281J IV C2.12–15 'La Révolte de l'*Austria*', press cuttings from *L'Humanité*, 30 September–4 October 1933.
123 ADSSD AM 281J IV D1.20 Jean Carrière to editor of *L'Ordre Communiste*, 27 September 1921.
124 ADSSD AM 281J V A3.12 *Dans les Antilles* (this is in the same handwriting as an account of protests in Toulon. Marty wrote a marginal note with the initials AB, suggesting that this might be Alex Barillon).

4

Age, time and personal memory

Though Marty's *Révolte* was ostensibly an act of collective memory or even collective autobiography, he reduced the imagination of participants to a monological didacticism. A re-examination of the personal memories of mutineers allows Marty's imposed uniformity to be unpicked. The mutiny, as Bakhtin might have put it, was dialogical: it entailed a multiplicity of subjectivities unevenly communing through collective action, everyday practices, song, symbolism and language.[1] Overlapping with public commemorative practices, though not entirely at one with then, shifting between private and public spheres, this dialogue also underwent its own patterns of fragmentation, network reconstruction, cognitive decline and mortality. Although intergenerational transmission might refresh the mutiny's place in French political culture, it could not rejuvenate the mutineer cohort. Moreover, their testimonies reveal a temporal directionality, being backward- or forward-facing, or, indeed, occupying an amnesiac present.[2]

The pleasure and pain of personal memory

André Marty sought to write the history of the mutiny with a missionary zeal. As a historian, he gathered witness accounts of the events in the same spirit as many of those who served in the trenches, who came forward to testify to their experiences in the bourgeoning combat literature of the Great War. As his appeal for witnesses in *L'Humanité* illustrates, Marty wanted factual accounts – without mutineer subjectivity, which he perceived to be peripheral detail:

Avoid useless details. Cite facts, statistics and dates. Send photos, documents, indicating whether they must be returned or whether they can be kept. Indicate whether the comrade wishes to be cited in the book or remain anonymous.[3]

Mutineer testimony was quite different from that of Marty's ideal of a singular, linear and factual narrative. Memory was suffused with emotion and shaky on detail. A mutineer aboard Vice-Admiral Amet's flagship, the battleship *Jean Bart*, Jean Carrière, described this 'memorable day' as the 'best day of our lives'.[4] 'LC' from Marseille wrote to *L'Humanité* about the 'happy initiative' to recall the memories of the Black Sea.[5] For Tillon, his memory of the outbreak of the mutiny on the cruiser *Guichen* was 'the most beautiful surprise of my life'.[6]

Such unambiguous positive recall of the events is rare. It is not so much that the episodes were not memorable or did not have joyous hope-filled moments, but, for many, it was difficult to separate the mutiny or war from their attendant personal costs. Most mutineers did not share Marty's drive to recall the mutiny. Many associated the mutiny with difficult – even traumatic – experiences of war or the price that they paid for participation in the revolt.[7] René Ascoet described his mistreatment after the mutiny as 'transcend[ing] the horror that the human brain can conceive as torture that one can inflict on another human being'. He and his colleagues were stripped and beaten one by one and then returned to the cells; he remained unconscious for twenty-four hours.[8] He would not be able to relate the entire story. Painful memories had a psychological and even a physiological effect. In his account of the 'emotional brain', the neuroscientist Joseph Ledoux observed that fear stimulating the amygdala region of the brain could create indelible emotional memories and in the most intense forms leading to anxiety disorders.[9] A police surveillance report about Georges Wallet, Roger Rolland and Henri Alquier, who had been recently released from Clairvaux prison after three years of incarceration, noted that they seemed to be suffering from depression as a consequence of their long detention.[10] Whether, how and when to remember the rebellion were emotionally burdensome dilemmas for mutineers. Encountering other mutineer testimony confronted peers with the limits of their own knowledge, experience and memory of the events. Both Tillon and Marty annotated their copies of mutineer testimony in their private papers with underlinings, question marks and marginal comments. Reading fellow *Guichen* mutineer Théo Le Coze's account in a local newspaper, Tillon underscored the attitude of Senegalese riflemen to the mutiny to denote either his disagreement or the additional insight it provided him. He added a long marginal comment emphasising the difference in perspective of Le Coze, who escaped discipline and had said nothing of the court martial, condemnation and imprisonment of mutineers such as Tillon.[11] For another *Guichen* mutineer, reading Tillon's *La Révolte Vient de Loin* (1969) prompted a real emotion and sincere gratitude towards the author, because the former had not forgotten the *shock* of these events that marked his entire life.[12]

From a multidisciplinary vantage point, then, parameters of emotion, time and activation shape both memory formation and recall. Several mutineers experienced the repression after the events, twenty-six from the *France* alone. If the mutinying soldiers are included, the numbers reached into the hundreds. Typically, those with poor disciplinary records, those who acted as delegates or those identified by officers or their informants as ringleaders ('*meneurs*') were punished. Most mutineers went unpunished.

Punishment had a significant bearing on memory. The court martials were intended to instil fear. Mutineers had good reason to fear them. The prosecution in Marty's case called for the death penalty on three counts.[13] Mutineers did not feel that the authorities conducted the court martial justly. Marty believed that his defence counsel, the prosecution and the judge colluded to arrive at his guilty verdict at his second court martial aboard the *Condorcet* on 4–5 July 1919. He compared his experience to the equally unjust treatment of François Peronne of the battlecruiser *Waldeck-Rousseau*, who was tried in Cattaro on 8–10 June.[14] Several hundred mutineers were sent to the penal colonies that had already caused a series of scandals prior to the war.[15] On 18 April the Ministry of War decided that 225 mutineers of the 58th Infantry Regiment would perform hard labour in the penal colony of Meknes, which consisted of road-building in the Moroccan sun.[16] A Ministry of War note pleaded against future indulgence towards these men on the grounds that their action was of 'such a serious character that they could not remain unpunished'.[17] In terms of the mutineer hierarchy of respect, only those who lost their lives during the events, namely Jeanne Labourbe and the supposed victims of Morskaïa Road, had greater status than those who faced incarceration amongst the mutineers. This prestige of the mutiny's 'martyrs' possessed a symmetry with the cult of the dead during and after the Great War.[18] From the perspective of personal memory, however, court-martialled mutineers recalled the stress and suffering of their punishments.[19] Others sought to forget rather than relive these experiences, omitting the penal experience in their narratives. For mutineers, prison transformed what had begun as a collective action into a personal struggle for survival in which solidarity was barely imaginable.

The fallibilities and limits of personal memory

References to memory feature prominently in letters to Marty. The multiple aspects of the memory (such as sensory, emotional, linguistic or semantic dimensions) of the same subject might be uneven, fragmented or inconsistent. Several mutineers confused the sequence of events, lost the ability to narrate details, forgot elements or returned to other episodes.[20] A mutineer of the Danton-class battleship *Condorcet*, writing in 1934, illustrates this. Albert Cornier emotionally navigated 'moving memories', visualising the faces of fellow prisoners in Cherbourg and Istanbul but could not always summon their names. His loss of contact with his 'great friend' provoked palpable regret.[21] Cornier's experience confirms the recognition-recall distinction between two forms of memory: the capacious ability to recognise (faces) and the more limited nature of (linguistic) recall.[22] Likewise, Tillon believed that the 'disappeared' (i.e. dead mutineers) deposited sediment of their lives in his memory and that their voices and gestures were the truest and surest aspect of his duty-bound – if fragile – capacity to remember.

Ease of recall varied between mutineers. Writing in 1927, Joseph of a tank regiment doubted his own account, qualifying it with the phrase 'if my memory is faithful'.[23] For Lefebvre, who had mutinied at Kherson, so many memories persisted that they were impossible to relate.[24] Marty exchanged letters and had conversations with Lefebvre, considering him a 'good' source. In a second round of an exchange of letters in 1928 with Marty, Roger Benoist regretted not having taken notes at the time because of his struggle to remember details.[25] Writing eight years after the mutiny, despite asserting the veracity of his memories, Eugène Lefort admitted lapses in his ability to recapture aspects in his account. Thus, while he could remember the dates of his enlistment and discharge, even when he had leave in Corfu, he confessed that he could not be definite about the sequence of journeys between Odessa and Sevastopol in the Black Sea or the name of a torpedo boat that he boarded in early April. It may well be that he could refer to his military service record for these details but not the rest. He also found it difficult to recount events in chronological order, apologising for forgetting an episode relating to the mutiny's aftermath that he inserted just before his conclusion.[26]

Yet this same individual could reconstruct the events of 20 April in his spatial-cognitive imagination, drawing a map of Sevastopol that identified the route of the demonstration, the location of the Greek machine-gun emplacement and the sites of the shootings.[27] Leva, a gunner on the *république*-class battleship *Patrie*, struggled to remember the leader of the revolt on his ship, being only able to identify Ricci, the butler (*maitre d'hotel*) of the subaltern officers, who was living along the coast in Toulon. He was hazy about the others who were mostly engineers and stokers and a few from above deck.[28] In his memoir published in 1969, all too aware of the gaps in his memory, Tillon apologised for the strengths and weaknesses of his multiple attempts to recollect, articulating his sense of obligation to his fellow mutineers to arrive at the truth.[29]

Understanding mutineer memory requires an appreciation of how memory changes with time. Here again, insights of neuroscience indicate useful directions. The threshold between short-term or working memory and long-term or explicit memory is crucial, the former allowing the development of the latter. Working memory manifests as activity in the frontal cortex, notably in the language region known as Broca's area. The act of recall activates working memory. Working memory draws on visual areas for visual memories, motor areas for memory of physical activity, temporal areas for facial recognition and a configuration of cortical areas concerned with abstract concepts. Thus storage of stable traces of explicit memory ranges widely across the brain. These elements are summonsed into working memory with recall, illustrating the connected, multiple and flexible character of memory, which works through the passage of neurotransmitters through the synaptic connections formed with various levels of intensity during the events.[30] Thus, memory is more than the simple associative phenomenon that Donald Hebb, the pioneer of the study of memory and synapses, suggested. Instead, memory can also possess a more advanced nature, having a goal-seeking or hypothesis-making quality. Equally, it analyses and synthesises spatial cues, in the stage after the formation of synapses connecting neurons, as Lefort's map of Sevastopol illustrated. In this, specific pathways are reinforced through repetitious pulses of neurotransmitters, allowing more complex memory, learning and cognition known as hippocampal long-term potentiation.[31]

An exchange between two mutineers of the *Guichen* reveals the gaps, uncertainties and redrafts of memory. In the summer of 1966, Germaine Douvrin and Tillon had met on their holidays and reminisced about their common past. Writing to Tillon some weeks later, Douvrin wanted to address a detail that remained obscure to him. Awaiting the verdict of their court martial, Douvrin struggled to recall which group of workers were demonstrating. He sensed it was striking arsenal workers but could not be sure. They certainly sang the *Internationale* but he could not recall whether there was any connection to the mutineers' court martial.[32]

Such uncertainty contrasted with very full memoirs written several decades after the event such as Le Ramey and Vottero's accounts in *Mutins de la Mer Noire* (1973) and Tillon's *La Révolte Vient de Loin* (1969). These were no doubt given a framework of detail from previous accounts (notably Marty's) and commemorations, into which personal reminiscence was interlaced. The dynamics of memory help to explain this. Repetition facilitates recall and learning. So group reminiscence would have strengthened and rendered a coherent narrative of events from the fragmentary traces in earlier iterations of recall, as would opportunities to recount memories for any audience keen to listen.[33] Given Tillon's position as president of the mutineer association, he doubtlessly was called upon several times to narrate his experiences, in a sense thereby rehearsing *La Révolte Vient*. He also consulted archival materials to assist in the recovery of memory (though these are not very helpful as no official investigation followed the mutiny on the *Guichen*). The relationship between memoirs and personal memory is therefore not a straightforward one.

The pattern that emerges is that although aspects of the mutiny returned to mutineers vividly, many basic details escaped them. Despite Marty's guidance that prioritised factual reconstruction, the accounts that he received proved weak in this matter but rich in the subjectivity and emotion that he deemed to be of marginal interest. In this regard, Marty misunderstood human memory. It is no accident that the testimonies suffuse emotion. Despite their differences, for scholars from a range of backgrounds, not only does the intensity of emotional experience correlate to the strength of memory formation but also the recovery of events might dredge up their associated emotional register.[34] That said, even emotionally intense memories could be prone to inaccuracy.[35]

Experts in memory offer a catalogue of reasons for this fallibility. From the perspective of neuroscience, events most strongly committed to memory are those experienced with emotional intensity (or to use the neuroscientific term, with the greatest level of activation).[36] As biochemist Steven Rose put it, personal memory acts as an internal record of experience being a 'most treasured – but fragile – of possessions'.[37]

Consequently, for Rose, crude materialist understandings of memory that use metaphors of data retrieval and computer memory are misleading. Mutineers could not access their pasts in such a straightforward manner.

Instead, as individuals tortured by an inability to forget reveal, human memory is a filtering process and requires active remembering.[38] Moreover, memory degrades over time through forgetting. This was somewhat of a blind spot for Maurice Halbwachs, who wrote the seminal sociological account of collective memory.[39] In contrast, Ernest Renan pointed to the centrality of forgetting (and historical error), even above memory, in the making of a nation.[40] Moreover, forgetting has its own generational dynamics.[41] The phenomenological philosopher Paul Ricoeur elaborated the complex modalities of forgetting: as traces effaced or persisting, as an instrumentalisation of the past, as the blockage of memory, as manipulated memory and as commanded forgetting (amnestying the past).[42] Each of these manifest in the progressive erosion of the mutiny in personal and shared memory. An illustration of the forgotten aspects of the mutinies was the participation or otherwise of colonial subjects.

Psychologists Hermann Ebbinghaus in the 1880s and Frederick Bartlett in the 1930s conducted classic studies of forgetting, which found that losses began shortly after an event, deteriorating progressively, and that after several months, modifications, omissions and altered sequences and details were noticed. Bartlett therefore judged that recall entails 'an effort to understand' to render the traces of memory that persist both consistent and comprehensible.[43] Memory can thus carry distortions, even (unwitting) falsehoods.[44] Oral historians addressed this problem head-on in the 1970s and 1980s when conservative opponents seized upon memory's fallibility as the fatal flaw of this new methodology. For Portelli, memory did not reconstruct the detail of a factual past, nor did it need to, as it did something more important: it revealed how past experience remained meaningful for interviewees in the present.[45] This implied that history is meaningful to us all, to our sense of self. Portelli thus provided a persuasive rationale for the value of oral history and, by extension, the value of mutineer testimony. It is worth noting that pre- or non-literature cultures, according to Walter Ong, make considerable effort to remember experiences through the orality of fables, poetry and song.[46] For Ong and the Toronto school, modernity entailed an epochal shift from orality to literacy. This perspective can lead to overlooking the persistence of oral sub-cultures, and privileging highly literary social groups. Ultimately, given their non-elite status, the mutineers had to rely upon a combination of oral, literary and artefactual means to recall their actions, as my suspicion about Lefort using his military service document to feign more accurate recall, suggests.

For some mutineers, life had moved on, the mutiny inhabiting a past (and increasingly alien) world. Writing about the mutiny on the *Condorcet* of 11–12 June 1919 fifteen years later, Albert Cornier opened his account for Marty with the observation:

> This is for me a return backwards, a voyage into my past! And each year, this incursion into the land of memory feels a little more melancholic![47]

Some mutineers recognised the changes in themselves when recalling the events. Eugène Lefort thanked Marty for copies of *Jean Le Gouin* and *La Caserne*, indicating that he was active in communist anti-militarist work amongst sailors eight years after the mutiny. He was happy to be of service to Marty but observed that he made his account according to 'the state of mind that I had at that moment for I was only 19 years old'. Lefort's testimony also revealed that mutineers had to deal with the mutiny's politically contentious afterlife. In Lefort's case, he had regularly defended Marty against friends who detested him.[48]

Emotion and personal memory

Emotion saturated the recall of the events. Neuroscientists believe that memories connect with two types of markers: one knowledge-based, the other emotional. The latter markers associate an event with pleasure, happiness, unhappiness or suffering. Emotion thus connects the valence and intensity of a memory.[49] Some mutineers had difficulties recalling the events because of the passage of time on grounds of the fallibilities of memory and their troubling character. Writing in 1926, Jean Camille of *Du Chayla* told Marty he would do all he possibly could to reassemble all his memories.[50] Joseph of the 301st Tank regiment witnessed the incidents at Tiraspol. Eight years afterwards, and having joined the Communist Party, he could say:

> After years of silence that have not extinguished the remorse, I come to accuse myself before you, to accuse us Frenchmen of the infamous role that we blindly played. I have for a long time kept these papers. I send them to you today, their title 'I blush to be a Frenchman'.[51]

Ribot's letters to Marty reveal the difficulty of memory from both the cognitive and emotional perspective. He was happy to write to Marty and pleased that he was not forgotten, but it is clear that the act of recall unlocked difficult memories. He took a fortnight's interruption in writing the letter because he found the whole process of trying to 'retrace the little details' very tiring and needed to stop. His account expressed a heavy burden of shame for France's role in the events, sharing experiences of witnessing summary executions as well as evoking his personal sense of desperation and isolation as an individual revolutionary amongst troops he had not long known and who did not trust him. It was anything but a fond memory of heroic comradeship.[52] Similarly, an emotional mix of regret and affection is apparent in fellow *Guichen* mutineer Denis Dupuit's letter to Tillon in 1966:

> I have often thought of you and yours, but having neglected you (I offer you a thousand apologies), I did not dare to write any longer [...]. You see that I have followed you in my thoughts always. Thank the gods! I have found my friend again![53]

In these illustrations, neuroscientist Joseph Ledoux's distinction between explicit memories of emotions (remembering fear) and implicit emotional memory (being afraid again) is apparent.[54] Thus, an involuntary sense of cold seized Eugène Ribot's body on recalling the traumatic experience of witnessing the summary execution of a Russian prisoner at the hands of his fellow French troops.[55] Charles Tillon reported that his hand trembled with anger as he set about writing his memoirs, given his mistreatment by his closest comrades within the PCF.[56]

Social theorist Walter Benjamin observed that for the generation of veterans, the Great War had destroyed the art of storytelling.[57] It was impossible, given the mechanised nature of the war and scale of killing, to fit it into the epic heroic conventions of autobiographical narrative. Likewise, historians have noted the traumatic quality of the war experiences, the interruptions of momentary discomposure and the prevailing silences. Most witnesses sought to articulate a truth about the war experience that was officially denied. Measured against this yardstick, the mutiny bears some comparison.[58] Joseph, who struggled with the guilt of French actions during the campaign and had remained silent about the events until Marty prompted him, sent Marty a photograph telling him to do with it as he pleased.[59] In contrast, some former mutineers expressed the pleasure of recalling events. A regimental musician fondly remembered the refusal of his military band to play for General Louis Franchet d'Espèrey on 14 July 1919 at a military ceremony in Istanbul.[60] Prompted to write down memoirs of the mutiny on the tenth anniversary, Lachurie of the Danton-class battleship *Vergniaud*, who had witnessed the mutiny and the demonstration of 20 April in Sevastopol, noted the pleasure of retelling the events.[61]

In *The Principle of Hope* (1995), Ernst Bloch posits that hope occupied a special vantage point in the revolutionary process. Others (such as Christopher Hill in *The Experience of Defeat*) have scrutinised hope's dancing partner despair. Hill associates despair with the ultimate defeat of the English Revolution. He found an undercurrent of this emotion in John Milton's poetry and in the religious trajectories of the millenarian milieu during the post-revolutionary era. Likewise, Leon Trotsky noted the dialectic of revolutionary hope and counter-revolutionary despair that animated the rise of fascism in Germany.[62] Reading the mutineer testimonies in this light, hope and despair gauge revolutionary expectation and its absence. As Bloch put it: 'The most tragic form of loss isn't the loss of security; it's the loss of the capacity to imagine that things could be different.'[63] Similarly, Walter Benjamin pondered the tragedy of revolutionary despair regarding Auguste Blanqui's last reflections from his prison cell, which were a 'renunciation without hope of a great revolutionary'.[64]

Precisely how mutineers navigated these two powerful emotions set the coordinates of their post-mutiny trajectories. The memory of hope lingered in the mutineer narratives amid a prevalent mood of despair and lost revolutionary opportunity. Disappointment when a cycle of contestation fails to deliver on its early expectations can yield to sadness and despair. Jean Riballet, of the 176th regiment, felt sufficient familiarity with Marty to talk of his marriage and child, allowing him to confide in his fellow mutineer. For Riballet, writing eight months after his release from prison due to the amnesty in January 1922, the war constituted a 'sad moment'.[65] His cryptic comment suggests a desire not to relive painful military experiences. For Pierre Vottero, of the battleship *Voltaire*, who was aged twenty-one in 1919, being abandoned in the sadistic prison regime at Clairvaux resulted in 'despair' and a 'terrible memory' of the prison chief that he retained five decades on.[66] Writing in 1927, Joseph, of the 301st Tank regiment, who to his shame, shelled opponent positions, stated that there was a 'very sad mentality' in his regiment and, consequently, maintained no contacts from the time.[67] Duport of the *France* also spoke of 'very sad things' in a letter written to his parents within a fortnight of the mutiny, going on to relate atrocities of the French intervention.[68] Yet Duport was more ambivalent, relaying the dual disillusions of intervention and mutiny to his parents.[69] Marius Fracchia, a former mutineer living in St Tropez, wrote to Marty of his joy to have real friends in such awful moments. The former local secretary of the *Confédération Générale du Travail Unitaire* (CGTU) dockers' union registered his sadness that workers did not understand the class struggle and that the socialist campaign against the Communist Party discouraged the workers. All in all, he had for some time despaired about the working class and he left the Communist Party.[70]

Sadness and despair permeated mutineer testimony reflecting upon their defeat through the longer lens of retrospection. Alex Barillon, of the *Waldeck-Rousseau*, hoped for a better understanding between peasants and workers but propaganda was insufficient where he was living. As he pithily put it, too much holy water was being drunk there.[71] This widespread despair also resulted from the dissipation of class struggle and the decline of the revolutionary left after 1919. It corresponded to a wider demoralisation on the left as a whole. Thus, an article in *Le Travailleur* lamented the post-mutiny odyssey of Badina, who had apparently abandoned the workers' movement.[72] In a memoir written three days before his death, in a hospital in Bicêtre, in January 1939, the gunner Alphonse Cannone of the *France* captured the sense of defeat and despair felt with the repression of the mutiny: 'Could we hope? Is a better future taking shape for the people? Alas, only illusions.' His despair corresponded not only with his failing health, but also his immediate experience as an FAI (Iberian Anarchist Federation) activist in the Spanish Civil War, taking flight with the thousands of others chased across the border by Franco's advance.[73]

While the act of recall summoned mixed emotions, regret provided a prevailing and many-sided emotional tone. Mutineer aboard the *France*, Duport regretted not counting the shells fired on Odessa, failing in his moral duty as a witness to atrocity.[74] The passage in Ribot's troubled testimony about the summary execution of a Russian prisoner at the hands of a French firing squad is laced with powerful regrets at his own impotence and his personal failure to start the movement of revolt to 'prevent the murder of a decent man, a hero.'[75] Equally, the spurned chance of revolution recurred in mutineer testimonies. Hindsight suggested a calculation of mistakes made and chances rued. A Leading Seaman gunner wrote to *L'Humanité* listing what they should have done during the revolt:

1. The nomination of a committee of sailors.
2. The possession of arms.
3. Seizure of the radio transmitter and all means of communication.
4. The complete isolation of the general staff under proper guard.
5. To not be dispersed in the boats and maintain a perfect cohesion.
6. Keep in contact the Russian workers and French workers to put our forces at the service of the revolution.[76]

Being asked as to the unforgettable quality of the events in an interview for *L'Humanité*, Marty reflected:

> Certainly! With a great regret however which had obsessed us during the years in the squalid prisons of the republic: 'Ah! If we had a communist party in France! Ah! If we had known the doctrine of Lenin! Ah! If we had learned to build secret cells on the ships, in the factories, soldiers, sailors and workers would have done more than stop the intervention! They would have engaged in the final struggle.[77]

It would be easy to dismiss this as a doctrinaire formula. Yet non-PCF former mutineers shared the feeling.[78] Regret centred on missed opportunities for action, including revolutionary action.

The long debate within neuroscience about the significance of two brain regions (the amygdala and the hippocampus) to memory again highlights the multiplicity and complexity of what we call memory. As lesion studies (where specific areas of the brain are damaged) have shown, both are highly significant for memory but of different types. As Ledoux observes, the amygdala acts as a triggering device for survival mechanisms, such as responses to danger (which developed earlier in evolutionary time), while the hippocampal circuits are stimulated with complicated memories taking place in time and space, sometimes described as cognitive mapping, that link to more complex learning through formulating hypotheses. Such dualities appear in the overlayering of memories in mutineer narratives: the mutiny provoked emotional impulses with recall, but it was also an experience from which mutineers learned.[79]

Memory and keepsakes: songs, photographs and letters

To restore dialogue to mutineer memory, Marty's monological account needs to be unpieced. In part, this can be done through re-examining the nature of his archive of the mutiny. This documentation has a dialectical quality, being both autobiographical, and therefore analogous to the collections of other mutineers, and collective, being the sum of materials that many mutineers gathered. As such, Marty's archive gives an insight into the relationship between personal memory and one's own possessions, artefacts, material and intangible culture.

A striking feature of Marty's collection of testimonies is the diversity of its form. Marty's archive is composed of letters, memoirs, photographs, songs and press cuttings. For instance, Jean Camille, an engineer aboard the battlecruiser *Du Chayla* was able to provide Marty with a pamphlet that Labourbe's circle had produced and, indicating its status for him, had written at the bottom of the last page '*Souvenir de Nicolaief, mars 1919*' (*Memories of Nicolaief, March 1919*).[80] Eugene Ribot provided him with a leaflet from the same group and 'Comrade B[ouryes]' had the fragment of another pamphlet as a memento.[81] Some of these items evidently possessed the aura of a heroic relic for their owners. Pierre Vottero, of the *Voltaire*, recalled how he enthusiastically imbibed the stories of the mutineers of the *France* when they arrived in Bizerte in May–June 1919, retaining the memory of the copy of a Russian leaflet that Frédéric Daucros had 'piously conserved' from the Black Sea.[82] For his part, Vottero treasured a leaflet and a song sheet from the campaign for the release of the mutineers, which he had lent to Marty, but which had not been returned (both still remain in the latter's papers).[83]

The most common documentary form in the mutineers' archive is epistolary. The letters vary in length from several pages long to a few lines. The addressee is most commonly Marty. Duport allowed Marty to use the letters he had written to his parents on his return journey from the Black Sea. When Marty is the addressee, this obviously frames a letter in two senses. First, the letter is an expression of the nature of the interpersonal relationship between Marty and the mutineer. Second, the author writes with the reconstruction of the mutiny in mind. In other letters, this is not the case and there is no eye to posterity. The timing of the letters varies considerably. The earliest letter in Marty's collection is from 1921, while Tillon's papers contain mutineer correspondence from as late as 1973.

If letters were the predominant form of mutineer testimony in the collection, they were not the only one. Several mutineers produced reports of their actions for newspapers.[84] Other mutineers sent Marty their journals of military service or the extracts relevant to the mutiny. Marius Jules Cyrille, a helmsman on the *Ernest Renan*, sent Marty extracts of a notebook of the journey, (*cahier de route*) with day-by-day entries from 25 February to 23 June 1919.[85] Lucien Godin of the *Bruix* also provided Marty with a travel diary (*carnet de route*) for the period 30 March–22 May 1919.[86] Beyond these forms, there are a few efforts to write memoirs of events from the first-person perspective. Nouveau wrote a lengthy memoir entitled *From Toulon to Calvi via Odessa: The riot on the Waldeck-Rousseau: its origin, its course, its end, its consequences*.[87] Similarly, Lachurie wrote a memoir of his experience of mutiny aboard the *Vergniaud*.[88] Ricros and Hurel wrote up their account of the court martial of the *France* a year after the event.[89]

The sample of mutineers in Marty's papers has reasonable coverage. There are accounts from all the major sites of mutiny with the exception of the Baltic, Famagusta and Archangel. The coverage, however, is uneven. The events in the Black Sea and on board the *France* have the greatest depth. Where the *France* is concerned, Marty assembled accounts from two of the three ships' delegates (Notta and Duport) as well as three others (Hurel and Ricros, Lagaillarde, and Pleurot). In addition, Marty could work from an official report into the events aboard the *France* that he managed to secure. These documents should not be seen simply as evidence of the mutiny; they should also be seen as evidence of how the mutineers remembered the event. Such written records indicate an attempt to make sense of the past and battle the slippages of memory. When Tillon sought to compile a brochure from the memories of those in the Association and Tondut offered his notes from the mutiny of the 58th Infantry that he had provided Marty, as well as an *Avant Garde* article to which he had contributed, he anxiously pleaded with Tillon to return them, being the last physical traces of the mutiny in his possession.[90]

Song, orality and memory

If song played a significant part in the mutiny, it also featured in mutineer memory. For unofficial or vernacular memory of events such as the mutinies, song functions as it did in oral cultures. It was a means to recall, perform, communicate and valorise an event. Such memory acted as a counter-current to official memory of the war and its aftermath.[91] Songs illustrate the passage from personal souvenir and individual memory to collective commemoration and the accumulation of public artefacts attesting to the mutiny.[92] One such song was an improvisation in the midst of the mutiny. In Marty's papers, an undated press cutting recorded a single verse that the crew of the battlecruiser *Waldeck-Rousseau* sang to Admiral Caubet on 27 and 28 April 1919. It was 'a song that must not be forgotten' according to the newspaper that printed it:[93]

> I've thought about it, I will not shoot!
> I'm a sailor, but a worker all the same!
> And on my rebel brothers down there,
> I will not shoot, I will remain myself.
> I am not the valet of the hangmen,
> Mad on opium, cocaine and morphine,
> Who hide their vices in the shadow of the flag,
> I will not move, preferring the sea.

The song registered a refusal to shoot on the grounds of class fraternity: 'I am a sailor but a worker all the same.' Refusing to be the 'valet of the hangmen', it denounced the ignoble officer class 'mad on opium, cocaine and morphine' who disguised their depravity through a hollow appeal to nationalism.[94] The crew of the battlecruiser *Waldeck-Rousseau* created the song during the effervescence that followed Marty's brief imprisonment aboard when the rumours of the Sevastopol mutinies reached them. Since 9 April the ship was patrolling the Black Sea near Odessa to protect Allied land forces.[95] On 23 April, the crew discovered that Marty was aboard, with Admiral Caubet removing him on 27 April. The revolt on the *Waldeck-Rousseau* signalled a second wave of mutiny only days after that in Sevastopol had subsided. Thus, capturing the collective mood of the time, this improvised song was retained in the memory of an individual mutineer to be transcribed and then shared with the movement. The dialectic of personal and collective memory manifests as mutually dependent mediations (creation, performance, transcription, publication and circulation) and spatial-temporal contexts.

Another song, *La Gloire aux Marins de la Mer Noire* became the standard of the mutiny sung at the Association's anniversary dinners. Marty's *La Révolte* carried the full text as an appendix. The publication overlooked the song's libertarian origins. Maurice Carlus authored the song, though Marty only attributed the editorship of the Committee of the Defence of the Sailors.[96] It was one of several songs to emerge during the amnesty campaign.[97] Which of these songs persisted within mutineer networks was arbitrary, probably relying upon inclusion in Marty's text.

The *Gloire aux Marins de la Mer Noire* borrowed the tune of *Gloire au 17e*, evoking the memory of the mutiny of the 17th regiment during the wine-growers' rebellion in Languedoc-Roussillon in 1907. This legendary event formed part of French radical culture and the song entwined with local and labour identity. Music historian Serge Dillaz described how all sections of the left quickly adopted *Glory to the 17th* as a standard. That *Glory to the Sailors of the Black Sea* borrowed the tune of its predecessor is significant.[98] Most immediately, the familiarity of the music aided those who wished to join in, particularly with the chorus, which bore the greatest similarity with its antecedent. Moreover, Chantegrelet and Doubis's music suggested an association between the two events in the mind of the audience or singer. This implied a connection to a longer tradition of song and militancy, lending an authenticity within French revolutionary traditions to the cause of the Black Sea mutineers who languished in military prisons and were accused in the right-wing press of being anti-French traitors.

The *Glory to the 17th* and the *Glory to the Sailors of Black Sea* bear more connections beyond their shared tune. In the refrain, the same opening line 'Salut! Salut à vous!' appeared but 'valiant sailors of the Black Sea' replaced 'brave soldiers of the 17th'. The chorus ended with their being asked to murder the republic in the first instance and communism in the latter. Beyond the chorus, intertextual borrowings were more subtle. Themes of virtue (honesty/clear conscience), the refusal, the (magnificent/sublime) gesture, the common enemy ('the great who are in power'/ 'capitalism' and 'tyrants of the earth'), the revolutionary day to come ('a day will come in France'/'surely one day') resonate between the texts.

The earlier song's explicit emotionality was stronger than that of the latter. In the *Glory to the Sailors of the Black Sea*, emotion was tacit with the exception of the 'sacred hope of revolution' that the sailors 'bore in their entrails'. Hence the *Glory of the Sailors of the Black Sea* sought to draw popular legitimacy from its association with its antecedent for the cause of communism and the imprisoned mutineers. The register shifted between the two revolutionary songs. The first made emotional appeals to family and the nation as well as a rational invocation of citizenship and the republic, whereas the latter solicited a corporate solidarity of the sailors ('*cols bleus*' (blue collars)) and the global borderless appeal of communism ('tyrants of the earth [...] frontiers of death, prison and money').

Finally, *The Glory to 17th* had a special significance for Marty. He wrote a book in tribute to the song.[99] Indeed, Marty was himself there on the day of this famous act. In memoirs about a trip on a torpedo boat that he made to Indochina in 1912 and colonial rule being for Michelin to export 'rubber that dripped with blood', Marty recalled singing *The 17th* during his return to France on a CGT dockers' demonstration on 1 May in Marseille.[100] *The 17th* continued to act as a musical template, providing familiarity and conferring the legitimacy of popular revolutionary tradition.[101] Being present during the wine-growers protests, the song was for Marty intangible heritage, signifying personal, family and regional belonging.

Photography, sight and memory

Both song and photography implied a relationship between the senses and memory. Memory and photography have several connections. Visual memory, visual metaphors and the equation between sight and truth suffuse mutineer narratives. Confiding in his parents, Duport's formulation 'my eyes have seen very sad things' suggested the visuality of his memory of the recent mutiny.[102] Recalling the scene when the commander of the north front of Sevastopol discovered the list of demands of the *France's* mutinous landing party, gunner Pierre Le Roux wrote: 'I can still see the officer holding the letter, asking for the author to come forward, giving his word of honour that no action would be taken.'[103] Seeing the red flag raised, or on a distant ship, or flying over Odessa, or tearing the red from the tricolour connected a visual memory to the reconstruction of narrative.[104] That mutineers lingered over the description of the size or colour of the flag suggests its visualisation in memory.[105] Indeed, as mutineers remarked, seeing the red flag rendered the mutiny 'unforgettable' or 'beautiful'.[106]

Reversing this relationship between recall and sight, oral historians and ethnographers have used photographs as a powerful prompt to memory.[107] Van Campen described the senses as 'doorways to lost memories'.[108] Paula Hamilton has suggested that the senses pervade testimony, noting the centrality of visual recall and description to many interviews. She also emphasised that the loss or absence of senses in testimony might be connected to trauma. Finally, she observed that place also held a great sensory significance for memory.[109]

Indeed, visual memory not only often includes the recall of particular photographs but resembles the photograph in eidetic memory, particularly associated with childhood.[110] With the transition to adulthood, from being fragmentary, imaged and timeless, memory becomes linear, temporal and largely imageless. Nonetheless, photography has become part of how we remember. Marty's photographic record of the mutiny assembled to illustrate his history is indicative of this process. Much more so than today, photography had a powerful association with authenticity and veracity. It was becoming much more common in publishing and associated with the success of those periodicals and newspapers that were able to deploy it more frequently. Indeed, the first edition of Marty's *Révolte* coincided with the birth of *Vu* and *Regards*, both landmarks in a French photojournalism informed by an epistemology of photographic realism.[111] Prompted by Marty, a tank regiment veteran of the intervention could recall seeing photographs of the evacuation of Kherson, describing them as 'faithful witnesses of the occupation'. One depicted a crowd of workers on the ramparts watching soldiers of his company destroying barrels of wine, pouring the liquid into the sea, and a little further colonial troops throwing grenades and munitions into the sea. Unfortunately, Marty's correspondent remarked, the owner of these photographs would not be sympathetic. As for the veteran himself, he regretted that he possessed nothing 'not images, nor leaflets, nor photographs of this time.'[112]

With Marty having collected the visual record for *La Révolte*, their reproduction in that volume allowed readers to visualise the mutineers, their ships, Sevastopol and Odessa; thus, a particular visualisation of the mutiny entered the collective imagination of the labour movement. Many mutineers possessed copies, allowing the publication to act as a visual and literary prompt to memory. The assembled images in *La Révolte* reappeared in other publications: newspapers, *Les Heures Glorieuses* and even the sale of these photographs as a collection of postcards in 1949. While they formed a relatively stable visual repertoire of the mutiny, their significance was adapted with each iteration of their publication, not to mention of their individuated reception.

Marty's ability to gather this photographic record ensured that these images had what Walter Benjamin called an 'afterlife', wherein the meanings of the photograph were not frozen in the social relations from which they initially emanated but evolved according to the changing milieu of their reproduction.[113]

Marty's photographic archive comprised a variety of forms. He used the commercial postcards to provide photographs of the Black Sea and the French battleships that participated in the mutiny. More poignant and interesting were the personal photographs of mutineers. These were professional portraits with a conventional head-and-shoulders composition that were a ubiquitous souvenir of military service and a rite of passage for all those who served in the Great War. Such images might offer those who lost loved ones in the war a precious token not just to render death meaningful but to forestall the anxiety of forgetting: an illustration par excellence of what Roland Barthes described as the personal pain ('*punctum*') that a photograph can inflict.[114] The meanings of this military portrait genre of photography radiated along different pathways from the images. The perspective of the observer was crucial.

First, for non-mutineers, the photographs signified the human face of the mutiny in the newspapers, whether the physiognomies were imagined as heroic or villainous. The revolutionary press used these images during the campaign for amnesty of the mutineers. Thus, a montage of five mutineers (Pierre Vottero, Dulout, Louis Badina, Gustave Champale and Marius Fracchia) was used in a report from a campaign meeting in Cherbourg in September 1922.[115] The French National Library holds this image of the Black Sea mutineers produced by the Meurisse photographic press agency.[116] These were also circulated as fundraising postcards, a form of commodity with a mass market at the time. Adapting this form through the new technique of montage, a report in *L'Humanité* on the mutiny aboard the *Voltaire* superimposed the headshots of seven mutineers onto the gates of Clairvaux prison.[117] Showing the diverse uses to which the visualisation of the mutiny were put, such composite images of mutineers entered the files of the Minister of the Interior, serving the purpose of political surveillance.[118]

Second, for mutineers themselves, these representations of a youthful self signified a reference point for the composition of identity: the sometimes nostalgic, sometimes ambivalent knowledge of who you were and therefore – according to the narrative reconstruction of self in the present – who you are. Edouard Daniel, who had participated in the agitation in Brest during the summer of 1919, was happy to assist Marty by supplying his photo but pleaded with him to return it.[119] For other mutineers, these images signified the loss of contact with old comrades and the entry into new patterns of everyday routine after the Navy. Equally, these photographs substituted for the loss of memory, a proof of participation in the context of a deficit of the powers of recall.[120]

Photographs were personally meaningful keepsakes that could defy the decades. Corresponding with Tillon in early 1970, *Guichen* mutineer Millerin told how he had 'preciously kept' the photograph from 1919 of 'all of us [...] with the bastard of a leading seaman engineer behind me'.[121] In this exchange, it appears that while the trauma of the events could not be forgotten, Millerin had lost several details that Tillon's book exposed to him. So, at least the photograph provided a comforting certainty, around which to render his past meaningful and coherent. At roughly the same time, for Paul Poisson of the *Mirabeau*, his photographs of Russian labourers doing salvage work – taken in Odessa or Sevastopol, he could not be certain – still filled him with enthusiasm. He looked forward to sharing his memories at the Association's fraternal meal in May 1969.[122]

The final form of image was the group photograph of mutineers. This was, by some distance, the rarest form, signalling the limited dissemination of photographic equipment amongst the sailors, who had to rely on others to capture these documents so invaluable to personal memory. Léon Hurel of the *France* provided a unique group photograph of five sailors in engineers' overalls in a relaxed pose of comradeship.[123] It would be tempting to think that this was taken during the period when the officers were not asserting their authority between the mutiny and the *France*'s arrival in Bizerte. They were certainly not observing formal military discipline at the time and were exercising an emotional liberty. It is not until the reunions of mutineers during the 1960s that a couple more group photographs of ageing veterans emerge.

That this photographic form is so uncommon underlines Walter Benjamin's insight into photography as symptomatic of capitalist modernity, being a dynamic medium of successive technological, commercial and creative transformations. Photography moved from the experiments of wealthy amateurs via the professional photographer's studio with its convoluted paraphernalia into the hands of those from all classes who – through ownership of small simple cameras – could both produce and consume photographs. The unusual character of Hurel's image signals that the mutiny stood at this last threshold and alerts us to the absence of the mutineer-photographer, or even the sympathetic photojournalist who appeared within a decade and amply documented comparable events such as the Popular Front or the liberation of Paris. This implies both an impoverished photographic record (even in comparison to the Great War) and a visual hegemony on the part of the military authorities, who are still able to constrain the photographic record of the mutiny. Mutineers, then, had to contest the afterlives of the two predominant conventional photographic forms: the portraiture of military service and the commercial postcards of their battleships.

Photographs have also served public memorialisation. The communist newspaper of the 13th Parisian *arrondissement* illustrates how the PCF visualised the mutiny during its thirtieth anniversary. It featured images of Jeanne Labourbe; two rail workers, Gorbatiouk and Pryschak, hanging from the iron structure of Odessa railway station, with a sign around their necks, declaring 'a warning to the Bolsheviks'; the battlecruiser *Waldeck-Rousseau*; and a photograph of a youthful Charles Tillon in uniform and André Marty in his cap and overalls. These photographs rendered the mutiny visible, human, credible and meaningful in a way that the accompanying text could not. Without the text, however, the photographs would have been open to interpretation. Each of these images visualises an aspect of the narrative, stressing the martyrdom and heroic status of participants as well as the military power of the French state. The image of Marty stressed his proletarian character, despite his officer status. That of Tillon underlined his youthful heroism. By 1949, this established repertoire, familiar to a more experienced communist milieu, had insinuated itself into visual inventory of the collective memory of activists.

A final photographic form, again rare, was the portrait of the revolutionary veteran, also being connected with memorialisation. In 1969, the PCF newspaper of Limoges, *Écho du Centre*, featured an article about Marcel Monribot of the *Condorcet*. The photographer carefully composed a domestic scene. In the foreground but off-centre, in suit and tie, the former rail worker sat on his bed, *L'Humanité du Dimanche* in his lap. In the background, still in sufficient focus to draw the eye, was a row of books on a shelf, upon which was placed a portrait of his younger self in sailor's uniform. This secondary picture-within-the-picture was looking into the camera in order to make eye contact with the viewer, inviting comparison and contemplation. As if these were not sufficient clues to understand the image, the caption read: 'Fifty years after, Marcel Monribot remains faithful to his combat of 1919'.[124]

Death, ageing and morbidity

From the late 1950s to the 1970s, age pressed upon the mutineer cohort. A preoccupation with the effects of age was ubiquitous in the letters between mutineers. They described, often at length, the sender's well-being or illness, enquiring about the health of (or wishing good health to) the correspondent and their loved ones. Such morbidity mixed with mourning and loss. This context surely explains the propensity for mutineer nostalgia, sometimes deployed alongside the trope of rejuvenation. In his apologies to the fraternal meal of the mutineers' association, Fichou noted how his health prevented him from attending but passed on his best wishes to those who 'participated in the event with all the élan of the heart of their youth'.[125] The letters of mutineers could talk of a 'rejuvenating past' or of 'becoming old' as repeated themes. Désiré Brest complimented Tillon as his 'character did not age', remaining his youthful combative self and drawing his son's admiration.[126] Age not only affected individuals, it sapped the collective capacities of the network. Tondut observed that Tillon's remark that time was passing quickly was correct and the 'more that one aged, the more this truth is affirmed'.[127] In late 1964, with the Association in the 'most complete doldrums', Tondut was acutely aware that in a movement with no place for the young, activity was taking a serious blow with the passage of time.[128]

The correspondence between mutineers revealed how the deaths of fellow mutineers, especially those from the same ships or regiments, were particularly difficult. On news of Le Moullec's death in a car crash, Tondut of the 58th Infantry reflected that, Thomas already having died, 'I remain alone of the trio and I have a lot of trouble coming to terms with his disappearance.' He conflated his survival with the survival of the mutineer network, 'if we want to survive, we must do something.'[129] The present offered little in the way of good news, 'life continues in its routine in this Paris, more and more mind-numbing and unhealthy'.[130]

The fiftieth anniversary revealed the increasing frailty of the mutineer generation and the troubles of maintaining their veteran organisation. Tillon's invitation elicited a host of apologies. 'Quite a few difficulties' prevented Louis Vauly from attending.[131] Charles Fréchard offered his 'great regret' at not being able to attend.[132] Chasseing explained that his wife was eighty-one and not able to travel.[133] Marcel Corbière was still bedridden and observed wistfully 'evidently we are not 20 years old'.[134] Thomas René could not attend due to pulmonary illness, possibly cancer.[135] For Daublin, too, illness prevented his attendance – which he regretted – asking Tillon to say hello to the comrades and signing off 'long live the Black Sea mutineers!'[136] Joseph Escola could not attend as he had been hospitalised on 14 April in the Rheumatology Department and he could no longer walk.[137] As a pensioner living in a place with poor rail services, Emmanuel Gillé could not come for financial and travel reasons.[138] On a happier note, Rollett apologised because the meeting coincided with the first communion of his grandson.[139] If mutineers wrote freely of heart disease, cancer and haemorrhoids with their peers, pathologies of memory and cognition – as opposed to physical ones – were a taboo. The erosion of memory entailed the loss of mutineer identity, for which the repeated invocations to remember their mutiny acted as an anxious overcompensation.

If some mutineers could not attend, the widows of others responded that their husbands had passed away. Jean Perez's widow told Tillon that her husband had died on 24 February that year, leaving her very tired.[140] Madame Chomel told Tillon that she received his letter only by chance, having moved in 1961 to Haute Loire and, then again, two years ago to Montgerou. After long illness, her husband had died in November 1964, which she had experienced as a cruel loss. Reading Tillon's invitation had moved her, remembering how very attached her husband was to his fellow mutineers. She asked if she should attend the meal as this would bring back the sadness of the last occasion that she had attended with her companion.[141] Jules Marin's widow also informed Tillon of her husband's 'last voyage without return'.[142] Tillon's draft reply to Madame Marin highlights the elegiac mixture of emotions amongst contemporaries witnessing the passing of their generation. He relayed his sorrow at her news, but stressed his memory of Marin as a 'comrade so strong, so full of combative experience and whose heart was brimming with friendship'. If the reference point of youth in old age and mourning featured as a trope among mutineers, the letter carried another common theme, that of forgetting and memory. He asserted that history would remember their glorious acts, despite the sadness of loss. In consoling Madame Marin, Tillon was obviously trying to redress the way Marin's death had passed unnoticed within the wider labour movement, without an obituary in the union or party press, as was happening with so many other mutineers.[143]

This nostalgia was more than a backward-looking refuge in the past. It was a way of dealing with grief and a critical working through the events of one's life for posterity. It thus fed into the desire for recognition of the mutiny amid the condescension of the labour movement in the supposed era of affluence. Rather than simply a self-indulgent focus upon the past, mutineers appealed as much to the future of the French labour movement, so as to renew its aspiration to emancipation. This found its fullest articulation, in the attempt to transform memory into history.

In apparently their last exchange, Vuillemin relayed in a letter to Tillon the news of 'my comrade' Albert Doublier's death and funeral in Lyon. He had been alongside Vuillemin, one of the crew's delegates aboard the *France* during the mutiny. He reflected:

One by one, the witnesses of this epoch disappear, a few years more and nobody will know that there was a mutiny in the Black Sea. Despite your efforts to perpetuate the memory.[144]

Tillon's reply recorded the deaths of two more of the faithful, the Association's treasurer Marius Fabre and 'our old friend' Jégou.

Conclusion

Reading mutineer testimony for the dynamics of personal or autobiographical memory underlines the fragile life-course of the trace memories of the mutiny. Indeed, that concept of the 'traces' of memory seems to satisfy the insights of several disciplines of brain and mind. Age confronted mutineers with their own mortality and those of their comrades. It threatened the mutineer generation with the deterioration of memory. Viewed together, mutineers' personal memories were not uniform and did not conform to Marty's or the Navy's assumptions. Neither were they inert, pristine and individual, confirming their dialogical character. Beneath the heroic veneer of Marty's account lay uncertainties, revisions, some who were working through or moving on, but many seemed to return to the mutiny as a powerful anchor of their political consciousness. The battle against forgetting the mutiny was thus both personal and a shared one, relying on artefacts, personal narrative and exchanges with fellow mutineers. More than acting as individuals, they sought also to respond to the threat of oblivion with their own collective mnemonic practices.

Notes

1 Bakhtin, *Dialogic Imagination*, pp. 288–97.
2 See for example, Nancy Wood, *Vectors of Memory: Legacies of Trauma in Postwar Europe* (Oxford and New York: Berg, 1999).
3 *L'Humanité*, 4 October 1928.
4 ADSSD AM 281J IV D1.20 Jean Carrière to editor of *L'Ordre Communiste*, 27 September 1921.
5 ADSSD AM 281J IV E3.8 Voyageur Marseille, Perpignan, 27 October 1927.
6 Tillon, *Révolte*, p. 247.
7 Dominique Fouchard, *Le Poids de la Guerre* (Rennes: Presses Universitaires de Rennes, 2013).
8 ADSSD AM 281J VI D4.40 *La Provence*, 17 April 1929.
9 LeDoux, *Emotional Brain*, pp. 251–2.
10 AN F7 13165 Mutineers of the Black Sea Report, 22 August 1922.

11 CHSP CT1 *Ouest Journal* (Reims), n.d., 1949.
12 CHSP CT1 Millerin to Tillon, 15 January 1970.
13 ADSSD AM 281J I B1 Marty, *Affaire*, pp. 33–4.
14 ADSSD AM 281J I B1 Marty, *Affaire*, pp. 33–4.
15 Dominique Kalifa, *Biribi: Les Bagnes Coloniaux de L'Armée Française* (Paris: Perrin, 2009).
16 SHD 7 N 800 Note on the affair of the 58th Infantry in southern Russia, n.d.; *L'Humanité*, 21 August 1919, includes a letter dated 5 April from a mutineer.
17 SHD 7 N 800 Note on the affair of the 58th Infantry in southern Russia, n.d.
18 Jay Winter, *Sites of Memory, Sites of Mourning: The Great War in European Cultural History* (Cambridge: Cambridge University Press, 1998).
19 Tillon, *Révolte*, pp. 329–413. ADSSD AM 281J V A2.10–11 One correspondent who was a radio operator reported on his imprisonment in a cell aboard a ship that apparently reached 67°C, with the result that he was hospitalised afterwards with nosebleeds, throbbing ears and fever. Regarding his incarceration, Tillon sent two letters to *La Vague*, 13 and 30 May 1920.
20 ADSSD AM 281J IV E1.13 Eugène Lefort, *Souvenirs sur les événements de la Mer Noire*.
21 ADSSD AM 281J V 3.24 & 38 Albert Cornier to Marty, May 1934.
22 Rose, *Making*, pp. 132–3.
23 ADSSD AM 281J III E8.2 Joseph to Marty, 3 May 1927.
24 ADSSD AM 281J III E2.8 Lefebvre to Mary, n.d. AM VI D4.7 Marty's list: 'Souvenirs de la Mer Noire'.
25 ADSSD AM 281J III E12.2 Roger Benoist to Marty, 4 April 1928.
26 ADSSD AM 281J IV E1.2–13 Eugène Lefort, *Souvenirs sur les événements de la Mer Noire*. For Lefort's membership of the Association, CHSP CT1 Liste des Adherents de l'association ('1949?'). CHSP CT1 Société fraternelle des soldats et marins de la Mer Noire ('1950'). CHSP CT1 Liste des adherents ('1958').
27 ADSSD AM 281J IV E1.3 Eugène Lefort, *Souvenirs sur les événements de la Mer Noire*.
28 ADSSD AM 281J III D2 4 Leva to Marty, 14 January 1931.
29 Tillon, *Révolte*, p. 11.
30 Donald Olding Hebb, *The Organization of Behavior: A Neuropsychological Theory* (New York: Wiley, 1949).
31 Rose, *Making*, pp. 262–70. Tim Bliss, 'The physiological basis of memory', in Steven Rose (ed.), *From Brain to Consciousness?: Essays on the New Sciences of the Mind* (Princeton: Princeton University Press, 1998), pp. 73–93. On memory as 'social learning', Jay Winter and Emmanuel Sivan (eds), *War and Remembrance in the Twentieth Century* (Cambridge: Cambridge University Press, 1999), p. 11.

32 CHSP CT1 Douvrin to Tillon, 21 August 1966.
33 Jean-Pierre Changeux and Paul Ricoeur, *What Makes Us Think? A Neuroscientist and a Philosopher Argue About Ethics, Human Nature and the Brain* (Princeton: Princeton University Press, 2000), p. 139.
34 Felicity Callard and Constantina Papoulis, 'Affect and embodiment', in Susannah Radstone (ed.), *Memory: Histories, Theories, Debates* (New York: Fordham University Press), pp. 246–62.
35 Bob Uttl, Amy L. Siegenthaler and Nobou Ohta (eds), *Memory and Emotion: Interdisciplinary Perspectives* (Oxford: Blackwell, 2006).
36 Reddy, 'Saying something new', pp. 8–23.
37 Rose, *Making*, p. 70.
38 Alexander Luria, *The Mind of a Mnemonist: A Little Book About a Vast Memory* (London: Cape, 1969).
39 Annette Becker, 'Memory gaps: Maurice Halbwachs, memory and the Great War', *Journal of European Studies*, 35 (2005), pp. 102–13.
40 Ernest Renan, 'What is a nation?' in Jeffrey K. Olick, Vered Vinitzky-Seroussi and Daniel Levy (eds), *The Collective Memory Reader* (New York and Oxford: Oxford University Press, 2011), pp. 80–3; for an influential anthropological essay upon forgetting, Marc Augé, *Oblivion* (Minneapolis, MN: University of Minnesota Press, 2004).
41 Howard Schuman and Willard L. Rodgers, 'Cohorts, chronology, and collective memory', *Public Opinion Quarterly*, 68, 2 (2004), pp. 217–54.
42 Paul Ricoeur, *Memory, History, Forgetting* (Chicago: University of Chicago Press, 2004), pp. 412–56.
43 Changeux and Ricoeur, *What*, p. 147. Rose, *Making*, pp. 124–5. Hermann Ebbinghaus, *Memory: A Contribution to Experimental Psychology* (Bristol: Thoemmes, 1998). F. C. Bartlett, *Remembering: An Experimental and Social Psychology* (Cambridge: Cambridge University Press, 1932).
44 Elizabeth F. Loftus, Julie Feldman and Richard Dashiell, 'The reality of illusory memories', in Daniel L. Schacter (ed.), *Memory Distortion: How Minds, Brains, and Societies Reconstruct the Past* (Cambridge: Harvard University Press, 1995), pp. 47–68.
45 Alessandro Portelli, 'The peculiarities of oral history', *History Workshop Journal*, 12, 1 (1981), pp. 96–107. Ronald Fraser, *Blood of Spain: An Oral History of the Spanish Civil War* (London: Pimlico, 1986), pp. 30–2. Debating objectivity in relation to witnesses, Thomas Treize, 'Between history and psychoanalysis: a case study in the reception of Holocaust survivor testimony', *History & Memory*, 21, 1 (2009), pp. 127–50.
46 Walter Ong, *Orality and Literacy* (London: Methuen, 1982).
47 ADSSD AM 281J V A3.14 Albert Cornier, May 1934.
48 ADSSD AM 281J VI D2.86-7 Eugène Lefort to Marty, 7 March 1927.
49 Changeux and Ricoeur, *What*, p. 141.
50 ADSSD AM 281J III E3.4-9 Jean Camille to Marty, 2 June 1926.

51 ADSSD AM 281J III E8.1 Joseph to Marty, 7 February 1927.
52 ADSSD AM 281J VI C1 13 Eugène Ribot.
53 CHSP CT1 Dupuit to Tillon, 20 April 1966.
54 LeDoux, Emotional Brain, pp. 200-1.
55 ADSSD AM 281J VI C1.18 Eugene Ribot. Rose, Making, pp. 122-4 on Ebbinghaus and the distinction between voluntary and involuntary memory.
56 Tillon, *Révolte*, p. 10.
57 Walter Benjamin, 'The Storyteller', in Walter Benjamin, *Selected Writings*, (Cambridge: Harvard University Press, 2006), Volume 3, pp. 143-66.
58 Penny Summerfield, 'Culture and composure: creating narratives of the gendered self in oral history interviews', *Cultural and Social History*, 1, 1 (2004), pp. 65-93. Marlene A. Briggs, 'Dis/composing the First World War in Britain: trauma and commemoration in the testimony of Harry Patch, 1998-2008', *History & Memory*, 28, 1 (2016), pp. 71-109. On the difference between official and vernacular memory in war, John Bodnar, *Remaking America: Public Memory, Commemoration, and Patriotism in the Twentieth Century* (Princeton: Princeton University Press, 1991).
59 ADSSD AM 281J III E8.1-12 P. Joseph.
60 ADSSD AM 281J IV E3.8 Voyageur Marseille (Perpignan), 27 October 1927.
61 ADSSD AM 281J III D2.12 Lachurie, *Vergniaud: Souvenirs d'un ancien matelot du cuirassé Vergniaud*.
62 Leon Trotsky, *Struggle Against Fascism in Germany* (New York: Pathfinder, 1971).
63 Ernst Bloch, *Principle of Hope* (Cambridge: MIT Press, 1995); Enzo Traverso, *Left-Wing Melancholia: Marxism, History, and Memory* (New York: Columbia University Press, 2016); David Harvey, *Spaces of Hope* (Berkeley: University of California Press, 2000).
64 Benjamin, *Selected Writings*, Volume 4, p. 93.
65 ADSSD AM 281J III E2.11 Jean Riballet to André Marty, 3 September 1922.
66 Le Ramey and Vottero, *Mutins*, p. 103.
67 III E8.1 Joseph to Marty, 3 May 1927.
68 ADSSD AM 281J III D2.26 Duport letter to parents, 25 April-1 May 1919. For Duport's membership of the Association, CHSP CT1 Société fraternelle des soldats et marins de la Mer Noire ('1950').
69 ADSSD AM 281J III D2.26 Duport letter to parents, 25 April-1 May 1919.
70 ADSSD AM 281J VI D4.54 Fracchia to Marty 8 December (n.y.).
71 ADSSD AM 281J VI D2.57 Barillon to Marty, 15 March 1926.
72 ADSSD AM 281J VI A5.1 Marceau, 'Le coup de groin du porc', *Le Travailleur*, 28 October 1928.
73 CHSP CT1 'Memoires de Cannone', *Contre-Courant*, 1953, p. 6.
74 ADSSD AM 281J III D2.26 Duport letter to parents, 25 April-1 May 1919.

75 ADSSD AM 281J VI C1 18-19 Eugène Ribot.
76 ADSSD AM 281J III D2.9-10 An ex-quartermaster gunner writes to us on the faults of the sailors of the Black Sea, *L'Humanité*, 25 August 1932.
77 ADSSD AM 281J V B.24 'Odessa 1919-Shanghai 1932 a bord du Waldeck-Rousseau', *L'Humanité*, 7 February 1932.
78 *L'Humanité*, 19 September 1926. On the desire for a Lenin in Paris by a libertarian novelist and former sailor, César Fauxbras, *Mer Noire: les Mutineries racontées par un Mutin* (Paris: Ernest Flammarion, 1935), p. 88.
79 LeDoux, *Emotional Brain*, p. 224. Rose, *Making*, p. 269.
80 ADSSD AM 281J VI B2.3 Groupe Communiste Français, *L'Entente et le Problème Russe*, February 1919.
81 ADSSD AM 281J VI B2.6 Eugene Ribot's leaflet. VI B2.8 comrade B's conclusion of a pamphlet carrying as title 'Proletarians of all countries unite'.
82 Le Ramey and Vottero, *Mutins*, p. 88.
83 Le Ramey and Vottero, *Mutins*, p. 103.
84 Amongst several others, VI D4.37 Morival Marceau, press cutting in *L'Enchainé*, 26 April 1929. VI D4.39 Salvarelli (*Waldeck-Rousseau*), 1921 in *La Provence*, 27 April 1929.
85 ADSSD AM 281J III D2.5 Marius Jules Cyrille, *Cahier de route*.
86 ADSSD AM 281J VI D2.89-98 Lucien Godin (*Bruix*), *Carnet de route*, 30 March-22 May 1919.
87 ADSSD AM 281J VI D2.63-74 R. Nouveau, *De Toulon à Calvi par Odessa*.
88 ADSSD AM 281J III D2.12 Lachurie, *Vergniaud: Souvenirs d'un ancien matelot du cuirassé Vergniaud*, n.d. Also, ADSSD AM 281J VI D2.24 Francois Perrone, *Memoire de la Mer Noire: Bord du Waldeck-Rousseau*, 28 January 1920.
89 ADSSD AM 281J IV D5.7-9 Huret and Ricros, *Report of Court Martial of France*, c. 18 July 1920.
90 CHSP CT1 Tondut to Tillon, 20 July 1964.
91 T. G. Ashplant, Graham Dawson and Michael Roper (eds), *Politics of War, Memory and Commemoration* (London: Routledge, 2000).
92 ADSSD AM 281J VI B2.9 A moving memory (newspaper cutting).
93 ADSSD AM 281J VI D2.78 press cutting, but no indication from where: 'A song that must not be forgotten'.
94 ADSSD Marty Fonds VI D2.78 press cutting but no indication from where: 'A song that must not be forgotten'.
95 Masson, *Marine*, pp. 349-60.
96 Brécy, *Florilège de la Chanson Révolutionnaire de 1789 au Front Populaire*, pp. 247-9. Marty, *Révolte*, pp. 665-6. *Le Libertaire*, 4 March 1921. Robert Brécy, *Autour de la Muse Rouge: Groupe de Poètes et Chansonniers Révolutionnaires: 1901-1939* (Saint-Cyr-sur-Loire: C. Pirot, 1991), pp. 99-100, 113, 123, 165-6. *Pour les marins* was published in *Le Libertaire*, 8 April 1921. *Les Marins de la Mer Noire* in ADSSD AM 281J II E24

L'Internationale, 13 March 1922. The songs also included *Clairvaux* and Clovys's *La Voix des Prisons*.
97 ADSSD AM 281J II E24 *L'Internationale*, 13 March 1922.
98 For a print version of the lyrics, ADSSD AM 281J III A2.57: *Gloire aux Marins de la Mer Noire*.
99 Marty and Calas, *A la Gloire des Lutteurs de 1907*.
100 André Marty, *Souvenirs d'Indochine* (Paris: Éditions de l'Avant-Garde, n.d.), p. 13. The pamphlet also reproduced Marty's speech in the Chamber of Deputies denouncing France's war in Indochina.
101 Brécy, *Florilège de la Chanson Révolutionnaire de 1789 au Front Populaire*, p. 260.
102 ADSSD AM 281J III D2.26 Duport.
103 CHSP CT1 press cutting *Contre-Courant*, n.d., 1953, p. 7.
104 ADSSD AM 281J II D2.29–30 Duport; VI D1.7 Notta; AM IV D1.20 Jean Carrière to editor of *Ordre Communiste*, 27 September 1921. SHD SS Ed 30 Admiral Legay, Report on the demonstration of 20 April 1919, 27 April 1919.
105 ADSSD AM 281J VI D2.63–4 R. Nouveau, *De Toulon à Calvi par Odessa*.
106 Le Ramey and Vottero, *Mutins*, p. 51. III D2.3 Leva, 29 November 1930.
107 Penny Tinkler, *Using Photographs in Social and Historical Research* (London: Sage, 2013). Penny Tinkler, '"When I was a girl...": women talking about their girlhood photo collections', in A. Thomson and A. Freund (eds), *Oral History and Photography* (Basingstoke: Palgrave, 2011), pp. 45–60. Tim Strangleman, 'Representations of labour: visual sociology and work', *Sociology Compass*, 2, 5 (2008), pp. 1491–1505.
108 Cretien Van Campen, *The Proust Effect: The Senses as Doorways to Lost Memories* (Oxford: Oxford University Press, 2014).
109 Paula Hamilton, *The Proust Effect: Oral History and the Senses* (Oxford: Oxford University Press, 2011).
110 Rose, *Making*, p. 122. At a threshold of nine or ten years.
111 Michel Frizot and Cédric de Veigy, *VU: Le Magazine Photographique, 1928–1940* (Paris: La Martinière Éditions, 2009). Danielle Leenaerts, *Petite Histoire du Magazine Vu (1928–1940) Entre Photographie d'Information et Photographie d'Art* (Brussels: Peter Lang, 2010). Jorge Ribalta (ed.), *The Worker Photography Movement (1926–1939): Essays and Documents: A Hard, Merciless Light* (Madrid: Museo Nacional Centro de Arte Reina Sofía, 2011).
112 ADSSD AM 281J III E8.2 Joseph to Marty, 3 May 1927.
113 Walter Benjamin, 'Little history of photography', in Walter Benjamin, *Selected Writings*, (Cambridge: Harvard University Press, 2005), Volume 2, part 2, pp. 507–30.
114 Roland Barthes, *Camera Lucida: Reflections on Photography* (London: Vintage, 2000).
115 *L'Humanité*, 3 September 1922.

116 BNF IFN-9038511 Les héros de la Mer Noire: Badina etc.: Paris: diff. par l'Agence Meurisse, 1922. This is an image of Badina, Fracchia, Champale, Dulout and Vottéro. http://catalogue.bnf.fr/ark:/12148/cb41581716p; IFN-9053769 For an image of Marty from 1921, http://catalogue.bnf.fr/ark:/12148/cb415800709 (last accessed 2 April 2018).
117 L'Humanité, 16 August 1922.
118 AN F7 13163 Mutineers of the Black Sea.
119 ADSSD AM 281J VI C2.3 Edouard Daniel to Marty, 14 January 1926.
120 CHSP CT1 Tondut to Tillon, 31 January 1967, 7 March 1967, 29 September 1967.
121 CHSP CT1 Millerin to Tillon, 15 January 1970.
122 CHSP CT1 Poisson to Tillon, 10 May 1969.
123 ADSSD AM 281J VI C4.6 'Du France, Léon Hurel'.
124 CHSP CT1 press cuttings, Écho du Centre, c. May 1969.
125 CHSP CT1 Fichou to Tillon (n.d. 1973). Also for trope of youth, CHSP CT1 Tillon to membership, n.d. (1969).
126 CHSP CT1 Brest to Tillon, 19 April 1967.
127 CHSP CT1 Tondut to Tillon, 29 December 1964.
128 CHSP CT1 Tondut to Tillon, 29 December 1964.
129 CHSP CT1 Tondut to Tillon, 14 October 1965.
130 CHSP CT1 Tondut to Tillon, 14 December 1966.
131 CHSP CT1 Louis Vauly to Tillon, 9 April 1969.
132 CHSP CT1 Fréchard to Tillon, 17 April 1969.
133 CHSP CT1 Chasseing to Tillon, 2 May 1969.
134 CHSP CT1 Corbière to Tillon, 4 May 1969.
135 CHSP CT1 Thomas René to Basset, 8 May 1969.
136 CHSP CT1 Daublin to Tillon, 13 May 1969.
137 CHSP CT1 Escola to Tillon, 21 May 1969.
138 CHSP CT1 Gillé to Tillon, 5 May 1969.
139 CHSP CT1 Rollett to Tillon, 8 May 1969.
140 CHSP CT1 Mrs Perez to Tillon, 6 May 1969.
141 CHSP CT1 Chomel to Tillon, 10 May 1969.
142 CHSP CT1 Madame Marin to Tillon, 6 May 1969.
143 CHSP CT1 Tillon to Madame Marin, n.d., May or June 1969.
144 CHSP CT1 Vuillemin to Tillon, 28 June 1973.

5

Associational memory

This chapter assesses the associational activity and the mnemonic practices of mutineers, as well as how these changed over time. Any event, not least one as significant for the participants as the mutinies of 1919, possesses an afterlife that unfolds in successive phases.[1] Initially, the unofficial knowledge of the Black Sea Mutiny spread, inspiring collective action amongst the armed forces and in France's port cities. This phase of collective action lasted until the autumn of 1919. Between then and 1923, the mutiny remained a matter of political actuality, returning to the news via reports concerning the courts martial, press attempts to smear or exonerate mutineers, the amnesty campaign and the electoral activity on behalf of imprisoned mutineers Marty and Badina. This phase ended with the release of Marty in July 1923.

After that point, the PCF sought to hegemonise understandings of the mutiny. Several former mutineers joined the party and their voices added to its anti-militarist campaigning. The mutiny served as an object lesson in fraternisation and revolutionary defeatism. The PCF deployed the mutiny pedagogically during the Ruhr occupation of 1923, the Rif War in Morocco in 1925 and its anti-militarist campaigns in the French armed services. By this time, the mutiny began to subside in the public attention and so began a long battle against oblivion on the part of its sympathisers and participants. The most concerted efforts in this regard were Marty's publications about the mutiny.

The Second World War transformed France's social memory, and this had profound implications for the mutiny. The resistance and liberation of France provided a new generation with its formative event.

The institutions of the French left, most notably the PCF, redefined themselves through this new reference point, contributing to the resistencialist myth. Looking through the prism of social memory, Pierre Nora distinguished between alienated 'sites [*lieux*] of memory' and the remembering milieu that connected participants to their past experiences. From this standpoint, the mutiny was increasingly distant, displaced and in danger of losing its status in the PCF *milieux* that had nurtured its memory. The mutineers needed to assert the revolt's continued relevance.[2] They confronted a new situation wherein even in the circles that had valorised their past, a threat of lost recognition and amnesia had materialised. The mutiny's place within the PCF's foundation myth increasingly ceded to the cult of Thorez expounded in his autobiography *Le Fils du Peuple* and within the official history of the party.[3]

Association Fraternelle des Anciens de la Mer Noire et de leurs Amis (1949–73)

More so than any other anniversary, the thirtieth anniversary elicited considerable commemorative activity. The PCF published new editions of *La Révolte de la Mer Noire* and *Les Heures Glorieuses de la Mer Noire*. Marty also produced an article for the *Cahiers du Communisme*, the PCF's theoretical journal. By June 1949, of the 200,000 print run of *Heures*, only 25,000 copies apparently remained, suggesting the commemorations generated considerable enthusiasm.[4] Yet, the party hierarchy was ambivalent, prioritising the dissemination of Thorez's *Fils du Peuple*, which probably sold 250,000 copies in 1949–50, while only 20,000 copies of *La Révolte* were printed.[5]

Although Marty had developed a network of correspondents so that he could write *La Révolte*, no formal organisation, until 1949, connected the mutineers of 1919. Then, with party support, a network of former mutineers took formal institutional shape. The first step towards this was taken on 17 April. The *Association Amicale des Anciens Soldats et Marins envoyés contre la Russie des Soviets en 1919* commemorated the 1919 mutinies at a meeting in Argenteuil. Insisting on the continued relevance of the mutiny, the secretariat of André Lavieu (of the *Waldeck-Rousseau*), Jean Le Ramey, Virgile Vuillemin and Emmanuel Gillé (all three of the *France*) sent a message of support to the International Peace Congress.[6] This act was 'faithful to the spirit that animated 1919 ... to the memory of the fallen 30 years ago'. They designated four delegates to attend the congress: Le Ramey, Marcel Tondut of the 58th Infantry, Marius Dumont of the *Waldeck-Rousseau* and François Basset of the *Justice*. They would represent (with a dash of rhetorical hyperbole) the '300,000 soldiers and sailors who refused to fight the Russia of the Soviets'.[7]

Emerging from this initiative, the *Association Fraternelle des Anciens de la Mer Noire et de leurs Amis* (AFAMNA, Fraternal Association of the Veterans of the Black Sea and their Friends) formed on 4 June 1949 at a general assembly with twenty-one in attendance. Vuillemin explained and gained approval for the Association's constitution. Tillon argued for a single organisation of former mutineers, like the *Forces Françaises de L'Intérieur* (FFI) veterans' movement, so as not to become a bureaucratic burden. The constitution specified that only those who had been condemned for mutiny could serve on the national committee. This restricted the potential candidates, given that, despite mass participation, only a minority had faced court martial. The meeting elected a national committee comprising André Marty (president), Charles Tillon (vice-president), Virgile Vuillemin (secretary), Jean Le Ramey (assistant secretary) and André Lavieu (treasurer).[8] Membership was to cost 250 francs a year. More funds were to be raised from the sales of postcards, songs and *Les Heures Glorieuses*. The assembly also enthusiastically adopted a motion calling for an official delegation to visit the Crimea.

Selected communist districts or regions also celebrated the 30th anniversary. On 26 April, the PCF of the 13th Parisian *arrondissement* organised a public meeting in the *Le Fagon* cinema. Two members of the Association (Louis Delamare and Antoine Paulet) lived in the area. Tillon chaired, with speakers including Raymond Bossus of the Central Committee and André Karman of the PCF's Seine Federation as well as the mayor and municipal councillors of the 13th. The meeting connected past and present struggles, honouring Salesse (a railway worker who refused to transport riot police to the Nord during the recent strikes), alongside the dozen survivors of the mutiny. Addressing railway workers in the 13th, Marty invoked the Black Sea Mutiny to illustrate how the peace campaign required action not just words. He reframed the group memory of the mutiny for the early Cold War, by comparing the military threat that US imperialism posed to the Soviet Union and the Allied intervention of 1919. Equally, he turned the mutiny to the purposes of condemning the post-liberation far left. According to Marty, the 'socialo-gaulliste' *Franc-Tireur* newspaper duped its readers into equating the US and the USSR.[9] In the 10th *arrondissement* at the CGT headquarters, rue des Granges-aux-Belles, Marty rehearsed the case for anti-militarist action to a capacity audience.[10] In similar style, *La Vie du XIIIe* implored members to undertake the 'imperious task in the grave hours' of reading and selling *Les Heures Glorieuses de la Mer Noire*, arguing that 'at a moment when our government is preparing a new war against the land of the Soviets for the millionaires of the dollar, it is particularly relevant to know and to make known how the crime of 1919 was broken'.[11] Local communist publications also joined in the commemorations. *La Vie du XIIIe* published extracts of Marty's *Cahiers du Communisme* article alongside Tillon's recollections of the *Guichen* mutiny and the lessons that they offered. The status of Tillon, mayor of Aubervilliers, had grown with the passage of time, having been head of the *Francs-Tireurs et Partisans* (FTP, military-wing of the communist resistance movement), and a minister in the post-war government.

Just as the memorialisation centred on selected Parisian *arrondissements*, beyond the capital too there was a marked spatial pattern to commemoration. In *Le Bretagne*, the Finistère PCF's newspaper, Marty reiterated the trope of going beyond rhetoric to defend the Soviet Union against the US war threat. Tillon also featured in the paper's three-page coverage of the event.[12] *Journal Ouest* (Reims) featured Théo Le Coze's account of the *Guichen* mutiny.[13] He had joined the ship on 28 January 1919 and witnessed the revolt. It was only when Tillon became the regional secretary of the *Confédération Générale du Travail Unitaire* (CGTU) that Le Coze realised the former's role in the mutiny and joined the PCF. The memorialisation in 1949 then was not an act of nostalgia but oriented on the present, with the history of the mutinies apparently offering its clear lessons for the communist movement.

The invitation list for a meeting (probably in Aubervilliers), which was later found in Tillon's papers, highlights the character of the commemoration even further: Paul Langevin's widow; Marcel Cachin, who had spoken out in the National Assembly in 1919 about the mutiny; anti-fascist artist Francis Jourdain, the President of the *Secours Populaire Français* (the communist philanthropic organisation); Jean Mérot, who had been condemned to death by a military tribunal at Toulon as part of the communist resistance during the Second World War for agitation amongst sailors; Tillon's principal private secretary when he was at the Ministry of Air, Pierre-Félix Le Gueinec; Yvonne Robert, who went to Spain with the International Brigades and was a close associate of Marty; and Tremellat, who led the movement of dockers and young workers of Marseille.[14] Alongside former mutineers, those present connected recent struggles with the movements of the Popular Front era and the resistance sharing the common thread of being Tillon and Marty's friends and allies. This suggests both the use of their patronage circle as well as, at best, inertia, on the part of other leading communists such as Maurice Thorez and Jacques Duclos with regard to the celebrations. This evidently had a spatial dimension with local networks of the 13th *arrondissement*, Tillon's municipal base in Aubervilliers as well as the latter's connections to his native Brittany. Already a pattern was emerging wherein memorialisation was becoming geographically uneven, reliant upon the human connection to events via ageing – usually communist – militants.

The outcome of the 30th anniversary was the Association. Notifying the Police Prefect, its assistant secretary Jean Le Ramey declared the *Association Fraternelle des Anciens de la Mer Noire et de leurs Amis* had been constituted, registering its headquarters as *Café Populaire*, rue Frémicourt, in the 15th *arrondissement*.[15] Though the Association's name was changed several times, it existed for the next 24 years. The membership in 1950 stood at 68.[16] When the list was compiled in 1958, of the eighty-two names, nine, having died, were scored out, and two were designated as 'ill'.[17] The membership combined those who were soldiers and sailors in 1919 and those who had been active in the *Comité des marins* that campaigned for the release of the mutineers. There were some exceptions to these criteria. Widows and sons featured in membership lists as did Henri Martin, a sailor and former FTP member, who had been jailed for agitating against the Indochina war.[18] Jacques Sadoul also appeared in the initial membership list for 1949.[19] In 1967, Tillon referred to a paying membership of 30.[20]

The Marty-Tillon affair of 1952

The Black Sea Mutiny's afterlife inevitably became embroiled in France's Cold War. In October 1952, René Pleven, the Minister of National Defence, sought to suspend the parliamentary immunity of five leading communists.[21] In Marty's case, Pleven cited his 1949 re-edition of *La Révolte* and *Les Heures Glorieuses* as well as pro-independence speeches against colonial oppression in North Africa as violent attacks on French foreign policy in justification of the proposed suspension. The subcommission investigating communist parliamentary privilege again cited these publications on 4 February 1953. This might have been expected but, to Marty's fury, five days later an article in *L'Humanité* repeated the claim that Marty had said to an officer (*officier instructeur*) in May 1919 that he had only been involved in the plot because of the intense stress he felt from overworking.²² For Marty, this echoed the long-standing campaign to disparage him and the Black Sea mutineers. It was the beginning of an internal witch hunt against him, which spilled out into a public controversy.²³

The Marty-Tillon affair is now well documented.²⁴ In 1952, the party conducted a campaign against Marty and Tillon apparently in order to shift blame for the debacle of 28 May 1952: the violent clashes with the police concerning the US general Rideway's visit and the Bonn–Paris Convention that ended the Allied occupation of West Germany. Marty and Tillon were already at this point under an internal party investigation that Mauvais was conducting. Mauvais delivered the report with its host of spurious accusations to the Political Bureau on 1 September and then to the Central Committee (CC) on 3 September.

A fortnight later the affair became public. The leadership deprived Marty and Tillon of their positions within the party one by one. Both were expelled from the Central Committee, the communist faction of the Aubervilliers council deprived Tillon of his mayoralty, the party transformed the FFI-FTP Association into the National Association of Veterans of the Resistance, making Tillon initial president at the inaugural congress in June 1952, then replacing him after the Mauvais report.

The communist press hounded them both. Jacques Duclos, in particular, spoke publicly of their crimes, comparing the affair to the Slansky and Doctors' Trials in Czechoslovakia and the USSR respectively. Both underwent self-criticism, namely the confession of false accusations and the humiliating declaration of party loyalty.²⁵ These were deemed to be insufficient. A further CC meeting occurred on 7 December, expelling Marty and returning Tillon to the party ranks.

Marty challenged the accusations, while Tillon remained publicly silent to avoid expulsion, hoping for the next 17 years that the party would return to its authentic revolutionary character. In his memoirs, Tillon described how he could escape to his new house in Monjustin, while matters were much worse for Marty 'wounded in his home, without refuge, trapped by perfidious relationships, retaining only the admiration of a few veteran sailors [Vuillemin, Monribot and Chenavaz] of 1919'.²⁶ Marty used his expulsion from the PCF to subject its leadership to a searching critique. He condemned the 'shameful compromise' of tripartism, in which communist ministers (including Charles Tillon) participated in the post-Liberation government, which in so doing betrayed the hopes of the resistance. In particular, he highlighted its culpability for re-establishing French imperialism in Indochina through the bombardment of Haipong on 24 November 1946. Despite such atrocities, the PCF had made no call to anti-imperialist action in contrast to the Rif campaign of 1925.[27] Marty also denounced Pierre Mendès-France's false peace of 1954 in Indochina, which allowed US imperialism sufficient respite to launch war against the Vietnamese people.

Inevitably, the campaign against Marty and Tillon reached the Association. According to Marty, Thorez had wanted to prevent its creation in 1946.[28] Maurice Foucault sent out a circular on behalf of the executive on 6 October 1952, calling a meeting for 25 October at 43 boulevard de Picpus in the 12th *arrondissement*. On the agenda of the meeting was the re-election of the executive and a treasurer's report.[29] On receiving the circular, Marty replied, saying that he would need five or six days to confirm his attendance but was shocked at the agenda: how could a committee re-elect itself? He also wondered why the minutes of the last general assembly of 20 April were not on the agenda.[30] A report of a meeting of the new executive held on 7 March 1953 found its way into Tillon's papers. With Sadoul, Le Ramey, Tondut, Dubreuil, Foucault, Gillé and Basset (all PCF members) present, the executive decided that Marty had adopted a shameful position 'systematically play[ing] the game of the worst enemies of the people'. He would be deprived of his functions and his membership of the Association would be put to the next general assembly. The executive initially included Tillon in this resolution but ultimately deleted his name. They evidently had trouble deciding whether to target Marty and Tillon together, ultimately deeming it wiser to restrict their accusations to Marty.[31]

Engaging in counter-denunciation, Marty questioned the credentials of those mutineers who replaced him. Le Ramey, the new President of the Association, was at the time of the mutiny the lowest rank of common sailor (*matelot sans specialité*) and had been acquitted in September 1919. Given that courts martial did not acquit without serious reason, Marty insinuated that Le Ramey had played some kind of double game. He alleged that a branch of the Ministry of the Navy had employed Le Ramey for 12 years. Moreover, Le Ramey had no active resistance record, only joining the party in April 1946. Indeed, his livelihood depended upon communist patronage, having been employed as a concierge in the *Maison des Metallurgistes*, rue Pierre Thibaud. Marty subjected the new secretary Maurice Foucault to similar scrutiny. Overlooking his resistance record, Marty observed that the photoengraver was unknown until 1946 when he joined both the party and the Association of Veterans of the 58th Infantry, which mutinied at Tiraspol, for which he was not even court-martialled. Marty may have borrowed the tactics of smear being used against him but the political standing of the new executive could not match those of Tillon, Marty and Vuillemin, whom they replaced.

Within the Association, the Marty-Tillon affair had a corrosive effect. From the PCF's perspective, the Association served little purpose in the second half of the 1950s.[32] The Association's inactivity ensured Tillon's isolation. Thus, it took until 1966 for Germaine Douvrin to apologise to Tillon for '20 years of silence', last having seen his fellow *Guichen* mutineer alongside Marty and other comrades.[33] Even as late as 1971, a former mutineer wanted to meet 'my old friend' Tillon for a 'friendly and frank discussion about your activity'.[34] Virgile Vuillemin and Joseph Chenavaz offered individual acts of solidarity and consolation. Vuillemin resigned from the PCF. An undercurrent of bitterness against the party persisted amongst some mutineers. Thus, Désiré Brest, in a letter in 1973, ironically charted the tragicomic biography of Tillon: 'mutineer of 1919, minister of 1945, hero of the PC from 1921 to 1951, PC heretic since 1951, excommunicated since then for perseverance in error according to the diabolical theologians!'[35]

1959: missing the 40th anniversary and the Chenavaz affair

It was not until 1958, with the 40th anniversary approaching, that the Association revived, electing a new executive. By this time, Marty was dead. The PCF leadership hoped that the Association could underline the party's revolutionary credentials, challenged by the emerging new left coalescing around Algerian solidarity. It could also emphasise the historical connections between the Russian revolution and the French labour movement during the high Cold War. Its symbolic value could be deployed during commemorations of the October Revolution and 1919. While the party was practically entwined with the institutions of the Fourth Republic via municipal and trade union administration, the memory of the mutiny afforded it a certain symbolic flexibility. Tillon became Association President in 1958; without him the venture might have stalled from the outset. For the Association's sake, he was willing to overlook publicly his personal sense of grievance. Nevertheless, smears had left their mark. The editor of the *Nouvel Humanisme*, Monstier, who claimed once to have admired the heroism of the Black Sea Mutiny, now wrote to Tillon denouncing him for a 'veritable con trick'.[36]

Frustrations dogged the Association's relaunch after the 20 April general meeting.³⁷ The new bureau sought to sell anniversary membership cards, stage fraternal banquets in Paris and Marseille and hold a national general assembly. Although there was an announcement in *L'Humanité* on 8 March 1958 that elicited some interest, the communist press *L'Humanité* and *Réveil des Combattants*, despite promises, failed to take the Association's press releases. Equally, efforts to find a venue for the 40th anniversary banquet entailed a seven-month wild goose chase around communist municipalities from Ivry to Gennevilliers to Bobigny.³⁸ That Tillon lived in Aix complicated matters, leaving much of the day-to-day business of finding venues and publishers in Tondut and Basset's hands in Paris, both PCF loyalists. By April and May 1959, Tillon's bitterness that the Association would miss the anniversary as a consequence of this obstruction showed in his correspondence with Tondut. The latter reciprocated this sentiment and expressed surprise at the appearance of Marcel Veyrier's article commemorating the mutiny without advertising the details of the Association.³⁹ In the fashion of the PCF during the Cold War, Veyrier emphasised that the Black Sea sailors' internationalism and patriotism were inseparable, being centred on Franco-Soviet solidarity.⁴⁰ This tricolour internationalism constituted an electoralist appeal to Frenchness. Thus, for the PCF, it was one thing to make the connection to the October Revolution: it was quite another to establish a live dialogue between participants and a new generation regarding contemporary events. The party marked the 40th anniversary by giving voice to a journalist with no connection to the events and by ensuring that the focus did not fall on the mutineers themselves.

Tondut complained that it took ten days for Foucault's widow to inform them that the print run for the anniversary cards and the Association's bulletin could not take place.⁴¹ The Association even received a categorical refusal from the *Association Républicaine des Anciens Combattants* (ARAC) for a stall at the communist festival *Fête de L'Humanité* (not wanting to be 'marked'), adding insult to injury *L'Humanité* prohibited the sale of the Association's anniversary cards.⁴² By August, Tillon was describing Thévenin's failures (and those of other senior PCF officials) to deliver on the publication of press releases (as the text was 'misplaced') or finding a banquet venue as sabotage.⁴³ The anniversaries of the major mutinies from Sevastopol to Itea had now passed. Tillon proposed the date of 4 October so as to benefit from a mobilisation of the veterans' movement.

The general assembly and fraternal meal did eventually occur on 4 October 1959. Only Tillon, Basset, Tondut, Chapotat, Dubreuil, Thomas, Le Moullec, Prochasson, Laurent and Fabre attended. The PCF Central Committee delegated Georges Frischmann to observe. The municipality of Ivry, of which Georges Marrane was the long-time communist mayor, hosted the event. Basset circulated an upbeat report of the meal – 'worthy of Pantagruel' – and the convivial atmosphere, which ended as usual in songs.[44] The offer of a visit to the Soviet Union equally had the imprint of Stalinist manoeuvring. Thévenin was to judge whether delegates were 'politically responsible'.[45] Tillon suspected that the delegation 'exclusively of veterans of the Black Sea' was a 'turn of phrase' to disguise the exclusion of the veterans of 1919.[46]

The re-emergence of the Association in 1959 re-ignited the Marty affair, at least in the press of the revolutionary left. Mutineer Joseph Chenavaz was disgusted at Marty and Tillon's treatment at the PCF's hands. In October 1955, Chenavaz had written privately to Tillon describing how the party in Isère had repeatedly visited him to poison him against Marty and his fellow *Guichen* mutineer. He declared that Tillon was an inspiration to him and that he would always remain true to his revolutionary politics. Their common experiences of mutiny and the unforgettable prison in Salonika meant that – despite his revulsion at those who spread lies against them in the PCF – he remained 'faithful to the revolutionary ideal which we arrived at together on 25 June 1919 aboard the *Guichen* at Itea'.[47] Four years later, in May 1959, *La Voie Communiste*, a Trotskyist periodical, published Chenavaz's letter denouncing the party's instrumentalisation of the Association.[48] At this time, the Algerian War was in full swing with the small far left of intellectuals and student radicals leading the opposition to it in France.[49] Revelations about the French army's widespread use of torture had become a political scandal in 1958, with the PCF embarrassingly having voted for special powers for the Mollet government. At the same time, opposition from the French Algeria lobby (an alliance of the far right settlers, Gaullists and the military elite) had precipitated the Fourth Republic's unseemly demise and de Gaulle's return to power.

Chenavaz, a long-time PCF member, complained that the party's 'immovable and infallible' leaders had done nothing to commemorate the mutiny's 40th anniversary precisely because they had substituted parliamentary for revolutionary action and that this constituted a form of class treachery. In 1919, he continued, the mutineers stopped war through action, now the PCF sought to stop war through signatures. He defended André Marty for remaining a revolutionary to his last breath and condemned Fajon, Mauvais and Duclos who described Marty as a traitor and a police spy. In particular, stating that he was present during Marty's last moments, Chenavaz asserted that Duclos's article in L'Humanité 'killed' Marty. Chenavaz complained that it was now impossible to find Marty's La Révolte because the PCF had suppressed its publication and distribution. He implied that the party wished to repress the mutiny's memory for politically expedient reasons. He had been a founder member of the Association in 1949 until 1953 'when the demolitionists liquidated everything'.

Chenavaz explained the sequence of events that precipitated his letter. In January 1959, the newly formed bureau sent him a circular and an invitation to join. He replied that he would only do so on condition of Marty's rehabilitation. In response, on 25 January, Tillon said nothing about Marty but that the bureau would answer him in due course. Unbeknown to Chenavaz, the bureau met on 14 February 1959 to plan the 40th anniversary and discussed the letter there. Basset could not attend but sent a letter stating that they could not discuss a matter that pertained to a particular party because of their non-partisan status.[50] Consequently, the bureau did not feel that it could decide such a course of action and so deferred to the judgement of a future general meeting. Thus, no response was forthcoming by the time Chenavaz's letter to La Voie Communiste was published in May. He concluded his piece in the Trotskyist monthly on the need for a new revolutionary party, as both the SFIO and the PCF had betrayed the working class. Chenavaz's resignation letter from the Association of 13 June complained that the bureau's silence indicated that it remained undemocratic and that Tillon was still acting on the orders of those who insulted Marty, himself and others.[51] Writing to Tondut in August, Tillon mentioned Chenavaz's letter in La Voie Communiste and that Basset had referred to it as that of a 'provocateur' in previous correspondence.[52]

Chenavaz's letters were read at the Association's general meeting of 4 October 1959. The meeting regretted his violent tone but agreed that democracy had been neglected. The general meeting noted that it was an error to expel the president and vice-president (Marty and Tillon) without a hearing. At the same time, the general meeting confirmed the principle of non-interference in the affairs of parties and that therefore they could not revise the decision without undermining this principle. Reacting no doubt to Chenavaz's observation that the PCF was repressing the memory of the revolt, and in particular Marty's publications,

Tillon commented that the meeting acknowledged the right to criticise. In the spirit of working together, the assembly planned a pamphlet about the mutinies that would be a non-partisan history of each regiment and ship as well as the agitation in the ports and arsenals. Basset's circularised report presented a misleading version of the meeting's contents. It failed to mention Chenavaz, instead stating that Tillon was delegated to reply to letters asking about the 'resignation of certain members such as [Emmanuel] Gillé'.[53] Such misrepresentation fuelled the tensions between Tillon and Basset.

It was not until 21 October 1959 that Tillon sent a reply to Chenavaz.[54] Tillon started with an account of the reception of his letters and democratic discussion that they had provoked at the general meeting. Rebuking Chenavaz, Tillon observed that the 'periodical of opposition' to which the former sent his letter did nothing to defend Marty in 1952 (it did not exist until 1958). What counted, Tillon asserted, was to 'stay faithful to his past'. More sympathetically, he appealed to Chenavaz's sense of nostalgia, recalling their risking their liberty at the 'most beautiful time of their lives'. The letter played on the shared sentiment of mutineers: 'How happy would we be that this cause had triumphed over all …?' Unlike Chenavaz, who condemned PCF leaders in Grenoble for asking demonstrators to disperse, Tillon made no mention of present politics, except the progress that the Soviet Union had attained.

The slumbering 1960s

Pierre Viansson-Ponté's *Le Monde* article entitled 'France is bored' written two months before the events of May 1968, summing up the apparent political calm of the 1960s, might have been written with the Association in mind.[55] The next sign of life after the Chenavaz affair in the 'slumbering' Association appears to have been the visit of a delegation (consisting of Basset, Dubreuil, Fernand Lauze and Émile Quesnel) to Moscow in April 1961.[56] This prompted Tillon to inquire about the status of the organisation. In June, he wrote to the executive, asking to be replaced because he could not attend meetings in Paris, all the more so as his wife, a former deportee, was ill.[57] Since the general meeting of October 1959 on the 40th anniversary, Tillon continued, some executive members had hastily circulated the membership in misleading fashion, reflecting neither the decisions nor the spirit of the meeting. After this, the executive had fallen silent, only interrupted in May 1961 with the Moscow visit to represent, as Tillon observed caustically, 'a memory that no longer has any interest in France'. Tillon found this situation highly unsatisfactory, wanting the Association to be transformed from 'a small sect of windbags [*radoteurs*]' to 'the chroniclers [*évocateurs*] of a History written with the numerous men still living'. He implored the executive to respect the statutes and abide by the decisions of the general meeting. No reply was forthcoming. The executive of the Paris region under Basset's leadership circulated the membership about the Russian trip, proposing a fraternal meal on 25 June depending on the response.[58] It appears that this did not happen.

The following year on 26 June, the date of the *Guichen* mutiny, Tillon again wrote to the executive, asking for his membership cards for 1961 and 1962 – unless, he observed, he had been expelled, as in 1952. He wanted information about the composition of the executive and the decisions taken at meetings, to which he presumed that he had not been invited.[59] A year later, Tillon repeated the process, quoting his previous letter in its entirety, saying that he had received no reply. On this occasion, he sent the letter to both Basset and the secretariat of the PCF.[60]

If Tillon kept his papers assiduously, it appears that the next major effort to regroup the Association (now using the title *Association des Anciens Soldats et Marins de la Mer Noire et de 1919*, ANASM) was in 1964. In February, Tillon as President and Basset as Vice-President sent a circular indicating that they had received considerable approval for the Association's continuation. Again, the officers used the discourse of remaining 'faithful to the memory' of 'events of our lives'. They set the date of their fraternal banquet and general meeting for Sunday 19 April, namely the 45th anniversary of the mutiny on the *France*, rendering this once more the epicentre of the sequence of mutinies.[61] Recognising the difficulties of travelling to the capital, comrades in the south envisaged a second banquet in Toulon. A follow-up letter indicated that the Parisian venue would be the *Gavroche* restaurant, on rue Rougement in the 9th *arrondissement*. It stressed that regions should at least send delegates so that 'we will remain faithful to our memories and friendship'.[62] The year 1964 was significant for the PCF as its general secretary of more than three decades passed away. While committee members joined the funeral procession and laid a wreath in Maurice Thorez's honour, mutineers continued to feel belittled as *L'Humanité* declined their press release expressing condolences.[63]

PCF's obstruction aside, the infrequency of the meetings attests to the difficulties of maintaining a network of ageing mutineers. No general assembly and meal occurred in 1965. Basset explained in the name of the executive that they did not wish to tarnish the success of the 1964 event. Tondut forwarded the circular to Tillon, with an apologetic note indicating that Basset had missed Gal and Tillon from the list of the committee, in whose name he claimed to speak.[64] In December 1965, when the secretary of the Association requested a meeting with Duclos, given the promises that the latter had made at the last banquet, Gaston Plissonnier offered Tondut a meeting.[65] On Tondut's arrival, it was Werthlé who spoke to him, explaining that the election period prevented the insertion of the Association's press releases.[66] In a letter to Tillon about the meeting with Werthlé, while Tondut believed that he was listened to, he did allow himself the sarcastic remark that he hoped he would not have to wait for the third ballot of the election of March 1967 for the election period to end.[67] Two months later, Tondut was still waiting.[68] He was not alone in experiencing this frustrating evasion. After having received the enthusiastic agreement from Fajon and Carrel that they could carry an article in *L'Humanité du Dimanche*, the Association's treasurer Lucien Dubreuil fell into bad humour and lethargy when no such outcome was forthcoming.[69]

The Association met on 24 April 1966 for a general assembly and fraternal meal at the *Tambour* café.[70] Tillon opened the meeting, wishing good health to all and excusing those unable to attend due to distance or indisposition. Several touching letters of apology were read with a minute's silence being held for the 'disappeared'. The assembly recounted their experiences of the mutiny and called upon the bureau to redouble efforts to commemorate the event the following year as it would be the 50th anniversary of the Russian Revolution. They suggested an exhibition at the Museum of Montreuil. All participants were invited to find witnesses who remembered the events. The committee renewed its mandate, having been enlarged through co-option. It undertook to make the 1967 commemoration 'unforgettable'. The fraternal meal followed, at which Jacques Duclos (of all people given his role in the Marty affair) was the guest of honour. Finally, the membership rates were reduced because all subscribers were now retired and many were infirm.[71]

Notes for Tillon's presidential address at the general assembly of 1967 began with the absence of interest amongst professional historians in the mutiny. He noted his obligation to pay homage to disappeared veterans, first among them Jeanne Labourbe. He reflected that there was 'only one book that offered a historical guarantee for the whole of the movement'. He thereby posed the urgency of committing the mutiny to the historical record, as well as, in oblique fashion, Marty's contentious rehabilitation. Tillon recalled the acts of fraternisation, refusal and mutiny amongst 100,000 soldiers and sailors, concluding that, despite the lack of money for a publication, one duty remained: that of being the 'guardians of memory'. The general assembly took place on 16 April. Bulgarian and Russian journalists attended, no doubt because of the anniversary of 1917. Basset noted how the Association would participate in the events to mark the 50th anniversary of the October Revolution in the Museum of Montreuil. Dubreuil had enlarged Marty's collection of photographs and Le Ramey had gathered pamphlets of the mutiny, appealing to those who possessed souvenirs, photographs or postcards to loan them to the exhibition.[72]

The Association also appealed to the generation of 1919 to come forward with memories to assist the curation of the exhibition. Tondut privately confided in Tillon that, as he feared, although a few members approved of the idea of the exhibition, nobody possessed memories that could be used.[73] Thus, for all the Association's rhetoric of faithfulness to the memory of the past or the 'recall of the rejuvenating past', personal memory was frail and fickle in the face of public exposure.[74] Tillon himself was reluctant to cooperate with the exhibition given that it was a PCF event, accusing Basset of being too closely aligned with 'the 44' (the PCF headquarters at 44 rue Le Peletier, 9th *arrondissement*). Tillon objected to the presence behind the scenes of a *Trud* journalist who had snubbed him at their meal and 'other robots of the 44' who sought to ignore the mutinies beyond Russian territory, including those in Romania, Greece and France. He wanted to withdraw his photo and questioned whether they could use Marty's.[75] The Parisian communist members of the executive (Dubreuil, Basset and Tondut) met to discuss the matter and deplored Tillon's 'refusal' to cooperate with the exhibition. Tondut wrote to him, fearing that Tillon's attitude to Basset would destroy the '*Amicale*'. Tondut attempted to mediate between Tillon and Basset, stating that he too had been victim of Stalinist manoeuvring when he was ousted from *Inter-Presse-Publicité* that he had founded in the difficult circumstances of 1945; despite this, he had continued to remain a party activist.[76]

Tillon penned a response. On the basis of their long friendship, Tillon articulated his private frustrations that he would not air publicly. He had not refused to collaborate with the exhibition but that he would not perform the tasks (*corvées(!)*) that the 'masters of the communist museum of the PCF' had asked of him: he could not summarise Marty's book in a few lines. He objected to the 'perfect Thorezian' distortion of their history that the Museum of Montreuil, the party's historical manual and its historical institute were conducting. This reduced the complex participation of sailors and soldiers in a mature revolutionary process to the Black Sea revolt alone. Likewise, the Soviet authorities recalled October but not what followed: just as the Black Sea was cursorily remembered, the years in jail suffered by mutineers were forgotten. Tillon objected to the idea that he was the source of discord, having respected all opinions in the Association and bearing no grudge against those acting under party discipline during the Marty affair. In his view, the exhibition and the delegation to Moscow were hollow ways to commemorate their actions and he owed it to the largesse of their stance in 1919 not to diminish its memory for the sake of keeping 'bureaucrats' at museums or in Moscow happy. Observing the irony involved, he said that while he would like to visit Greece, the site of the *Guichen* mutiny, he could not, as Stalin had abandoned the Greek revolution to the British Empire in 1945.[77] The drafted and redrafted letter bore Tillon's repressed anger at the injustices that the PCF had committed against the memory of the mutiny. Ultimately, in another act of abnegation, he did not send it.

Tondut wrote again on 8 November, reading Tillon's silence as a deterioration in their relations, imploring him to reply. Confirming Tillon's understanding of the party's attitude, Tondut reported that the exhibition had been a minimal affair: a single window display with photos of ships, Vuillemin and Labourbe as well as a few leaflets, not even using the photographs that Dubreuil had enlarged and framed. Tondut believed implausibly that there would be a second exhibition at Montreuil. He did assert two grounds for enthusiasm, however. First, he, Basset and Prochasson had attended a colloquium at the *Institut Maurice Thorez* and encountered Pierre Vottero, the *Voltaire* mutineer, who spoke to the audience and received a rapturous reception. Second, having heard of the colloquium, a mutineer contacted him, donating 1,500 francs to their organisation.[78]

On this occasion, Tillon did respond. He stated that he had not replied because he found Tondut's first letter incomprehensible and the second one even more so, reminding him of the demands for self-criticism that the Association expected from himself and Marty in 1952. Given that there was no rancour at the last meeting, and the only criticism was that Basset had shared the membership list with a PCF official, Tillon wondered how the idea of damaging divisions within the Association had emerged. He asked what the party had done with the list and whether the party was organising a faction within the Association. He proposed a meeting of the executive on his visit to Paris later that month. He signed off as a 'former mutineer of the *Guichen* condemned to five years of hard labour for solidarity with the October Revolution'.[79] In the meantime, the Soviet embassy honoured Lavieu, Le Ramey, Daucros, Sevret, Pauly, Fabre and Tondut with medals for their participation in the mutinies, with Tillon notably being ignored in the ceremony.[80]

In Tondut's next missive to Tillon, after news of Dubreuil's hospitalisation, the former regretted the bitter-sweet exchange of views between them, and said that he could not express himself freely and put his thoughts effectively into words. He repeated that he too had been a victim of bureaucratic manoeuvres and that therefore he sympathised with Tillon's expulsion from the Central Committee. Moreover, Tondut continued, Lavieu too had also suffered similarly at the hands of the bureaucrats. He remained with the party because he believed that the bureaucrats did not represent the party itself. With news of the ceremony at the Soviet Embassy, Tillon's repressed emotions gave way. He described the executive as the puppet show of the communist faction, patiently liquidating the Association and dishonouring the dead. He warned that 1968 was not 1952 and he would not go quietly. Czechoslovakia and the student movement prompted this transformation of attitude, finding the juxtaposition of Prague and the medals ceremony obscene:

> the crime against Czechoslovakia, which for someone condemned to the military prison for solidarity with the Russian Revolution has a different meaning than for those who receive Stalinist decorations 50 years afterwards.[81]

On 3 January 1969, Basset wrote to Tillon asking for his thoughts on the 50th anniversary. With Dubreuil dead and Tondut having resigned, Basset proposed a new 'democratically elected' bureau; Tillon underlined this phrase and scribbled a question mark in the margin.[82] A meeting was set for 18 January 1969. In Tillon's meeting notes in advance of the executive meeting, he rehearsed his arguments. He would open with his long-standing motifs of the mutiny's forgotten status, the affirmation of the mutiny's essential truth as well as the years of prison faced by the mutineers. He would pay tribute to individual mutineers, Vuillemin, Marius Fracchia, Tondut and Lucien Terion (who had died as a consequence of deportation during the Vichy regime). Tillon expected a showdown over PCF factionalism and with Basset in particular. When it came to the meeting itself, Chapotat was absent because of a serious illness, leaving Vice-President Basset and Tillon. Basset read Tondut's resignation letter and declared himself in agreement. Tillon believed this to be an attempt to provoke his resignation after his disagreement with the 'Stalinists' over the events in Czechoslovakia.[83] Underlying this manoeuvre, Tillon assumed, the PCF wanted to celebrate the mutiny's 50th anniversary in line with the Soviet Embassy's wishes.[84]

Despite this, in 1969, signs appeared that the events of May 1968 had re-energised the memory of the mutiny. The growth of the revolutionary left and a desire to interrogate France's revolutionary past prompted new interest in 1919. Indeed, rumours circulated widely during May of a mutiny aboard the aircraft carrier *Clemenceau*.[85] For the 50th anniversary, prominent PCF figure Raoul Calas briefly introduced a series of documents in the *Cahiers de Maurice Thorez*, reformulating the foundation myth of the PCF. This was still a 'glorious page of the revolutionary French workers' movement'. He talked of three elements of the revolt. First, the soldiers and sailors who mutinied held a variety of motives: desire for demobilisation, a return to France or conviction that the war was illegal. Politically, some were anarchists or anarcho-syndicalists but did not belong to a 'really revolutionary party'. The second element was the 'intelligent and heroic propaganda of Bolshevik revolutionaries'. Finally, a genuinely revolutionary current emerged within France after the capitulation of reformist socialists in August 1914, leading to the formation of the PCF in December 1920. The hero of the party's birth was thus not Marty (whom Calas did at least mention in his introduction) but Cachin:

> It was the representatives of this current amongst whom the strong and noble personality of Marcel Cachin who was naturally the most ardent in showing their active solidarity with the triumphant Russian revolution.[86]

Amongst the documents was an extract from the party's official history *Histoire du Parti Communiste Français* (1964).

An exchange of letters between Virgile Vuillemin and Charles Tillon demonstrated the way the events of 1968 reframed mutineer memory. Vuillemin wrote excitedly to Tillon for his opinion on an approach from the anarchist author Daniel Guérin and Daniel Anselme, editor of the *Cahiers de Mai*, a periodical inspired by 1968. Both were interested in commemorating the mutiny during its 50th anniversary.[87] They wanted Vuillemin to record his experiences for *Cahiers* and Guérin was interested in penning a history. Indeed, the anniversary seemed, at last, to be precipitating historical interest from several directions. The communist publication *Nouvelle France* as well as the *Moniteur de la Flotte* produced articles about the mutiny and courts martial.[88] Vuillemin was considering writing his memoirs, seeking Tillon's advice on sources and access to the archives. Tillon was himself planning to write an account of the mutiny based on Marty's book. Moreover, Vuillemin heard that Philippe Masson was in the process of writing a doctorate on the Black Sea intervention, using ministerial archives that had recently become fully accessible. Tillon travelled to Besançon in February 1969 to visit Vuillemin, re-cementing their friendship that had been forged during resistance activity in Toulouse and confirmed with the solidarity Vuillemin showed for Marty and Tillon in 1952.[89] The whole recrudescence of interest in the mutinies sparked hope amongst these former mutineers that their revolt would finally get the audience that it deserved.

At the same time, tension increased between, on the one hand, Tillon and Vuillemin and, on the other, the PCF 'Basset-Tondut' faction, who sought to liaise with the Soviet Embassy to render the commemoration propaganda for the Soviet Union. For Tillon and Vuillemin, the repression in Prague meant that they wished to emphasise that the mutiny was an anti-war act, rather than stressing solidarity with the current Soviet regime, and that the mutiny occurred before the formation of the PCF and therefore the Association should stress its independence from the party. That Duclos chaired the previous general meeting still rankled with Vuillemin. Their last encounter had been unpleasant, after Vuillemin had written a protest letter during the Marty affair.[90]

Moreover, Tillon recalled that at the commemoration of 1957, the high-handed Montreuil council had not offered them the council building but a squalid attic (*'soupente crasseuse'*).[91] He wanted to widen the appeal of the Association and extend its reach to the *Comité des marins*. The organisation's lack of resources was starker than Tillon might have expected. On the Association's treasurer Lucien Dubreuil's death, Basset learned from his widow that it had only 40 francs and several outstanding debts.[92] Complicating the preparations, Basset and Le Ramey's trip to Odessa and Moscow took place between 14 and 21 April. This included a march for Jeanne Labourbe and a commemorative event at a sailors' hostel. With Basset and Le Ramey leaving for Odessa on 14 April, Tillon was to send out the first notices for its meal and general meeting. On Basset's return from the USSR, he wrote to Tillon rebuking him for not informing him about the circular regarding the anniversary event. Of fifty-three invitations, thirty-three had signed up, including fourteen veterans.[93] With similar terseness, Tillon replied that he could not circulate the membership without knowing the venue.[94] In a further letter, Basset blamed the mayor of Pantin for imprecision about the venue and moving the meal an hour to 12 noon because of a demonstration.[95]

Weakening Tillon's position further, Vuillemin decided that he would not after all attend the general meeting as the balance of forces would not be sufficient to wrestle back the Association from Basset. The best that they could hope for would be to become president and vice-president, leaving the crucial role of secretary in PCF hands. Basset would always have columns in *L'Humanité* and *La Nouvelle France* at his disposal.[96] Vuillemin regretted not seeing Tillon, wishing him a good meeting and saying that they should get together either in Aix or Besançon. Vuillemin offered to put in a resignation letter if Tillon thought it useful. Vuillemin, however, thought this to be unnecessary as this would be the last meeting of the Association that was

> dead like most of the sailors of the Black Sea. At this last meeting, for I am certain it will be the last, there will be only one of those who was sentenced for his part in the action of 1919: that will be you.[97]

If Vuillemin's assessment of the Association was pessimistic, he did offer grounds for a more positive attitude, proposing to send Tillon copies of the *Cahiers de Mai* and looking forward to reading Tillon's 'book of memories' when it was finished.

Despite Vuillemin's doubts, Tillon succeeded in passing a resolution rehabilitating Marty at the Association's 50th anniversary meeting at the festival hall of Pantin council. Tillon reported that the constrained resources of their modest organisation did not permit them giving the event the importance for which they had hoped at the last meeting. As their small numbers were yet further reduced, this rendered the duty of memory all the more significant. While still mentioning the 'young revolution of workers, soldiers and sailors of the land of the soviets', the discourse shifted towards that of May. Now their action signified a fight 'for freedom of peoples to self-determination, and for friendship between all the peoples and the independence of all!' Through this formulation, Tillon invoked solidarity with the Vietnamese people against

US imperialism as well as providing a coded rebuke to the Thorezian wing of the Central Committee that had supported Soviet repression in Prague. Tillon also signalled the problem of the intergenerational transmission of memory as it remained impossible, he complained, to mention the mutiny to the youth in the classrooms.[98]

On the day after the general meeting, Tillon wrote to *Le Monde* with the text of the motion rehabilitating Marty.[99] Tillon also contacted *La Marseillaise*, *L'Humanité* and the PCF secretariat in response to an article in the former about the fraternal meal. Not only did it make the factual error of locating the Black Sea Mutiny in Odessa, and reduced the significance of the mutiny to a few 'survivors', it invited sympathisers to communicate with Paquet of the CGT bakers' union as secretary of the Association. This was the union of which Basset was the retired secretary. Tillon read this as a second attempt to expel him from the Association in line with the PCF's effort to diminish and falsify the history of the mutiny to the exclusion of Marty.

A further consequence of the meeting in Pantin was the reconciliation between Tondut and Tillon. The former invited them to 're-find' their friendship, hoping they could forget their differences. He wanted the new resolve within the Association to provide the basis, as Tillon had argued, for a more efficacious committee. He proposed that due to his own infirmity, he could be Douvrin's assistant secretary rather than the other way around. As regards Basset, Tondut had seen him with PCF Central Committee member Jean Fabre the day prior to writing to Tillon.[100] Basset had resigned from his position as vice-president and would forgo any responsibilities. Later, Tillon observed to Bernard Fabre that Basset had abandoned the Association to take a place on the secretariat of George Marchais's PCF and, despite this, would be representing the mutineers of the Black Sea in the USSR (his third such visit).[101]

The new committee appeared to be taking shape. Marcel Monribot accepted a position on the new committee, though voicing his misgivings on the grounds that he doubted that he could attend all the necessary meetings in Paris given that he was living in Périgeux, Dordogne. He was surprised that only two of the PCF members present had voted against the resolution, describing it as a homage to Marty. He was waiting on a letter from Vuillemin (hence his delay in writing to Tillon), who he believed would join the committee.[102] Vuillemin replied three days later, saying that he would not be against his inclusion on the new committee, whose composition he was keen to find out. He warned that

Basset could not be trusted. If Basset was saying that Vuillemin was no longer a member, the latter asserted that this was incorrect as he had paid his membership fees. Vuillemin regretted not attending the general assembly, asking if André Lavieu had attended and saying that he had just heard of the loss of Chenavaz, who was a 'good comrade'.

The last supper and the duty of memory

Released from the 'complex' about Marty's expulsion, Tillon's victory did allow mutineer correspondents to consider the wider sweep of history. Tondut observed that they were no further forward than 50 years ago, the exception being the achievements of the Popular Front era (40-hour week and paid holidays). He took solace in the fact that they would not be there to see what was to come, as he feared that it would not be pretty.[103] In a similar retrospective mode, Maurice Gleize opined wistfully that if Tillon had been told how complicated the revolution would be during the Black Sea revolt, he would not have believed them.[104] In Tillon's draft letter to Madame Marin, he reflected upon Louis Marin's sense of duty as a free man to act during great historical events such as 1919 and the resistance.[105] This clearance of the burden of the past also allowed historical work on the part of Tillon and others. The long-stated goal of recording the memories of mutineers in a publication now materialised, if only through individual endeavours.

The efforts to elicit the memories of mutineers for a brochure had been an unfulfilled goal of the Association throughout the period since its relaunch in 1958. Ultimately, Tillon recognised that this project was holding back the history of the mutinies and set about writing his own memoir of the revolt on the *Guichen* published in 1969. He encouraged Vuillemin to do likewise. Vuillemin responded that several others had also asked him to write a memoir but he had always replied that he would do this when he was old, knowing that this trapped his interlocutor. He knew well that Tillon would not fall for the ruse and would be willing to call him decrepit. The mutineer of the *France* instead did not want to write a propaganda account but something more serious akin to Tillon's but this would require consultation of the archives, citations, a proper context and precisely the resource he did not have: time.[106] They exchanged views on Le Ramey and Vottero's publication and Gacon's introduction to it. Vuillemin wanted to know who this 'Stalinist Gacon' was and what gave Le Ramey and Vottero the authority to speak of the prison experience. Tillon was even more scathing.

Le Ramey was now usurping Marty, just as he had done within the Association in 1952. The book was 'destined to teach history according to Stalin to the new members of Marchais's party under the cover of the union of the left [the electoral pact with Mitterrand's Socialist Party signed in 1972]'.[107]

By March 1970, Tillon's hope to revitalise the Association was not bearing obvious fruit. There would be no general meeting that year. Undeterred, a final meeting of the old comrades did take place, defying expectations to the contrary. The Association (now assuming the name *Amicale des Marins et Soldats de 1919*') met up for its fraternal meal on 17 June 1973 for a final time, four years after Vuillemin had pronounced its demise. This in itself was a considerable tribute to Tillon's efforts to reorganise the organisation in 1969. Time's decimation continued, disrupting the organisation and necessitating morbid exchanges of information within the network. For instance, François Collet updated Tillon on the address and state of health of Morvan and Jean Fichou, asking what had become of Marius Grignon of the *France*, who must have left his address, while Robillard of Parthenay and Chéri Marbic of St Brieuc had 'disappeared'.[108] At the meal itself, the old comrades ate their way through a first course of stuffed mussels and palm hearts, before moving on to roast beef or leg of lamb with flageolet beans, *dauphinoise* potatoes and green salad. The dessert consisted of a cheese plate, pastries or fruit bowl. They washed this down with a *rosé de provence*, a *sauvignon* and a *côtes du Rhône*. The gastronomy signalled the political shift away from the high Stalinism of the Cold War. In 1950, they had a Russian-themed hors d'oeuvre: speciality pies of the Caucasus, Siberian dumplings and Moscovite blinis.[109] Tillon's presidential address followed suit. The post-1968 trope of a revolution for liberty replaced the tighter identification with the Soviet regime.

After the celebration in his last exchange with Vuillemin, Tillon exercised a degree of emotional liberty in stark contrast to the years of managing his emotions inside the Association, reflecting on the state of affairs, in which Le Ramey and Marchais had become France's most worthy salesmen of Russian vodka, and that the 'psychiatric case Brejhnev' and the 'cowboy Nixon' dined together at 'banquets for atomic peace'. Amid all this, he had to suppress his regret at being condemned to spend his life in a world gone mad, with Pompidou saying: 'the army is the last resort of liberalism.'[110]

Conclusion

At the end of the Association's existence, there is a very clear sense of how generational time intersected with an institutionalised duty of memory. At this moment, the Association was able to undertake two actions that signalled its emancipation from the bureaucratic shackles and obstruction that the PCF had imposed upon it. First, the ageing mutineers were able to commune together freely at their final meal, which was the work of the new committee that had rehabilitated Marty. Second, they contributed to the renewal of interest in the mutiny in connection with the 1968 generation via the special edition of *Cahiers du Mai*, *La Révolte vient de loin* and Le Ramey and Vottero's book. Their contribution to their own history was perhaps not what they had envisaged in the late 1950s and, for the historian, there is something tragic that mutineers like Vuillemin, whom the authorities had deemed was the principal ringleader of the mutiny on the *France*, failed to complete his memoirs. That said, their historical production was a last expression of mutineer subjectivity. Ironically, this threshold also signalled the interest of non-mutineer historians who deployed the conventions of professional and archival research that, in effect, silenced the mutineers once again. A new form of oblivion formed in the shadow of the *Château de Vincennes*, in which the official documentation lies.

Notes

1 Jeffrey K. Olick and Joyce Robbins, 'Social memory studies: from collective memory to the historical sociology of mnemonic practices', *Annual Review of Sociology*, 24 (1998), pp. 105–40.
2 Pierre Nora, 'Between memory and history: les lieux de mémoire', *Representations*, 26 (1989), pp. 7–24.
3 Reappearing in several re-editions from 1937, 1954, 1960, Maurice Thorez, *Fils du Peuple* (Paris: Éditions Sociales, 1949). Commission d'Histoire, *Histoire du Parti Communiste Français: Manuel* (Paris: Éditions Sociales, 1964). John Bulatis, *Maurice Thorez: A Biography* (London: I.B. Tauris, 2015). Claude Pennetier and Bernard Pudal, 'Stalinism: workers' cult and cult of leaders', *Twentieth Century Communism*, 1, 1 (2009), pp. 20–9. Kevin Morgan, *International Communism and the Cult of the Individual Leaders, Tribunes and Martyrs under Lenin and Stalin* (London: Palgrave Macmillan, 2017).
4 *La Bretagne*, 11 June 1949.
5 Marie-Cécile Boujou, 'André Marty et les éditions du PCF', in Boulland, Pennetier and Vaccaro (eds), *André Marty*, pp. 69–75, p. 71.

6 Gillé lived in Argenteuil.
7 Centre d'Histoire Science Charles Tillon Papers (henceforth CHSP CT) 1 Lavieu and secretariat to Vigné, secretary of the Comité d'initiative Français du Congrès de la Paix, 1949.
8 CHSP CT1 report on AFDMNA general assembly, 4 June 1919.
9 *La Vie du XIIIe*, 1 May 1949.
10 CHSP CT1 *La Vie Ouvrière*, n.d., 1949.
11 *La Vie du XIIIe*, 1 May 1949.
12 CHSP CT1 *La Bretagne*, 11 June 1949.
13 CHSP CT1 *Journal Ouest*, n.d., 1949.
14 CHSP CT1 *Liste des invités connus à l'heure actuelle* (in pencil '1949?'). Also on the list were Teff (just acquitted, from Hérault); Barralle of Hérault; Dougnac; Ghislaine Villiers; Allemand of Vaucluse; Roger Villiod, former Calvi mutineer of the 4th *arrondissment*, and his wife the deputy Denise Ginollin; and Eugène Noiret and Perrier, both Calvi mutineers. Finally there was Lejaud, an engineer whom Le Ramey invited.
15 CHSP CT1 Le Ramey to Prefet de Police, 18 July 1949.
16 CHSP CT1 Société fraternelle des soldats et marins de la Mer Noire ('1950').
17 CHSP CT1 Liste des adhérents ('1958').
18 Axelle Brodiez, 'Le Secours Populaire Français entre Marty et Martin: deux mythes et deux affaires', in Boulland, Pennetier and Vaccaro (eds), *André Marty*, pp. 77–84.
19 CHSP CT1 Liste des adhérents de l'Association ('1949?'). *L'Affaire Henri Martin* (Paris: Gaillmard, 1953).
20 CHSP CT1 Tillon to Tondut, 20 November 1967.
21 André Marty, *L'Affaire Marty* (Paris: Éditions Norman Bethune, 1972), pp. 268–75.
22 *L'Humanité*, 10 February 1953.
23 Marty, *L'Affaire Marty*, pp. 57. *Action Française*, 17 June 1919; *Liberté*, 8 February 1929; *Gringoire*, 16 January 1939, 2 February 1939, 9 February 1939, 16 February 1939, 16 March 1939, 30 March 1939.
24 Stéphane Courtois and Marc Lazar, *Histoire du Parti Communiste Français* (Paris: Press Universitaires de France, 2000), pp. 263–5. Yves Le Bras, *Les Rejetés: L'Affaire Marty-Tillon* (Paris: La Table Ronde, 1974). Boulland, Pennetier and Vaccaro (eds), *André Marty*. Michel Dreyfus, *PCF: Crises et Dissidences* (Brussels: Éditions Complexe, 1989).
25 Charles Tillon, *Un 'Procès de Moscou' à Paris* (Paris: Seuil, 1971).
26 Charles Tillon, *On Chantait Rouge* (Paris: Laffont, 1977), p. 504.
27 Slavin, 'The French left and the Rif war, 1924–5', pp. 5–32.
28 Marty, *L'Affaire Marty*, p. 67.
29 CHSP CT1 Foucault circular, 6 October 1952.
30 CHSP CT1 Marty to Foucault, 9 October 1952 (A carbon copy sent to Tillon).

31 CHSP CT1 Meeting of the executive, 7 March 1953.
32 The mutiny served the purposes of the anniversaries of 1917, *L'Humanité*, 21 December 1957.
33 CHSP CT1 Douvrin to Tillon, 12 April 1966.
34 CHSP CT1 Fouges to Tillon, 6 June 1971.
35 CHSP CT1 Brest to Tillon, 16 May 1973.
36 CHSP CT1 Monstier to Tillon, 8 April 1958.
37 CHSP CT1 Tondut to Tillon, 12 May 1958, 11 June 1958.
38 CHSP CT1 Tondut to Tillon, 9 March 1959, 18 April 1959, 29 April 1959, 17 May 1959. CHSP CT1 Tondut to Maranne, 6 April 1959.
39 CHSP CT1 Tondut to Tillon, 5 May 1959.
40 CHSP CT1 press cutting Marcel Veyrier article in *L'Humanité*, 21 April 1959.
41 CHSP CT1 Tondut to Tillon, 12 June 1959.
42 CHSP CT1 Tondut to Tillon, 28 August 1959.
43 CHSP CT1 Tillon to Tondut, 24 August 1959.
44 CHSP CT1 *Trait d'union* 3, October 1959.
45 CHSP CT1 Tondut to Tillon, 23 April 1959, 5 May 1959.
46 CHSP CT1 Tondut to Tillon, 28 August 1959.
47 CHSP CT1 Chenavaz to Tillon, 3 October 1955.
48 CHSP CT1 *La Voie Communiste*, May 1959.
49 Irwin Wall, 'The French communists and the Algerian War', *Journal of Contemporary History*, 12, 3 (1977), pp. 521–43.
50 CHSP CT1 bureau report, 14 February 1959.
51 CHSP CT1 Chenavaz to Basset, 13 June 1959.
52 CHSP CT1 Tillon to Tondut, 24 August 1959.
53 CHSP CT1 *Trait d'union* 3, October 1959.
54 CHSP CT1 Tillon to Chenavaz, 21 October 1959.
55 *Le Monde*, 15 March 1968.
56 CHSP CT1 Tondut to Tillon, 15 April 1961 and Tillon to Tondut, 21 April 1961.
57 CHSP CT1 Tillon to bureau, 18 June 1961.
58 CHSP CT1 Executive of the Paris region, (1961?).
59 CHSP CT1 Tillon to executive, 26 June 1962.
60 CHSP CT1 Tillon to Basset, 4 June 1963.
61 CHSP CT1 Tillon and Basset to the membership, 17 February 1964.
62 CHSP CT1 Tillon and Basset to the membership, 17 February 1964.
63 CHSP CT1 Tondut to Tillon, 20 July 1964.
64 CHSP CT1 *Trait d'Union*, 1965.
65 CHSP CT1 Tondut to Tillon, 23 November 1965.
66 CHSP CT1 Tondut to Tillon, 7 December 1965.
67 CHSP CT1 Tondut to Tillon, 28 December 1965.
68 CHSP CT1 Tondut to Tillon, 13 February 1966.

69 CHSP CT1 Tondut to Tillon, 14 December 1966.
70 CHSP CT1 Tondut, secretary, circular, 13 November 1965. *Trait d'Union*, 1965.
71 CHSP CT1 Basset's circular, 6 May 1966.
72 CHSP CT1 *Procès verbal de L'Assemblée Générale du 16 avril 1967*.
73 CHSP CT1 Tondut to Tillon, 7 March 1967. For other discussion of the exhibition, Tondut to Tillon, 31 January 1967, 29 September 1967.
74 CHSP CT1 *Trait d'Union* (Basset), 1965.
75 CHSP CT1 Tillon to Tondut, 2 October 1967.
76 CHSP CT1 Tondut to Tillon, 10 October 1967.
77 CHSP CT1 Tillon to Tondut, 18 October 1967 (unsent).
78 CHSP CT1 Tondut to Tillon, 8 November 1967.
79 CHSP CT1 Tillon to Tondut, 9 November 1967.
80 CHSP CT1 Tondut to Tillon, 16 November 1967.
81 CHSP CT1 Tillon to comrades, (November 1968).
82 CHSP CT1 Basset to Tillon, 2 January 1969.
83 For Tondut's resignation letter, CHSP CT1 Tondut to Tillon, 18 October 1968. Courtois and Lazar, *Histoire du Parti Communiste Français*, pp. 337–41. Indeed, Tillon was eventually expelled in 1970 from the PCF for signing a statement alongside Roger Garaudy, the Central Committee member who had been most critical of Warsaw Pact intervention into Czechoslovakia on 21 August 1968.
84 CHSP CT1 Note, 18 January 1969. For the way the controversy within the party reached Tillon, CHSP CT1 Fréchard to Tillon, 26 December 1968.
85 *Action*, 14 June 1968. *Canard Enchaîné*, 19 June 1968.
86 Raoul Calas, 'Pages glorieuses de l'internationalisme proletarian: La révolte de la Mer Noire', *Cahiers de l'Institut Maurice Thorez*, 14, 2 (1969), pp. 92–4.
87 CHSP CT1 Vuillemin to Tillon, 23 January 1969.
88 CHSP CT1 *Nouvelle France*, 29 January 1969; *Moniteur de la Flotte*, n.d.
89 CHSP CT1 Vuillemin to Tillon, 14 February 1969.
90 CHSP CT1 Vuillemin to Tillon, 6 April 1969.
91 CHSP CT1 Tillon to Vuillemin, 1 April 1969.
92 CHSP CT1 Basset to Tillon, 5 April 1969.
93 CHSP CT1 Basset to Tillon, 26 April 1969.
94 CHSP CT1 Tillon to Basset, 26 April 1969.
95 CHSP CT1 Basset to Tillon, 30 April 1969.
96 Featuring an account by Jean Le Ramey, *La Nouvelle France*, 29 January 1969.
97 CHSP CT1 Vuillemin to Tillon, 8 May 1969.
98 CHSP CT1 Tillon to membership, n.d. (1969). Emile Quesnel produced a banner for the Association in favour of peace in Vietnam which he displayed at the *Fête de l'Humanité* in 1966. CHSP CT1 Quesnel to Tillon, 5 December 1966.

99 CHSP CT1 Tillon to Legris, editor of *Le Monde*, 19 May 1969.
100 CHSP CT1 Tondut to Tillon, 30 May 1969.
101 CHSP CT1 Tillon to Fabre, 10 May 1972.
102 CHSP CT1 Monribot to Tillon, 16 June 1969. Monribot mentions articles in *L'Echo du Centre*, 1969 and *Cahiers du Mai*, 1969; *Les Nouvelles* (Bordeaux), 1949.
103 CHSP CT1 Tondut to Tillon, 27 March 1970.
104 CHSP CT1 Maurice Gleize to Tillon, n.d., 1969.
105 CHSP CT1 Tillon to Madame Marin, n.d., May or June 1969.
106 CHSP CT1 Vuillemin to Tillon, 8 November 1973.
107 CHSP CT1 Tillon to Vuillemin, 3 November 1973.
108 CHSP CT1 Collet to Tillon, 1 May 1973.
109 CHSP CT1 *Repas fraternel des anciens marins de la Mer Noire*, 30 April 1950.
110 CHSP CT1, Vuillemin, 3 November 1973. For an obituary of Vuillemin, *Le Réfractaire*, August–September 1981.

Conclusion

When the war was over
Each of us expected
That we would soon embark
For France as our destination
In playing our family duty
We would became part of its joy
To return to the family
We left over 20 months before.

The Odessa Waltz[1]

Just as with the notorious lament *Chanson de Craonne* in the mutinous trenches of 1917, the *Odessa Waltz* was enormously popular with the French forces of intervention.[2] The military authorities supposedly offered 100,000 francs and immediate demobilisation for the denunciation of the *Odessa Waltz's* author, whose identity nonetheless remained undiscovered. The General Staff's comic pursuit of the elusive *Odessa Waltz* apparently caused much amusement amongst French troops.[3] Its authors entered the Black Sea mythology, which was conjured, on one side, by official denial and, on the other, by an oral sense-making process of hearsay and rumour. Years later, mutineer of the Second Mountain Artillery, Louis Espagnet, who ran a cinema in Juvisy in the Parisian *banlieue*, reported to Marty that two soldiers in his regiment and a sailor named Gaton penned the *Odessa Waltz*. He suggested that one of them, Doux, was a law student, who was arrested but subsequently released.[4]

The slippery authenticity of the *Odessa Waltz* says much about mutineer subjectivity, blending the propositional reason of its words with the non-propositional elicitation of emotion of its music.[5] As counterpoint to the 'slow, muted, slightly discordant' sadness of its melody, its lyrics opened with the joyous expectation of return to France and to family at war's end. Addressing those classic emotional well springs of nationalism that Benedict Anderson identified, the song blurred obligations to family and nation, articulating the pain of separation from family and the nostalgia for homeland.[6] Set to a musical form (the waltz) associated with dancing, its chorus focused on the sentimental and sexual yearning for wives and mistresses, nurturing the 'hope and joy' for renewed intimacy. The final verse registered the emotional reversal of continued military service after the Armistice and anticipated a demobilisation ambiguously described as 'liberation'. The song's profoundly cathartic quality rested upon both the performative release of repressed emotions and the articulation of a euphemistic 'gift' for the French political elite, a 'day of decision', which (as with 'liberation') evasively hinted at revolution.[7] Future gatherings of the former mutineers sang the *Odessa Waltz*, which assisted reminiscence about the events of their youth, being a fragment of 1919 that resisted the erosion of time. It helped them to make sense of their past, just as it had in 1919 helped them to make sense of their present. The *Odessa Waltz*, then, illustrates the emotion-laden reason of mutiny and how attention to mutineer emotion enriches our understanding of the events.

Mutineer consciousness: emotion and learning

In the conjuncture of 1919, mutineers constructed their own conceptions of the world, rejecting those of their superiors. Mutineers relied upon their senses, emotions, reasoning and memory so as to comprehend alien surroundings. The voices and sights of multitudinous peers came to dominate the mutiny's sensuous environment, displacing the unfamiliar territories of the East or the horrors of war that had previously estranged their senses. The humanising experience of mutiny assailed the senses, replacing the military sensorium of bugle-call routine and shouted orders or the visual semiotics of rank and authority. The red flag flew at the bowsprit where the admiral's colours had flown. The mutinous soundscape attuned to the improvised patterns of contention through silence, murmurings, volume, pitch, cries, shared slang, mutineer laments and revolutionary anthems. The senses imbibed the collective contest with the officers.

These altered sensual relations aroused powerful emotional responses, which also energised and were constitutive of the revolt. The mutiny thereby broke the institutional emotionology of the military establishment. The pattern of protest entailed an emotional sequence, as did its demoralising aftermath heavily charged with regrets and despair. The senses and emotions met in the chambers of consciousness, facilitating a subjectivity of new possibilities in both thought and action, followed by their disappointing closure. This subjectivity surged through great transnational circuits of hearsay, letters, press and mass displacements in a moment when the fixed and naturalised boundaries of empires and nation-states were in exceptional flux. Emotion was a mercurial contradictory feature of the revolt: being both personal and social, being communicated information between protagonists and motivational resource.

On their journeys to the East, or, in later phases of the protest, in the port cities, mutineers grappled with why they were not returning home, what the purpose of their mission was, what the nature of the Bolshevik regime was. Their emotionality and reliance upon their own eyes and ears did not imply unreason. In studying the mutinous crowd, Gustave Le Bon's dichotomy of emotion and cognition is no longer tenable; neither should we assert reason at the expense of emotion. Framed within their own political-cultural traditions, mutineer testimonies reveal an affective sense-making process, putting the recovery of truth at the centre of their outlooks. So for Nouveau of the *Waldeck-Rousseau*, the mystery of their mission prompted intense discussions amongst comrades who found the situation 'more and more bizarre'.[8] Equally, according to an engineer on the *Jean Bart*, the average sailor's mind became an 'abacus', adding the progressive revelations about their route to each instance of military preparation. The final confirmation arrived when officers selected a landing party. Its members counted the 128 cartridges placed into their hands: this was a war against the Bolsheviks.[9] Likewise, more so than being a fully formed ideological commitment from the outset, fraternisation emerged organically as a mundane fluid practice through a mixture of curiosity and empathy, being politicised over time. At least initially, then, it did not resemble the communist policy of fraternisation of the 1920s that purported to emulate it.

Mutineers exercised a democratic wisdom of crowds, comprising of measured response, collective discussion and a deliberative trust in their delegates. Given the likely consequences, this acumen entailed collective hesitation before violence. On hearing cries of 'to the rifles, to the mines', Notta, a delegate of the *France*, intervened to avoid tragedy. Greeted with hurrahs in response, he argued that they did not want to spill blood and they were not scared of the officers and their revolvers.[10] In this and other instances, the precipice of violence and threat of bloody repression was palpable.[11] The widespread avoidance of violence was not simply a lack of militancy, but managed emotions and the calculation of the balance of forces. Such a process viewed from within has significant implications regarding interpretation of the events. The absence of violence is used to formulate the widespread historical assessment that the mutinies were simple refusals akin to a routine breakdown in industrial relations. Viewing the revolt in terms of mutineer subjectivity challenges these conclusions that are based on outward behaviour and the conventional categories of the military such as 'morale'.

Crucially, mutineer consciousness constituted a common endeavour and this consciousness persisted after the events, despite repression and dislocation (though such certainly had an impact). Just as they tried to discover the nature of their mission to Russia, some mutineers spent their entire lives engaged in a shared effort to uncover the truth about the Sevastopol demonstration and the death of Jeanne Labourbe or, simply, to have their actions remembered. Their outrage at these events does not register in the scholarly literature. As such, the mutinies should not be seen a collapse of morale but the reverse: a powerful moral independence, an ethical questioning of the political motives of the general staff and government. Neither did the mutineers see themselves as traitors because the government and the officers acted unconstitutionally and betrayed the universal values of French republicanism.

Mutineer grievance and the historical record

If a history of mutineer subjectivity requires the reconstitution of their dialogue, then that history ought to attend to their preoccupations. The vantage point of a wider documentation allows us knowledge they could not access about Labourbe and Morskaïa Road. An abiding aspect of the Labourbe legend was the accusation of complicity in murder against French military authorities. The murder of 'Jeanne Laborde' first caused concern in French military circles only six months after her death, when *L'Humanité* alleged that French officers had played a part in her murder.[12] On the day following the article, General Alby, the chair of the council of the Ministry of War, requested information from the relevant authorities.[13] Upon this request, two accounts were forthcoming. The first was a report, presumably from Lieutenant-Colonel Freydenberg (though the signature is illegible) to General d'Anselme, and the second a note combining information from the two of them.[14] The formulation is very similar. The Moscow government hatched a 'Bolshevik plot' sending 'notorious terrorists' to Odessa to 'make propaganda among French troops and make them lead a rising in Odessa' or, in the other version, 'to start a riot amongst Allied troops'. Denikin's governor of police in Odessa, General Sannikoff, learned of the plot, arrested the conspirators at one of their meetings, seized their papers and summarily executed them. The French commander of Odessa had no knowledge of the affair because it was before the declaration of a state of siege so all authority resided in White Russian hands at that point. Produced within a week of the article, the rebuttal stated:

> No French civilian or French woman during the stay of French troops in Odessa went before a council of war. No French officer executed a French person or a foreigner. The allegations of the newspaper *L'Humanité* are without any foundation.[15]

However, the secret correspondence denying knowledge of the affair raises lingering doubts. Reading Lieutenant-Colonel Freydenberg's report to General d'Anselme suggests Freydenberg suspected that d'Anselme was feigning ignorance of the matter.

> [... T]his took place during the night and the next day the SR [Russian Section] reported that the Russians had executed those seized. I learned at the same time that one of the persons executed had a French name and that according to all probability she was a Frenchwoman. This was Mrs or Miss Laborde. *I reported this fact to you.*
>
> *You will certainly recall, my General*, that this summary execution made a fair amount of noise in the popular districts and that the disaffection of the people for the AVR [Russian Volunteer Army] only grew. It was on this execution that the metalworkers focused [...]. [My italics].

Indeed, the Lieutenant de Carsalade, Chief of the Navy's Russian Section, had written this rather casual paragraph in a report sent to the Ministry of the Navy on 2 March 1919.

> Following surveillance exercised around the Bolshevik centre of propaganda close to French soldiers and sailors, several raids took place on 1 to 2 March. All the principal agents, including the editor-in-chief and the printer of the newspaper *Le Communiste* were arrested. Searches and arrests continue.[16]

Clearly, the report is entirely nonchalant towards the identity or fate of the 'editor of *Le Communiste*', or that she was a French citizen, who was apparently tortured and summarily executed. Although the only proof of the French officer comes from Radkov, a member of the group, who had escaped, the French military was entirely unabashed about the actions of its White allies.[17]

Mutineers found the rumour of a French officer's presence entirely plausible. It conformed to the experience of those who had recoiled before the naval bombardment of civilians and the individual brutality of French officers or White forces during the occupation. At times, in the official documentation of the intervention, the imperial mask of civilisation drops. Thus, Captain Gaillard could write in a secret report to the Army general staff:

> Communist in the soul, communist inherited from the social institution of the '*mir*' [village], [...] imprinted with a mysticism going in all its expressions to the absolute limit, the Russian people today must be brought from savagery to modern civilisation by force. But this can only be done at the price of a great deal of blood spilt and a veritable extermination of those who foment disorders.[18]

Many of the mutineers suspected something similar. If the French military authorities struggled to get their story straight, the uncertainties about Labourbe's life troubled the left as well. A 'confidential' note in Marty's personal papers casts doubt on Marie/Jeanne Laborde/Labourbe's identity. It corrected the view that Labourbe was an intellectual, as some sentimental portraits of her had it. Marty observed that she did not have a university qualification; indeed, she failed her certificate and went to Poland as a governess with her friend Jeanne Laborde's certificate. Marty used Labourbe's photographs in his publications that her brother – a cooper from Roanne – sent him and this brother stated that the executed militant's real identity was Marie Labourbe.[19]

If Jeanne Labourbe's killing resulted in a decades-long search for the truth, so too did the French sailors' deaths on the Sevastopol demonstration on 20 April 1919. The news of this event had a tremendous psychological effect upon the sailors aboard the ships. While the Minister of the Navy, Georges Leygues emphasised that there were no murderers amongst the sailors, a French officer ordered Greek troops to fire on the demonstration in Sevastopol, at which there were apparently French deaths. To mark the ten-year anniversary of the event, the Soviet regime erected a monument where the French sailors were killed. Marty's *La Révolte* was dedicated to the French soldiers and sailors as well as Russian workers killed in Odessa and Sevastopol by 'the valets of French capitalism'.[20]

For years, Marty had tried to ascertain the names of those French sailors who had been shot on the Morskaïa Road, but to no avail. In November 1932, Marty even appealed to the Revolutionary Military Council of the Soviet Fleet in the Black Sea to investigate. Presumably expecting official exhumations, he told his Russian comrades that the sailors were buried in the French cemetery in Sevastopol and would have been wearing aluminium name tags with the matriculation number and date of birth.[21] Even his final 1949 edition of the book was unable to identify the French sailor (or sailors) killed on Morskaïa Road. Philippe Masson, relying on the official (previously confidential) reports, produced a very different account of the events, noting the confused circumstances of the shooting, but stating that 50 were wounded, of whom six were French sailors, one of these mortally so.[22] Masson did not provide a name, though he did consult the files of the Navy that contain the sailor's identity. So, during the mutineers' long quest for the truth, the military authorities knew and did not divulge the information. They had their own eyewitness reports concerning the Morskaïa Road events, including that of Ensign Pommier who ordered the Greek troops to fire on the demonstration.[23]

Indeed, the French Navy had conducted its own secret inquiry into the events of that day. Admiral Lejay wrote the report that comprised submissions from military intelligence and ten officers from four ships. One hundred and twenty eight crew members, including officers, were ashore from the *Vergniaud* on 20 April. Lieutenant Vaublanc interviewed 111 of them.[24] Vaublanc identified the victim of the shooting to be Morvan of the *Vergniaud* who was struck by three bullets.

After being shot, Grisset carried Morvan to the pharmacy. The transport ship *Duguay Trouin* that took the wounded confirmed Raymond Firmin Morvan's identity, a third class sailor and apprentice *fourrier* (quartermaster), a nineteen-year-old Parisian, whose parents lived in rue Langier of the 17th *arrondissement*. This was precisely the kind of urban working-class background about which the Navy complained in its investigations into the causes of the mutiny.

Why does this matter? To understand mutineer subjectivity, we have to comprehend the sense of injustice that animated their revolt. Far from being an emotional overreaction to insinuations and rumours, the truth about the deaths of 'Jeanne Labourbe' and Raymond Morvan was buried under official denial. After this, historians largely accepted the assumptions of the authorities. If memory mixed with legend, the mutineers were torn between the pressures of oblivion and a sense of obligation. They felt a duty to remember the Black Sea martyrs and to draw out the lessons of the mutiny for posterity. The return to democratic normality set in place a consensus that diminished the mutiny, with even the PCF succumbing over time to the conformity of electoral politics. In such circumstances, the mnemonic practices of mutineers were bent to the interests of the Soviet Union or the PCF. Over their life course, the meanings of the mutiny shifted for its participants for personal, shared and conjunctural reasons. Ageing itself interacted with this dialogue between past and present, as did the fortunes of their networking and the context of the Cold War and 1968. The last battle of the mutineer generation was to rescue their own history from these structural and personal pressures to forget or distort the past.

Method and consciousness

Despite the shared experiences during the mutiny, participants did not express a single voice. This was even less so after the event. For instance, in his court appearance, François Peronne of the *Waldeck-Rousseau* tried to distance himself from the 'criminal element that worked in the shadows' and denounced the revolutionaries on board.[25] The conflicted attitudes of mutineers returns us to the methodological problem of consciousness. The testimonies reveal the ambivalences, contradictions and inconsistencies of memory and consciousness. It would be tempting to follow Daniel Dennett's notion of consciousness as decentred 'multiple drafts' or Francisco Varela's rejection of the substantial unitary self.[26] Here, the historian's instinct cautions against the dangerous path that might lead to the denial of agency, to behaviourism, or to unmitigated structuralism. Instead, the hypothesis of a dialogical or contradictory consciousness seems like a good starting point for multidisciplinary discussion. Such a perspective combines conscious human agency with internal multiple and parallel processes, over which we do not exercise absolute control, yet is bound together through dynamic interaction with our social and natural environment. The insistence on conscious agency has been axiomatic to this study and finds ample substantiation throughout mutineer testimony. Indeed, mutineer agency can even be observed in the achievements of the last battle of the mutineer generation. As a consequence of maintaining an association into the 1970s, through the collective encouragement to generate autobiographical texts and witness statements, mutineers ensured that historians had (admittedly mediated) access to their dialogue.

This research draws upon the theoretical resources of a generation of Marxist scholars (Gramsci, Benjamin, the Bakhtin school, Lefebvre) to bridge existing fields of emotions, senses, space and memory. These theoreticians are particularly useful regarding these current research concerns and it is worth re-examining their works that have previously been mined according to past agendas. For instance, educationalists are much more familiar with Vygotsky than historians. Even amongst the former, his unfinished essay on emotions is overlooked. Uncertainties about authorship within the Bakhtin circle have lessened their appeal of late. Bakhtin's focus upon on the novel has meant that he is much more known to literature specialists than historians or linguists. He is more routinely turned to for his concepts of 'carnival' and 'heteroglossia' than emotions or consciousness. Equally, while Gramsci has been undoubtedly influential in social history, this has been primarily for hegemony rather than scrutiny of his concept of split or contradictory consciousness. Further reasons for neglect exist. The historians of emotion in particular have defined themselves as reformulating social and cultural history purged of Marxist influence. Arguably, this has closed off theoretical resources that assist our understanding of emotions and their relationship to consciousness.

Methodological implications of this expanded dialogical approach to subjectivity depend upon your disciplinary standpoint. For historians, those specialising in the senses, emotions, or history from below might go beyond the specialisations of their field and become more aware of the trap of compartmentalisation. This might curb the reductionist temptations within these research programmes. The claims of the historians of the emotions about the status of emotion in history illustrate this. Regarding mutineer testimony, it certainly looks like emotion was the 'substrate' of their actions or, equally, after the events their despairing incapacity. However, we might ask: are not emotions (at least in part) internal reactions to external environment, reactions over which we do not entirely have conscious control? Emotions might therefore be understood as an unconscious internationalisation of external structures, or limits upon agency, translated into the subjective processes of the mind. These affective impulses are consciously negotiated and culturally mediated or, as Reddy puts it, 'navigated'. Viewed in this way, emotion is not the real basis of each historical epoch but rather a crucial and revealing mediation between human agents and their material environment.

Dialogues between historians of the senses and the emotion might be particularly fruitful, given sensory-affective feedback loops. A bilateral approach between specific senses and specific emotions might have been more fruitful than the chapter structure adopted here. We might consider, for example, the way that positive emotions (joy) interacted with the sight of the red flag, with these emotions arousing visual attention, stimulating cognitive innovation and motivating broader repertoires of action, with this building into memory. The difficulty of assigning aspects of the mutiny such as song neatly into chapters on either the senses or emotions illustrates the connectedness of these components of consciousness.

Perhaps reconsideration of the validity of the category of consciousness within history is overdue and that it offers non-reductive grounds to cope with both interdisciplinary debates and the dangers of specialisation into fields of emotions, senses, memory and constructions of space and place. At the same time, the insights of these fields should be respected and each aspect of consciousness studied in a disaggregated manner into order reassemble in complex systemic ways. The result of a recognition of the disciplinary fragmentation around these fields should not be an excuse for a bland synthesis but rather a careful aggregation of connections, mediations and dissonances.

The outward-looking perspective of conversations with other disciplines, especially the natural sciences regarding the brain, as Reddy has done, is both important and perilous. This requires a recognition that these disciplines are themselves subject to major controversies, which non-experts access in condensed and simplified forms. Historians should inch forward cautiously in terrain like an evolutionary past shared with mammals providing insights into joyful play (and therefore the liberation of apparent victory of the mutiny), or universal emotions revealed in facial expressions (and therefore the smile as lingua franca of fraternisation). These provide interesting hypotheses but a sensitivity to the limits of the evidence needs to be retained. To avoid a hasty conclusion, consideration of disciplines attentive to cultural specificity can balance the universalising claims of the natural sciences.

1919: one hundred years on

Behind the scenes, the authorities knew 1919 was an exceptional year regarding social contestation. Clemenceau had access to the situation reports of French military intelligence (*deuxième bureau*) on the mood in France. While much of small-town and rural France was 'calm' or in 'good spirits', the *deuxième bureau* also relayed troubling news of anxiety, nervousness and agitation elsewhere. The cost of living, the eight-hour day, demobilisation, the Russian and Hungarian revolutions, the state of the labour market all perturbed the mood around the time of the mutinies. Social tensions intensified among the trade unions and emergent veterans' groups. The balm of victory was not able to soothe social hostility targeted towards women, foreigners, 'shirkers' and those who profited from the war.[27]

The attempt to apply a materialist understanding of mutineer consciousness and the connectivity of its constituent parts would evidently benefit from a sense of the wider material circumstances in which mutineers found themselves. Their subjectivity had such a striking character precisely because they were a microcosm of the century's most unruly year, usually viewed through the lens of the year of peace-making at Versailles.

Yet, viewing that year through their eyes leaves much out of sight. Jeanne Labourbe notwithstanding, mutineers say little about women or colonial troops who are absent, off-stage. For all the inability of the authorities to comprehend the mutineers' world, those in power worried about the potential of transgressive solidarities between women or colonial troops and the rebellious soldiers, sailors and the workers of port cities. Thus, time and again, reports such as that of Ensign Hainguerlot in Galați reported to his superiors about the proliferation of propaganda amongst service personnel through the intermediary of women in the cafés and bedrooms of the city, combining anxieties about revolution and sexual morality. Marty's co-conspirator Badina escaped with the help of 'Anika', his Romanian mistress.[28] Equally, French military authorities reported from Algeria in March 1919 that amongst ethnically Algerian troops, there was indifference to the progress of military operations, being preoccupied with social and religious rights, especially unjust payments to their families while they were in military service.[29] The context of the Russian Revolution and the Versailles Peace Conference meant that such grievances in Algeria and elsewhere were being re-framed into revolutionary anti-colonialism.

The mutineers constituted in miniature a chaotic conjuncture of profound global unrest. They were typical in the sense that they were forged by the great structural dynamics then at play. Ever since the moment that news of the mutiny prompted debate in the Chamber of Deputies and commentary in the press, a dispute about scale has plagued the mutiny. Participation in this movement was uneven. This is partly because the mutiny's (or mutinies') scope and meaning were ambiguous. The movement could be read as both a 'handful of leaders' and a mood that ran through much of the armed forces awaiting demobilisation. The Black Sea Mutiny became a synecdoche for a geographically and temporally expanded cycle of protest that lasted roughly eight months. Enumerating participants is equally problematic. Several hundred mutineers faced court martial. Thousands participated in protest. More still were probably caught up in the atmosphere though did not participate in events. Indeed, the events might profoundly influence even outside observers like César Fauxbras who wrote a novel *Mer Noire* (1932) about the mutiny or those in the campaign for amnesties for imprisoned mutineers. The dismissive trope that the revolt was two 'bad' or 'mad' days conducted by a 'handful of traitors' emerged because the mutiny did not fit with the official narrative of victory in war.

The memory of the event relied upon the smaller cohort closest to the revolt. Examining the dynamics of the mutineer generation and their network, two features – emotional intensity and memory – interplay at multiple scales. Those with the least emotional connection with the mutiny formed a vague attachment to it. They were likely to neglect its memory (perhaps even forget it) and shun its network. Even those with the strongest emotional investment in the mutiny might feel the pressure of despair or regret most keenly and resist public association with the mutiny. Other mutineers summoned the emotional energy to learn from the mutiny to grasp hope from the narrative of their past and undertook the 'duty' to remember. That generation has now passed away, transforming the commemorative impulse of the mutiny. However, they did bequeath sufficient testimony to transmit, however partially, their understanding of the mutinies.

This book is due for publication at the centenary of the Black Sea Mutiny. It will certainly not attract the attention that the peacemakers of Versailles will draw. Yet the actions of Woodrow Wilson, David Lloyd George and Georges Clemenceau are better understood if the unruly context of 1919 is appreciated. This unique global conjuncture refracted through the mutiny all its complexities, instabilities and ambiguities. Given that it marked the high waterline of global contention, of which the French mutinies were one manifestation, 1919 should not be reduced to the year of Versailles peace-making. The year left a powerful and uneasy impression. When mutineer Lagaillarde emerged in 1921, after two years of incarceration, some of which he had spent with Marty, he wrote as if nothing had changed. Little did he know that he had resurfaced in a different world; the moment of 1919 had passed, despite its lasting legacy. His letter to Marty's mother signed off with the misplaced confidence about the immediate future:

> Long live Marty, long live Badina, long live the sailors of the Black Sea, vengeance approaches, long live the revolution.[30]

Lagaillarde lived in a lost and forgotten time. However, there have been conjunctures, as in 1968, when the mutiny appears once more to be timely and relevant. When, as Walter Benjamin put it, historical agents subjectively 'blast open the continuum of history', reaching out to such moments – just as the mutineers did before them – for inspiration, hope and insight into their own predicament.

Notes

1 SHD SS Ed 30 untitled version of Odessa Waltz.
2 Robert Brécy, *Florilège de la Chanson Révolutionnaire de 1789 au Front Populaire*, p. 247. Raymonde Lefebvre and Paul Vaillant-Couturier, *La Guerre des Soldats: Le Champ d'Honneur, Conseils de Guerre aux Armées l'Hôpital* (Paris: Ernest Flammarion, 1919), pp. 143–50.
3 Rolland, *Odessa*.
4 ADSSD AM 281J I 2.3 Espagnet's declaration of 1927; Marty's comment, 6 January 1933. It was the subject of correspondence with another mutineer, ADSSD AM 281J VI D2.84–5 Eugene Lefort to Marty, 1 June 1927.
5 P. N. Johnson-Laird and Keith Oatley, 'Emotions, music, and literature', in Lisa Feldman Barrett, Michael Lewis and Jeannette M. Haviland-Jones

(eds), *Handbook of Emotions* (New York: Guilford Publications, 2016), pp. 102–13.
6 Benedict Anderson, *Imagined Communities: Reflections on the Origin and Spread of Nationalism* (London: Verso, 1991).
7 SHD SS Ed 30 untitled Odessa Waltz.
8 ADSSD AM 281J VI D2.63 R. Nouveau, *De Toulon à Calvi par Odessa*.
9 ADSSD AM 281J IV E1.3–5 Eugène Lefort, *Souvenirs sur les événements de la Mer Noire*.
10 ADSSD AM 281J IV D1.5 Notta.
11 SHD SS Ed 30 Commander Robez-Pagillon report, 23 April 1919. SHD 20 N 273 Colonel Trousson's report on the occupation of Sevastopol.
12 *L'Humanité*, 11 August 1919.
13 SHD 7 N 800 General Alby to Commander-in-Chief of the Allied Armies of the Orient, 12 August 1919.
14 SHD 7 N 800 Note sur la femme Jeanne Laborde, Information sent by General d'Anselme and Lt-Col Freydenberg, 18 August 1919. [Illegible] to d'Anselme, 14 August 1919.
15 SHD 7 N 800 Note sur la femme Jeanne Laborde, Information sent by General d'Anselme and Lt-Col Freydenberg, 18 August 1919.
16 SHD SS Ea 164 Lieutentant de Vaisseau de Carsalade, Chef de SR Naval, SR Marine (Odessa), Note de renseignements, 3 March 1919.
17 Marty, *Révolte* (1949), pp. 193–7.
18 SHD 7N 798 agent 337a report: Russia and the questions of the liberated Slavic peoples, 6 November 1918.
19 ADSSD AM 281J I 2.2 Confidential note by Marty, 6 January 1933. *Dictionnaire Biographique du Mouvement Ouvrier Français*, www.maitron-en-ligne.univ-paris1.fr (last accessed 12 April 2018).
20 André Marty, *La Révolte de la Mer Noire* (Paris: Editions sociales, 1932), n.p.; André Marty, *La Révolte de la Mer Noire* (Paris: Editions sociales, 1939), p. 11.
21 ADSSD AM 281J A4 2.2 Marty to the Military Revolutionary Council of the Black Sea Fleet, 4 November 1932.
22 See Masson's footnote about the legend that Pommier committed suicide in front of Amet. Masson, *Marine*, p. 264.
23 SHD 20 N 273 Colonel Trousson's report on the occupation of Sevastopol, appendix 17: Major de Villepin's report on the events of 20 April 1919.
24 SHD SS Ed 30 Vessel Lieutenant Vaublanc's report, 24 April 1919.
25 ADSSD AM 281J VI D2 20 François Peronne, *Memoire de la Mer Noire*, 28 August 1920.
26 Daniel Dennett, *Consciousness Explained* (London: Penguin, 1991), Francisco Varela, Evan Thompson and Eleanor Rosh, *The Embodied Mind* (Cambridge: MIT Press, 1993).
27 SHD 5 N 268 État des ésprits à l'interieur, March 1919.

28 SHD SS Ed 30 Enseign de vaisseau Hainguerlot to Commandant Supérieur (*Galatz*), 7 June 1919. SHD 20 N 273 Berthelot's report on the situation in southern Russia, 18 February 1919. 'Even women participate and one could say that the propaganda of brothels is perhaps the most dangerous.' SHD 7 N 802 Diverse information from a former agent of the SR in Russia arrived recently from southern Russia, 15 January 1919. 'On the ground propaganda is above all made by women, French schoolmistresses (... illegible) in the service of the Bolsheviks, Russians and Jews speak French, German well-dressed demimondaines, café singers, etc. enter into relations with the men and the NCOs, try to turn them from their duty and make them desert.' On Anika in Badina's memories, *L'Humanité*, 18 October 1922–1 January 1923.
29 SHD 5 N 268 État des ésprits à l'interieur, Alger, 3 March 1919.
30 ADSSD AM 281J IV D2.8 Lagaillarde to M. Marty, 14 November 1921.

Bibliography

Archives Nationales, Paris

AN F7 13163–5 Mutineers of the Black Sea.
AN F7 13349–51 Anti-militarism.
AN F7 13952 Amnesty campaign for mutineers.
AN F7 13960 On homosexuality in the navy.

Bibliothèque National de la France

IFN-9038511 Les héros de la Mer Noire: Badina etc. (Paris: l'Agence Meurisse, 1922). http://catalogue.bnf.fr/ark:/12148/cb41581716p.
IFN-9053769 For an image of Marty from 1921, http://catalogue.bnf.fr/ark:/12148/cb41580070 9 (last accessed 2 April 2018).

Service Historique de la Defence, Vincennes (SHD)

Conseil Supérieur de Guerre, Section Française
(Higher Council of War, French Section)

4 N 2 Correspondence, including military intervention in Murmansk and Archangel.
4 N 17 Correspondence from 2nd Bureau, including fortnightly bulletins.
4 N 25 Correspondence from 2nd Bureau, diverse notes and studies, including Siberia.
4 N 40 Russo-Rumanian Front, including situation in the Ukraine.

Cabinet du Ministre (Ministerial Cabinet)

5 N 159–60 Telephone messages and Telegrams, including mutinies.
5 N 181 Russia, including the mutiny of the 21st Colonial (3–23 March), collective indiscipline of the 73rd Battery (2 April).
5 N 183 Documents coming from mission in Russia, Poland and the Baltic Countries.
5 N 185 Southern Russia, the Caucasus and Siberia.
5 N 202 Hungary, Serbia, Yugoslavia and Bulgaria: notably Fiume.

Operations, Military and Diplomatic Information

5 N 268 Interior Morale: confidential Bulletins summarising the internal situation of morale coming from military intelligence, October 1917-August 1919.

Fonds Clemenceau (Clemenceau Papers)

6 N 54 Files of the Prime Minister.
6 N 93 Diverse information concerning military personnel, including discipline and leave.
6 N 220 Russia: Reports of military attachés concerning the situation.
6 N 221 Telegrams from military attachés.
6 N 225 Military Liaison with Denikin's Army.
6 N 226 French Military Mission in the Caucasus.
6 N 230 Telegrams coming from Northern Russia, including the mutiny of the 21st Colonial Battalion.
6 N 231 Telegrams coming from Siberia.
6 N 232 Internal and economic information on Russia 1917–21.
6 N 233 Political and Military Situation in Russia.
6 N 287 Daily synthesis of Telegrams.
6 N 289 Telegrams from the Navy.

État-Majeur de l'Armée, Deuxième Bureau (Army General Staff, Military Intelligence)

7 N 393 Siberia, including colonial battalion, November 1918–April 1919.
7 N 441 Colonial Infantry and Black Army, including reports on the use of black shock troops.
7 N 681 General situation in 1919: includes Germany, Hungary, Morocco, Spain, Hungary, Italy, etc.
7 N 796–99: Soviet Russia, 1917–20.
7 N 800 Southern Russia: including the 58th Infantry 'affair'.
7 N 801 Ukraine, including Odessa.
7 N 802 Ukraine: internal economic situation.

7 N 803 Ukraine: state of opinion in Odessa, report on evacuation.
7 N 817 Northern Russia, including on troop morale and propaganda.
7 N 972 Workers, social and industrial questions.

Armées – Front Oriental (Armies Eastern Front)

20 N 273 Information concerning Albania, Rumania and Russia, including Colonel Trousson's Report on Occupation of Sevastopol.
20 N 770 3rd Bureau Correspondence, including 58th Infantry, Berezan Island.

Etat-Major général, 1re section (renseignements, marines étrangères) (Ministry of the Navy-General Staff (information and foreign navies).)

SS Ea 157–164.

Etat-Major général, 4e section (forces navales, opérations) (Ministry of the Navy-General Staff (Naval Forces and Operations).)

SS Ed 30 Black Sea Mutiny.
SS Ed 61 Baltic correspondence.
SS Ed 98 EMG 4e section: Adriatic correspondence received: April 1919–December 1920.
SS Ed 113 Correspondence.
SS Ed 117–120 Correspondence.

Centre d'Histoire Centre d'Histoire de Science Po (CHSP), Paris

CHSP CT 1–2 Charles Tillon Papers.

Archives Départementales de Seine-Saint-Denis (ADSSD), Bobigny

ADSSD AM 281J André Marty Papers.

Periodicals

Action Française.
Cahiers du Mai.
L'Echo du Centre.
L'Humanité.
Le Libertaire.
La Nouvelle France.
Les Nouvelles.
La Vague.

Secondary Literature

Ageron, Charles-Robert, *"L'Algérie Algérienne": de Napoléon III à de Gaulle* (Paris: Sindbad, 1980), p. 101.
Ageron, Charles-Robert, 'La presse parisienne devant la guerre du Rif (avril 1925-mai 1926)', *Revue de l'Occident musulman et de la Méditerranée*, 24, 1 (1977), pp. 7-28.
Aminzade, Ronald R., Goldstone, Jack A., McAdam, Doug, Perry, Elizabeth J., Sewell, Jr, William H., Tarrow, Sidney, Tilly, Charles (eds), *Silence and Voice in the Study of Contentious Politics* (Cambridge; New York: Cambridge University Press, 2001).
Anderson, Benedict, *Imagined Community: Reflections on the Origin and Spread of Nationalism* (London: Verso, 1991).
Antier, Jean-Jacques, 'Révolte des équipages de la flotte à Toulon', *Les Dossiers Histoire de la Mer* (February-March 1980), pp. 73-86.
Ashplant, T. G., Dawson, Graham and Roper, Michael (eds), *Politics of War, Memory and Commemoration* (London: Routledge, 2000).
Ashworth, Tony, *Trench Warfare, 1914-1918: The Live and Let Live System* (London: Macmillan, 1980).
Audoin-Rouzeau, Stéphane and Becker, Annette, *14-18 Understanding the Great War* (New York: Hill and Wang, 2002).
Audoin-Rouzeau, Stéphane and Prochasson, Christophe (eds), *Sortir de la Grande Guerre-Le Monde et l'Après 1918* (Paris: Tallandier, 2015).
Augé, Marc, *Oblivion* (Minneapolis, MN: University of Minnesota Press, 2004).
Austin, John L., *How to Do Things With Words* (London: Clarendon, 1962).
Bailey, Peter, *Leisure and Class in Victorian England: Rational Recreation and the Contest for Control, 1830-1885* (Oxford: Routledge, 1978).
Bakhtin, Mikhail Mikhaïlovich, *The Dialogic Imagination: Four Essays* (Austin: University of Texas Press, 2010).
Bakhtin, Mikhail Mikhaïlovich, *Towards a Philosophy of the Act* (Austin: University of Texas Press, 1992).
Bakhtin, Mikhail Mikhaïlovich, *Speech Genres and Other Late Essays* (Austin: Texas University Press, 1986).
Balbirnie, Steven, '"A bad business": British responses to mutinies among local forces in Northern Russia', *Revolutionary Russia*, 29, 2 (2016), pp. 129-48.
Barbusse, Henri, *Le Feu: Journal d'une Escouade* (Paris: Flammarion, 1965).
Barbusse, Henri, *Paroles d'un Combattant: Articles et Discours 1917-20* (Paris: Flammarion, 1920).
Barthas, Louis, *Poilu: The World War I Notebooks of Corporal Louis Barthas, Barrelmaker, 1914-1918* (New Haven, CT: Yale University Press, 2014).
Barthes, Roland, *Camera Lucida: Reflections on Photography* (London: Vintage, 2000).
Bartlett, F. C., *Remembering: An Experimental and Social Psychology* (Cambridge: Cambridge University Press, 1932).

Bartov, Omer, *Murder in Our Midst: The Holocaust, Industrial Killing, and Representation* (New York: Oxford University Press, 1996).

Becker, Annette, 'Memory gaps: Maurice Halbwachs, memory and the Great War', *Journal of European Studies*, 35 (2005), pp. 102–13.

Bell, Christopher M. and Elleman, Bruce A., 'Naval mutinies in the twentieth century and beyond', in Christopher M. Bell and Bruce A. Elleman (eds), *Naval Mutinies of the Twentieth Century: An International Perspective* (London: Frank Cass, 2003), pp. 264–76.

Benjamin, Walter, 'Little history of photography', in Walter Benjamin, *Selected Writings* (Cambridge: Harvard University Press, 2005), Volume 2, Part 2, pp. 507–30.

Benjamin, Walter, 'The storyteller', in Walter Benjamin, *Selected Writings* (Cambridge: Harvard University Press, 2006), Volume 3, pp. 143–66.

Benjamin, Walter, *Selected Writings* (Cambridge: Harvard University Press, 2003).

Bidwell, Robin, *Morocco under Colonial Rule: French Administration of Tribal Areas 1912–1956* (London: Routledge, 2012).

Bijsterveld, Karin, 'The diabolical symphony of the mechanical age: technology and symbolism of sound in European and North American Noise Abatement Campaigns, 1900–40', *Social Studies of Science*, 31, 1 (2001), pp. 37–70.

Bliss, Tim, 'The physiological basis of memory', in Steven Rose (ed.), *From Brain to Consciousness?: Essays on the New Sciences of the Mind* (Princeton: Princeton University Press, 1998), pp. 73–93.

Bloch, Ernst, *Principle of Hope* (Cambridge: MIT Press, 1995).

Bodnar, John, *Remaking America: Public Memory, Commemoration, and Patriotism in the Twentieth Century* (Princeton: Princeton University Press, 1991).

Boujou, Marie-Cécile, 'André Marty et les éditions du PCF', in Boulland, Pennetier and Vaccaro (eds), *André Marty*, pp. 69–75.

Boulland, Paul, Pennetier, Claude and Vaccaro, Rossana (eds), *André Marty: l'Homme, l'Affaire, l'Archive* (Paris: CODHOS Editions, 2005).

Bourke, Joanna, *Fear: A Cultural History* (Emeryville, CA: Shoemaker & Hoard, 2006).

Bourke, Joanna, 'Fear and anxiety: writing about emotion in modern history', *History Workshop Journal*, 55, 1 (2003), pp. 111–33.

Boym, Svetlana, *The Future of Nostalgia* (New York: Basic Books, 2001).

Brécy, Robert, *Autour de la Muse Rouge: Groupe de Poètes et Chansonniers Révolutionnaires: 1901–1939* (Saint-Cyr-sur-Loire: C. Pirot, 1991).

Brécy, Robert, *Florilège de la Chanson Révolutionnaire de 1789 au Front Populaire* (Paris: Éditions de l'Atelier, 1990).

Brennan, Timothy, 'Subaltern stakes', *New Left Review*, 89 (2014), pp. 67–87.

Briggs, Jean L., *Never in Anger: Portrait of an Eskimo Family* (Cambridge: Harvard University Press, 1970).

Briggs, Marlene A., 'Dis/composing the First World War in Britain: trauma and commemoration in the testimony of Harry Patch, 1998-2008', *History & Memory*, 28, 1 (2016), pp. 71-109.

Brodiez, Axelle, 'Le Secours Populaire Français entre Marty et Martin: deux mythes et deux affaires', in Boulland, Pennetier and Vaccaro (eds), *André Marty*, pp. 77-84.

Bruel, Gaetan, 'L'oreille amputée', in Florence Gétreau (ed.), *Entendre la Guerre: Silence, Musiques et Sons en 14-18* (Paris: Gallimard, 2014), pp. 120-7.

Buch, Esteban, 'Silences de la Grande Guerre', in Florence Gétreau (ed.), *Entendre la Guerre: Silence, Musiques et Sons en 14-18* (Paris: Gallimard, 2014), pp. 128-33.

Bulatis, John, *Maurice Thorez: A Biography* (London: I.B. Tauris, 2015).

Burrow, J. A., *Gestures and Looks in Medieval Narrative* (Cambridge: Cambridge University Press, 2002).

Burstein, Andrew, *Sentimental Democracy: The Evolution of America's Romantic Self-Image* (New York: Hill & Wang, 1999).

Calas, Raoul, 'Pages glorieuses de l'internationalisme proletarian: La révolte de la Mer Noire', *Cahiers de l'Institut Maurice Thorez*, 14, 2 (1969), pp. 92-4.

Callard, Felicity and Papoulis, Constantina, 'Affect and embodiment', in Susannah Radstone (ed.), *Memory: Histories, Theories, Debates* (New York: Fordham University Press), pp. 246-62.

Carew, Anthony, *The Lower Deck of the Royal Navy, 1900-39: The Invergordon Mutiny in Perspective* (Manchester: Manchester University Press, 1981).

Carley, Michael Jabara, *Revolution and Intervention: The French Government and the Russian Civil War, 1917-1919* (Buffalo: McGill-Queen's University Press, 1983).

Carley, Michael Jabara, 'The origins of the French intervention in the Russian Civil War, January-March 1918: a reappraisal', *Journal of Modern History*, 48 (1976), pp. 413-39.

Carlisle, Janice, 'The smell of class: British novels of the 1860s', *Victorian Literature and Culture*, 29, 1 (2001), pp. 1-19.

Cassagne, Jean-Marie, *Le Grand Dictionnaire de l'Argot Militaire* (Paris: Éditions LBM, 2007).

Castells, Manuel, *Networks of Outrage and Hope: Social Movements in the Internet Age* (Cambridge: Polity, 2012).

Chack, Paul, *Marins à la Bataille: Méditerranée 1914-1918* (Paris: Gerfaut, 2001), 3 Volumes.

Chack, Paul, *Tu Seras Marin* (Paris: Éditions de France, 1939).

Chack, Paul, *Deux Batailles Navales: Lépante-Trafalgar* (Paris: Éditions de France, 1935).

Chack, Paul, *Branlebas de Combat* (Paris: Éditions de France, 1932).

Chack, Paul, *Pavillon Haut* (Paris: Éditions de France, 1929).

Changeux, Jean-Pierre and Ricoeur, Paul, *What Makes Us Think? A Neuroscientist and a Philosopher Argue about Ethics, Human Nature and the Brain* (Princeton: Princeton University Press, 2000).

Chatard, Jean, *Les Marins: Chants des Équipages* (La Rochelle: La Décourance, 2011).
Classen, Constance, Howes, David and Synnott, Anthony, *Aroma: The Cultural History of Smell* (New York: Routledge, 2002).
Classen, Constance, *Worlds of Sense: Exploring the Senses in History and Across Cultures* (London: Routledge, 1993).
Commission d'Histoire, *Histoire du Parti Communiste Français: Manuel* (Paris: Éditions Sociales, 1964).
Constable, Marianne, *Just Silences: The Limits and Possibilities of Modern Law* (Princeton: Princeton University Press, 2009).
Corbin, Alain, *Histoire du Silence: de la Renaissance à nos jours* (Paris: Albin Michel, 2014).
Corbin, Alain, *Le Miasme et la Jonquille: L'Odorat et L'Imaginaire Social xviiie-xixe* (Paris: Aubier Montaigne, 1982).
Corbin, Alain, 'Charting the cultural history of the senses', in Howes (ed.), *Empire*, pp. 128–40.
Courtois, Stéphane and Lazar, Marc, *Histoire du Parti Communiste Français* (Paris: Press Universitaires de France, 2000).
Cremadeills, Jacques, 'Le mot d'ordre de fraternisation pendant la guerre du Rif (1924–1926)', *Cahiers de la Méditerranée*, 14, 1 (1977), pp. 53–64.
Cru, Jean Norton, *Du Témoignage* (Paris: Allia, 2008).
Cru, Jean Norton, *Témoins: Essai d'Analyse et de Critique des Souvenirs de Combattants Édités en Français de 1915 à 1928* (Paris: Les Étincelles, 1929).
Damasio, Antonio R., *Looking for Spinoza: Joy, Sorrow, and the Feeling Brain* (Orlando: Harcourt, 2003).
Damasio, Antonio R., *The Feeling of What Happens: Body and Emotion in the Making of Consciousness* (New York: Harcourt, 1999).
Damasio, Antonio R., *Descartes' Error: Emotion, Reason, and the Human Brain* (New York: G.P. Putnam 1994).
Dartige de Fournet, Vice-amiral Louis, *Souvenirs de Guerre d'un Amiral, 1914–16* (Paris: Plon, 1920).
Darwin, Charles, *The Expression of the Emotions in Man and Animals* (London: John Murray, 1872).
Daucros, Frédéric, 'Comment les marins français d'Odessa ont connu Jeanne Labourbe', *Cahiers de L'Institut Maurice Thorez*, 5, 21 (1971), p. 86.
Davis, Mike, *Old Gods, New Enigmas: Marx's Lost Theory* (London: Verso, 2018).
Dechlette, François, *L'Argot des Poilus: Dictionnaire Humoristique et Philologique* (Paris: Éditions de Paris, 2004).
Delumeau, Jean, *Sin and Fear: The Emergence of a Western Guilt Culture 13th-18th Centuries* (New York: St. Martin's Press, 1991).
Dennett, Daniel, *Consciousness Explained* (London: Penguin, 1993).
Dictionnaire Biographique du Mouvement Ouvrier Français, www.maitron-en-ligne.univ-paris1.fr (last accessed 12 April 2018).

Drake, David, 'The PCF, the Surrealists, Clarté and the Rif War', *French Cultural Studies*, 17, 2 (2006), pp. 173-88.
Dreyfus, Michel, *PCF: Crises et Dissidences* (Brussels: Éditions Complexe, 1989).
Eagleton, Terry, 'Ideology and its vicissitudes in Western Marxism', in Slavoj Žižek (ed.), *Mapping Ideology* (London: Verso, 1994), pp. 179-226.
Ebbinghaus, Hermann, *Memory: A Contribution to Experimental Psychology* (Bristol: Thoemmes, 1998).
Eley, Geoff and Nield, Keith, *The Future of Class in History: What's Left of the Social?* (Ann Arbor, MI: University of Michigan Press, 2007).
Elias, Norbert, *The Civilizing Process: Sociogenetic and Psychogenetic Investigations* (Oxford: Blackwell Publishers, 2000).
Eustace, Nicole, 'Emotion and political change', in Matt and Stearns (eds), *Doing Emotions History*, pp. 163-83.
Eustace, Nicole, *Passion is the Gale: Emotion, Power, and the Coming of the American Revolution* (Chapel Hill, NC: University of North Carolina Press, 2008).
Facon, P., 'Les mutineries dans les corps expéditionnaires français en Russie Septentrionale (décembre 1918-avril 1919)', *Revue d'Histoire Moderne et Contemporaine*, 24 (1977), pp. 455-74.
Fauxbras, César, *Jean Le Gouin: Journal d'un Simple Matelot de la Grande Guerre* (Louviers: L'Ancre de Marine, 2004).
Fauxbras, César, *Mer Noire: Les Mutineries Racontées par un Mutin* (Paris: Flammarion, 1935).
Fink, Leon, *Sweatshops at Sea: Merchant Seamen in the World's First Globalized Industry from 1812 to the Present* (Chapel Hill, NC: University of North Carolina Press, 2011).
Fischer-Tiné, Harald (ed.), *Anxieties, Fear and Panic in Colonial Settings: Empires on the Verge of a Nervous Breakdown* (Cham, Switzerland: Palgrave Macmillan, 2017).
Fouchard, Dominique, *Le Poids de la Guerre* (Rennes: Presses Universitaires de Rennes, 2013).
Fournier, Eric, '"Crosse en l'air": l'insaisissable motif d'une histoire effilochée (France, 1789-1871)', *Romantisme*, 4 (2016), pp. 121-31.
Fox, Pamela, *Class Fictions: Shame and Resistance in the British Working-Class Novel, 1890-1945* (Durham, NC: Duke University Press, 1994).
Fraser, Ronald, *Blood of Spain: An Oral History of the Spanish Civil War* (London: Pimlico, 1986).
Frémeaux, Jacques, *Colonies dans la Grande Guerre: Combats et Épreuves des Peoples d'Outre-mer* (Cahors: 14-18 Éditions, 2006).
Frizot, Michel and Veigy, Cédric de, *VU: Le Magazine Photographique, 1928-1940* (Paris: La Martinière Éditions, 2009).
Gerwarth, Robert, 'The Central European counter-revolution: paramilitary violence in Germany, Austria and Hungary after the Great War', *Past & Present*, 200, 1 (2008), pp. 175-209.

Gerwarth, Robert and Manela, Erez, 'The Great War as a global war: imperial conflict and the reconfiguration of the world order, 1911–23', *Diplomatic History*, 38, 4 (2014), pp. 786–800.

Geslin-Ferron, Anne, 'Des fluctuations du consentement patriotique à travers les trêves et les fraternisations (1914–1918)', *Cahiers d'histoire. Revue d'Histoire Critique*, 127 (2015), pp. 95–114.

Goodman, Steve, *Sonic Warfare: Sound, Affect and the Ecology of Fear* (Cambridge: MIT Press, 2010).

Goodwin, Jeff, Jasper, James M. and Polletta, Francesca (eds), *Passionate Politics: Emotions and Social Movements* (Chicago: University of Chicago Press, 2001).

Gould, Stephen Jay, *Mismeasure of Man* (New York: Norton & Co, 1981).

Gramsci, Antonio, *Selections from the Prison Notebooks of Antonio Gramsci* (New York: International Publishers, 1971).

Großmann, Johannes, '1914, un lieu de mémoire européen? de la commémoration nationale à l'émergence d'un consensus mémoriel', *Guerres Mondiales et Conflits Contemporains*, 1 (2017), pp. 119–32.

Guigni, Marco, McAdam, Doug and Tilly, Charles, *How Social Movements Matter* (Minneapolis, MN: University of Minnesota Press, 1999).

Hamilton, Paula, *The Proust Effect: Oral History and the Senses* (Oxford: Oxford University Press, 2011).

Harris, William V., *Restraining Rage: The Ideology of Anger Control in Classical Antiquity* (Cambridge: Harvard University Press, 2002).

Harvey, David, *Spaces of Hope* (Berkeley: University of California Press, 2000).

Hathaway, Jane (ed.), *Rebellion, Repression, Reinvention: Mutiny in Comparative Perspective* (Westport, CT: Praeger, 2001).

Hazareesingh, Sudhir, 'Conflicts of memory: Republicanism and the commemoration of the past in modern France', *French History*, 23, 2 (2009), pp. 193–215.

Hebb, Donald Olding, *The Organization of Behavior: A Neuropsychological Theory* (New York: Wiley, 1949).

Heywood, Colin, 'The Catholic Church and the formation of the industrial labour force in nineteenth-century France: an interpretative essay', *European History Quarterly*, 19, 4 (1989), pp. 509–33.

Hibbitts, Bernard J., 'Making sense of metaphors: visuality, aurality, and the reconfiguration of American legal discourse', *Cardozo Law Review*, 16 (1994), pp. 229–356.

Hill, Christopher, *The Experience of Defeat: Milton and Some Contemporaries* (London: Faber and Faber, 1984).

Hirschkop, Ken, 'The classical and the popular: musical form and social context', in Christopher Norris (ed.), *Music and the Politics of Culture* (London: Lawrence and Wishart, 1989), pp. 283–304.

Hochschild, Arlie Russell, *The Managed Heart: Commericalization of Human Feeling* (Berkeley: University of California Press, 2012).

Hood, Ronald Chalmers, III, *Royal Republicans: The French Naval Dynasties between the Wars* (Baton Rouge, LA: Louisiana State University Press, 1985).
Hood, Ronald Chalmers, III, 'The French Navy and parliament between the wars', *International Historical Review*, 6, 3 (1984), pp. 386–403.
Howes, David (ed.), *Empire of the Senses: The Sensual Culture Reader* (Oxford: Berg, 2005).
Howes, David, 'Culture tunes our neurones', in Howes (ed.), *Empire*, pp. 21–4.
Howes, David, *Sensual Relations: Engaging the Senses in Culture and Social Theory* (Ann Arbour, MI: University of Michigan Press, 2003).
Howes, David and Classen, Constance, *Ways of Sensing: Understanding the Senses in Society* (New York: Routledge, 2013).
Huizinga, Johan, *The Waning of the Middle Ages: A Study of the Forms of Life, Thought and Art in France and the Netherlands in the XIVth and XVth Centuries* (London: Edward Arnold, 1937).
Ironside, Edmund, *Archangel, 1918–19* (London: Constable, 1953).
Isitt, Benjamin, 'Mutiny from Victoria to Vladivostok, December 1918', *Canadian Historical Review*, 87, 2 (2006), pp. 223–64.
James, William, *Principles of Psychology* (Bristol: Thoemmes, 1998).
Jasper, James M., *The Art of Moral Protest* (Chicago: University of Chicago, 1997).
Jaworski, Adam, *Silence: Interdisciplinary Perspectives* (Berlin: Mouton de Gruyter, 1997).
Jay, Martin, *Downcast Eyes: The Denigration of Vision in Twentieth-Century French Thought* (Berkeley: University of California Press, 1993).
Jenkinson, Jacqueline, *Black 1919: Riots, Racism and Resistance in Imperial Britain* (Liverpool: Liverpool University Press, 2008).
Jenkinson, Jacqueline, 'Black sailors on Red Clydeside: rioting, reactionary trade unionism and conflicting notions of "Britishness" following the First World War', *Twentieth Century British History*, 19, 1 (2007), pp. 29–60.
Johnson, Niall P. A. S. and Mueller, Juergen, 'Updating the accounts: global mortality of the 1918–1920 "Spanish" influenza pandemic', *Bulletin of the History of Medicine*, 76, 1 (2002), pp. 105–15.
Johnson-Laird, P. N. and Oatley, Keith, 'Emotions, music, and literature', in Lisa Feldman Barrett, Michael Lewis and Jeannette M. Haviland-Jones (eds), *Handbook of Emotions* (New York: Guilford Publications, 2016), pp. 102–13.
Joly, Danièle, *The French Communist Party and the Algerian War* (London: Palgrave Macmillan, 1991), pp. 20–41.
Jones, Adrian, 'The French railway strikes of January-May 1920: new syndicalist ideas and emergent communism', *French Historical Studies*, 12, 4 (1982), pp. 27–42.
Jonsson, Pernilla, Neunsinger, Silke and Sangster, Joan (eds), *Crossing Boundaries: Women's Organizing in Europe and the Americas, 1880s–1940s* (Uppsala: Uppsala University, 2007).
Jossifort, Tico, 'The Black Sea revolt', *Revolutionary History*, 8 (2002), pp. 99–114.

Julien, Jean-Rémy, 'Paris: cris, sons, bruits: l'environnement sonore des années pré-révolutionnaires d'après Le Tableau de Paris de Sébastien Mercier', in Jean-Rémy Julien et Jean-Claude Klein (eds), *Orphée Phyrgien: Les Musiques de la Révolution* (Paris: Éditions du May, 1989), pp. 39–60.

Kalifa, Dominique, *Biribi: Les Bagnes Coloniaux de L'Armée Française* (Paris: Perrin, 2009).

Kaye, Harvey J., *The British Marxist Historians: An Introductory Analysis* (Basingstoke: Palgrave Macmillan, 1995).

Keetley, D., 'From anger to jealousy: explaining domestic homicide in antebellum America', *Journal of Social History*, 42 (2008), pp. 269–97.

Kenez, Peter, *Civil War in South Russia, 1919–1920* (Berkeley: University of California Press, 1977).

Kiernan, Victor Gordon, *European Empires from Conquest to Collapse, 1815–1960* (Bungay: Fontana, 1982).

Knott, Sarah, *Sensibility and the American Revolution* (Chapel Hill, NC: Omohundro Institute of Early American History and Culture, 2008).

Krugler, David F., *1919, The Year of Racial Violence: How African Americans Fought Back* (New York: Cambridge University Press, 2015).

Le Bon, Gustave, *The Crowd: A Study of the Popular Mind* (New York: Penguin, 1977).

Le Bras, Yves, *Les Rejetés: L'Affaire Marty-Tillon* (Paris: La Table Ronde, 1974).

LeDoux, Joseph, *The Emotional Brain* (London: Phoenix, 1998).

Leenaerts, Danielle, *Petite Histoire du Magazine Vu (1928–1940) Entre Photographie d'Information et Photographie d'Art* (Brussels: Peter Lang, 2010).

Lefebvre, Henri, *The Production of Space* (Oxford: Blackwell, 1991).

Le Febvre, Lucien, 'Sensibility and history: how to reconstitute the emotional life of the past', in Peter Burke (ed.), *A New Kind of History: From the Writings of Lucien Febvre* (New York: Harper and Row, 1973), pp. 12–26.

Lefebvre, Raymonde and Vaillant-Couturier, Paul, *La Guerre des Soldats: Le Champ d'Honneur, Conseils de Guerre aux Armées l'Hôpital* (Paris: Ernest Flammarion, 1919).

Le Guennec, Nicole, 'Le Parti communiste français et la guerre du Rif', *Le Mouvement social*, 78 (1972), pp. 39–64.

Le Ramey, Jean and Vottero, Pierre, *Mutins de la Mer Noire* (Paris: Éditions Sociales, 1973).

Levin, David Michael (ed.), *Modernity and the Hegemony of Vision* (Berkeley: University of California Press, 1993).

Linebaugh, Peter and Rediker, Marcus, *The Many-Headed Hydra: Sailors, Slaves, Commoners, and the Hidden History of the Revolutionary Atlantic* (Boston: Beacon Press, 2013).

Loez, André, 'Les mots et cultures de l'indiscipline: les graffiti des mutins de 1917', *Genèses*, 59, 2 (2005), pp. 25–46.

Loez, André and Mariot, Nicolas (eds), *Obéir/Désobéir: Les Mutineries de 1917 en Perspective* (Paris: La Découverte, 2008).

Loftus, Elizabeth F., Feldman, Julie and Dashiell, Richard, 'The reality of illusory memories', in Daniel L. Schacter (ed.), *Memory Distortion: How Minds, Brains, and Societies Reconstruct the Past* (Cambridge: Harvard University Press, 1995), pp. 47–68.

Lunn, Joe, '"Les races guerrières": racial preconceptions in the French military about West African soldiers during the First World War', *Journal of Contemporary History*, 34, 4 (1999), pp. 517–36.

Luria, Alexander, *The Mind of a Mnemonist: A Little Book About a Vast Memory* (London: Cape, 1969).

MacMahon, Darrin M., 'Finding joy in the history of emotions', in Matt and Stearns (eds), *Doing Emotions History*, pp. 103–19.

Maier, Charles S., 'The two postwar eras and the conditions for stability in twentieth-century Western Europe', *American Historical Review*, 86, 2 (1981), pp. 327–52.

Maier, Charles S., *Recasting Bourgeois Europe: Stabilization in France, Germany and Italy in the Decade after World War I* (Englewood Cliffs, NJ: Prentice-Hall, 1974).

Manela, Erez, *The Wilsonian Moment: Self-determination and the International Origins of Anticolonial Nationalism* (Oxford: Oxford University Press, 2007).

Manela, Erez, 'Imagining Woodrow Wilson in Asia: dreams of east-west harmony and the revolt against empire in 1919', *American Historical Review*, 111, 5 (2006), pp. 1327–51.

Manela, Erez, 'The Wilsonian moment and the rise of anticolonial nationalism: the case of Egypt', *Diplomacy and Statecraft*, 12, 4 (2001), pp. 99–122.

Mann, Gregory, *Native Sons: West African Veterans and France in the Twentieth Century* (Durham, NC: Duke University Press, 2006).

Marival, Guy, 'La chanson de Craonne: de la chanson palimpseste à la chanson manifeste', in Nicolas Offenstadt (ed.), *Le Chemin des Dames: de L'Événement à la Mémoire* (Paris: Stock, 2004), pp. 350–9.

Marty, André, *L'Affaire Marty* (Paris: Editions Norman Béthune, 1972).

Marty, André, *La Révolte de la Mer Noire* (Paris: Editions sociales, 1932, 1939 and 1949), pp. 106–22.

Marty, André, *Les Heures Glorieuses de la Mer Noire* (Paris: Bureau d'éditions, 1932).

Marty, André, *Souvenirs d'Indochine* (Paris: Éditions de l'Avant-Garde, n.d.).

Marty, André and Calas, Raoul, *A la Gloire des Lutteurs de 1907* (Montpellier: Graille et Castelnau, 1947).

Masson, Philippe, 'The French naval mutinies of 1919', in Christopher M. Bell and Bruce A. Elleman (eds), *Naval Mutinies of the Twentieth Century: An International Perspective* (London: Frank Cass, 2003).

Masson, Philippe, *La Marine Française et la Mer Noire, 1918–1919* (Paris: Sorbonne, 1982).

Matt, Susan J., 'Current emotion research in history: or, doing the history from the inside out', *Emotion Review*, 3, 1 (2011), pp. 117–24.

Matt, Susan J. and Stearns, Peter N. (eds), *Doing Emotions History* (Champaign, IL: University of Illnois Press, 2013).

Maza, Sarah C., *Servants and Masters in Eighteenth-Century France* (Princeton: Princeton University Press, 1983).
McLuhan, Marshall, *The Gutenburg Galaxy* (Toronto: University of Toronto Press, 1962).
Memmi, Dominique, Raveneau, Gilles and Taïeb, Emmanuel (eds), *Le Social à L'Épreuve du Dégoût* (Rennes: Presses Universitaires de Rennes, 2016).
Milliot, Vincent, *Les Cris de Paris, ou, Le Peuple Travesti: les Représentations des Petits Métiers Parisiens (XVIe-XVIIIe siècles)* (Paris: Publications de la Sorbonne, 1995).
Morgan, Kevin, *International Communism and the Cult of the Individual Leaders, Tribunes and Martyrs under Lenin and Stalin* (London: Palgrave Macmillan, 2017).
Morgan, W. John, 'The pedagogical politics of Antonio Gramsci: "pessimism of the intellect, optimism of the will"', *International Journal of Lifelong Education*, 6, 4 (1987), pp. 295–308.
Nora, Pierre, 'Between memory and history: les lieux de mémoire', *Representations*, 26 (1989), pp. 7–24.
Olick, Jeffrey K. and Robbins, Joyce, 'Social memory studies: from collective memory to the historical sociology of mnemonic practices', *Annual Review of Sociology*, 24 (1998), pp. 105–40.
Olick, Jeffrey K., Vinitzky-Seroussi, Vered and Levy, Daniel (eds), *The Collective Memory Reader* (New York: Oxford University Press, 2011).
Ong, Walter, *Orality and Literacy* (London: Methuen, 1982).
Orr, Andrew, 'The myth of the Black Sea Mutiny: communist propaganda, Soviet Influence and the re-remembering of the mutiny', *French History*, 32, 1 (2018), pp. 86–105.
Palmer, Bryan D., *Descent into Discourse: The Reification of Language and the Writing of Social History* (Philadelphia: Temple University Press, 1990).
Parnavelas, John, 'The human brain: 100 billion connected cells', in Steven Rose (ed.), *From Brains to Consciousness?: Essays on the New Sciences of the Mind* (London: Penguin, 1998), pp. 18–32.
Paxton, Robert O., 'Darlan, un amiral entre deux blocs: réflexions sur une biographie récente', *Vingtième Siècle*, 36 (October–December 1992), pp. 3–19.
Pedroncini, Guy, *Les Mutineries de 1917* (Paris: Presses Universitaires de France, 1967).
Pennetier, Claude and Pudal, Bernard, 'Stalinism: workers' cult and cult of leaders', *Twentieth Century Communism*, 1, 1 (2009), pp. 20–9.
Perry, Matt, 'Vive la France! Death at sea, the French Navy and the Great War', *French History*, 26, 3 (2012), pp. 344–66.
Perry, Matt, *Memory of War in France, 1914–45: César Fauxbras, the Voice of the Lowly* (Basingstoke: Palgrave Macmillan, 2011).
Plamper, Jan, 'The history of emotions: an interview with William Reddy, Barbara Rosenwein, and Peter Stearns', *History and Theory*, 49, 2 (2010), pp. 237–65.
Portelli, Alessandro, 'The peculiarities of oral history', *History Workshop Journal*, 12, 1 (1981), pp. 96–107.

Racine, Nicole, 'The Clarté movement in France, 1919–21', *Journal of Contemporary History*, 2, 2 (1967), pp. 195–208.
Rancière, Jacques, *The Politics of Aesthetics: Distribution of the Sensible* (London: Bloomsbury, 2013).
Raphael-Leygues, Jacques and Barré, Jean-Luc, *Les Mutins de la Mer Noire* (Paris: Plon, 1981).
Reay, Diane, 'Beyond consciousness? The psychic landscape of social class', *Sociology*, 39, 5 (2005), pp. 911–28.
Reddy, William M., 'Saying something new: practice theory and cognitive neuroscience', *Arcadia-International Journal for Literary Studies*, 44, 1 (2009), pp. 8–23.
Reddy, William M., 'Emotional liberty: politics and history in the anthropology of emotions', *Cultural Anthropology*, 14, 2 (1999), pp. 256–88.
Reddy, William M., *The Invisible Code: Honor and Sentiment in Postrevolutionary France, 1814–1848* (Berkeley: University of California Press, 1997).
Reid, Donald, 'In the name of the father: a language of labour relations in nineteenth-century France', *History Workshop Journal*, 38, 1 (1994), pp. 1–22.
Reid, Donald, 'Industrial paternalism: discourse and practice in nineteenth-century French mining and metallurgy', *Comparative Studies in Society and History*, 27, 4 (1985), pp. 579–607.
Renan, Ernest, 'What is a nation?' in Olick, Vinitzky-Seroussi and Levy (eds), *The Collective Memory Reader*, pp. 80–3.
Ribalta, Jorge (ed.), *The Worker Photography Movement (1926–1939): Essays and Documents: A Hard, Merciless Light* (Madrid: Museo Nacional Centro de Arte Reina Sofia, 2011).
Ricoeur, Paul, *Memory, History, Forgetting* (Chicago: University of Chicago Press, 2004).
Robertson, George, Mash, Melinda, Tickner, Lisa, Bird, Jon, Curtis, Barry and Punam, Tim (eds), *Travellers' Tales: Narratives of Home and Displacement* (London: Routledge, 1994).
Roche, Jean-Marie, *Dictionnaire des Bâtiments de la Flotte de Guerre Française de Colbert à nos Jours: Tome II: 1870–2006* (France: Cloître, 2013).
Roeder, George H., 'Coming to our senses', *Journal of American History*, 81, 3 (1994), pp. 1112–22.
Rolland, P., *Odessa: Les Mutins de la Mer Noire* (Paris: Bureau d'Éditions, 1927).
Rose, Steven, *The Making of Memory: From Molecules to Mind* (London: Vintage, 2003).
Rosenfeld, Sophia, 'On being heard: a case for paying attention to the historical ear', *American Historical Review*, 116, 2 (2011), pp. 316–34.
Rosenwein, Barbara H. (ed.), *Anger's Past: the Social Uses of an Emotion in the Middle Ages* (Ithaca, NY: Cornell University Press, 1998).
Rosenwein, Barbara H., 'Worrying about emotions in history', *The American Historical Review*, 107, 3 (2002), pp. 821–45.

Rothstein, Andrew, *The Soldiers' Strikes of 1919* (Basingstoke: Palgrave MacMillan, 1980).
Rousseau, Frédéric, *Le Procès des Témoins de la Grande Guerre: l'Affaire Norton Cru* (Paris: Seuil, 2003).
Schafer, R. Murray, *The Soundscape: Our Sonic Environment and the Tuning of the World* (Rochester, VT: Destiny Books, 1993).
Schafer, R. Murray, 'Soundscapes and earwitnesses', in Smith (ed.), *Hearing*, pp. 128-33.
Schuman, Howard and Rodgers, Willard L., 'Cohorts, chronology, and collective memory', *Public Opinion Quarterly*, 68, 2 (2004), pp. 217-54.
Scott, James C., *Weapons of the Weak: Everyday Forms of Peasant Resistance* (Dehli: Oxford University Press, 1990).
Searle, John R., 'Austin on locutionary and illocutionary acts', *The Philosophical Review*, 77, 4 (1968), pp. 405-24.
Seeger, Anthony, *Why Suyá Sing: A Musical Anthropology of an Amazonian People* (Urbana, IL: University of Illinois Press, 2004).
Sennett, Richard and Cobb, Jonathan, *The Hidden Injuries of Class* (New York: Vintage, 1972).
Serres, Michel, *The Five Senses: A Philosophy of Mingled Bodies* (London: Continuum, 2008).
Slavin, David, 'The French left and the Rif war, 1924-5: racism and the limits to internationalism', *Journal of Contemporary History*, 26, 1 (1991), pp. 5-32.
Smith, Leonard V., *Between Mutiny and Obedience: The Case of the French Fifth Infantry Division during World War I* (Princeton: Princeton University Press, 1994).
Smith, Mark Michael, 'Producing sense, consuming sense, making sense: perils and prospects for sensory history', *Journal of Social History*, 40, 4 (2007), pp. 841-58.
Smith, Mark Michael, *Sensory History* (Oxford: Berg, 2007).
Smith, Mark Michael (ed.), *Hearing History: A Reader* (Athens: University of Georgia Press, 2004).
Snow, David A., Burke Rochford Jr, E., Worden, Steven K. and Benford, Robert D., 'Frame alignment processes, micromobilization, and movement participation', *American Sociological Review*, 51, 4 (1986), pp. 464-81.
Stearns, Carol Z., '"Lord help me walk humbly": anger and sadness in England and America, 1570-1750', in Carol Z. Stearns and Peter N. Stearns (eds), *Emotion and Social Change: Toward a New Psychohistory* (New York: Holmes & Meier, 1988), pp. 39-68.
Stearns, Peter N., *American Fear: The Causes and Consequences of High Anxiety* (New York: Routledge, 2006).
Stearns, Peter N., *American Cool: Constructing a Twentieth-Century Emotional Style* (New York: New York University Press, 1994).
Stearns, Peter N., *Jealousy: The Evolution of an Emotion in American History* (New York: New York University Press, 1989).

Stearns, Carol Zizowitz and Stearns, Peter N., *Anger: the Struggle for Emotional Control in America's History* (Chicago: University of Chicago Press, 1986).
Stearns, Peter N. and Lewis, Jan (eds), *An Emotional History of the United States*. Volume 4. (New York: New York University Press, 1998).
Stearns, Peter N. and Stearns, Carol Z., 'Emotionology: clarifying the history of emotions and emotional standards', *The American Historical Review*, 90, 4 (1985), pp. 813–36.
Stewart, Susan, 'Remembering the senses', in Howes (ed.), *Empire*, pp. 59–69.
Stovall, Tyler, *Paris and the Spirit of 1919: Consumer Struggles, Transnationalism, and Revolution* (Cambridge: Cambridge University Press, 2012).
Strangleman, Tim, 'Representations of labour: visual sociology and work', *Sociology Compass*, 2, 5 (2008), pp. 1491–1505.
Streets, Heather, *Martial Races: The Military, Race and Masculinity in British Imperial Culture, 1857–1914* (Manchester: Manchester University Press, 2004).
Stuart, Robert S., '"A 'de profundis' for Christian Socialism": French Marxists and the critique of Political Catholicism, 1882–1905', *French Historical Studies*, 22, 2 (1999), pp. 241–61.
Summerfield, Penny, 'Culture and composure: creating narratives of the gendered self in oral history interviews', *Cultural and Social History*, 1, 1 (2004), pp. 65–93.
Thomas, Martin, 'After Mers-el-Kébir: the armed neutrality of the Vichy French navy, 1940–43', *English Historical Review*, 112, 447 (1997), pp. 643–70.
Thompson, E. P., *Customs in Common: Studies in Traditional Popular Culture* (New York: New Press, 1991).
Thompson, Elizabeth, *Colonial Citizens: Republican Rights, Paternal Privilege and Gender in Syria and Lebanon* (New York: Columbia University Press, 2000).
Thorez, Maurice, *Fils du Peuple* (Paris: Éditions Sociales, 1949).
Tillon, Charles, *On Chantait Rouge* (Paris: Laffont, 1977).
Tillon, Charles, *Un 'Procès de Moscou' à Paris* (Paris: Seuil, 1971).
Tillon, Charles, *La Révolte Vient de Loin* (Paris: Juillard, 1969).
Tinkler, Penny, *Using Photographs in Social and Historical Research* (London: Sage, 2013).
Tinkler, Penny, '"When I was a girl..": women talking about their girlhood photo collections', in A. Thomson and A. Freund (eds), *Oral History and Photography* (Basingstoke: Palgrave Macmillan, 2011), pp. 45–60.
Traverso, Enzo, *Left-Wing Melancholia: Marxism, History, and Memory* (New York: Columbia University Press, 2016).
Treize, Thomas, 'Between history and psychoanalysis: a case study in the reception of Holocaust survivor testimony', *History & Memory*, 21, 1 (2009), pp. 127–50.
Trotsky, Leon, *Struggle against Fascism in Germany* (New York: Pathfinder, 1971).
Uttl, Bob, Siegenthaler, Amy L. and Ohta, Nobou (eds), *Memory and Emotion: Interdisciplinary Perspectives* (Oxford: Blackwell, 2006).

Van Campen, Cretien, *The Proust Effect: The Senses as Doorways to Lost Memories* (Oxford: Oxford University Press, 2014).
Van der Linden, Marcel, *Workers of the World: Essays Towards a Global Labor History* (Amsterdam: Brill, 2008).
Van Galen Last, Dick, *Des Soldats Noirs dans une Guerre des Blancs (1914–22): Une Histoire Mondiale* (Brussels: Éditions Université de Bruxelles, 2015).
Varela, Francisco, Thompson, Evan and Rosh, Eleanor, *The Embodied Mind* (Cambridge: MIT Press, 1993).
Volosinov, Valentin Nikólaievich, *Marxism and the Philosophy of Language* (Cambridge: Harvard University Press, 1986).
Voogd, Jan, *Race, Riots and Resistance: The Red Summer of 1919* (New York: Peter Lang, 2008).
Vygotsky, Lev S., *The Collected Works of L.S. Vygotsky, Vol. 6: Scientific legacy* (New York: Plenum Press Kluwer Academic, 1999).
Vygotsky, Lev S., *Thought and Language* (Cambridge: MIT Press, 1986).
Wall, Irwin, 'The French Communists and the Algerian War', *Journal of Contemporary History*, 12, 3 (1977), pp. 521–43.
Walraven, Maarten, 'History and its acoustic context: silence, resonance, echo and where to find them in the archive', *Journal of Sonic Studies*, 4, 1 (2013), http://journal.sonicstudies.org/vol04/nr01/a07 (last accessed 1 February 2018).
Wierzbicka, Anna, *Emotions across Languages and Cultures: Diversity and Universals* (Cambridge: Cambridge University Press, 1999).
Wimmer, Andreas and Schiller, Nina Glick, 'Methodological nationalism and beyond: nation-state building, migration and the social sciences', *Global Networks: A Journal of Transnational Affairs*, 2, 4 (2002), pp. 301–34.
Winter, Jay, 'Thinking about silence', in Efrat Ben-Ze'ev, Ruth Ginio and J. M. Winter (eds), *Shadows of War: A Social History of Silence in the Twentieth Century* (Cambridge: Cambridge University Press, 2010), pp. 3–31.
Winter, Jay, *Sites of Memory, Sites of Mourning: The Great War in European Cultural History* (Cambridge: Cambridge University Press, 1998).
Winter, Jay and Sivan, Emmanuel (eds), *War and Remembrance in the Twentieth Century* (Cambridge: Cambridge University Press, 1999).
Withers, Charles W. J., 'Place and the "spatial turn" in geography and in history', *Journal of the History of Ideas*, 70, 4 (2009), pp. 637–58.
Wood, Nancy, *Vectors of Memory: Legacies of Trauma in Postwar Europe* (New York: Berg, 1999).
A.Y., 'André Marty: Les heures glorieuses de la mer Noire', *Pensée*, 23 (April–May 1949), pp. 133–5.
Žižek, Slavoj, 'Lacan between cognitivism and cultural studies', in Rex Butler and Scott Stephens (eds), *Interrogating the Real* (London: Continuum, 2005), pp. 82–110.
Zolberg, Aristide R., 'Moments of madness', *Politics and Society*, 2 (1972), pp. 183–207.

Index

Amet, Vice-Admiral Jean-François-Charles (Commander of the Second Fleet) 29, 30, 33, 35, 38, 45, 61, 67, 116
anti-colonialism *see* colonialism
anti-Semitism 2
Archangel 3, 5, 8, 88, 104
Association Fraternelle des Anciens de la Mer Noire et de leurs Amis (AFAMNA, Fraternal Association of the Veterans of the Black Sea and their Friends) 19, 147–68, 180

Bakhtin, Mikhail 14, 15, 33, 36, 37, 59, 64, 65, 70–1, 95, 115, 181
Baltic Sea 7, 8, 87, 120, 128
Benjamin, Walter 14, 15, 28, 98, 123–4, 132, 134, 185
Bizerte vi, 5, 7, 36, 43, 67, 70, 86–9, 127, 134
Brest 7, 89, 93, 133
Bruix (Chanzy-class battlecruiser) 5, 6, 12, 33, 36, 56, 58, 60, 68, 85, 87, 128

Cachin, Marcel 148, 162
Cané, Albert 9

Cartesian dualism 17
Caubet, Rear Admiral Louis Alfred Marie (Commander of the *Waldeck-Rousseau*) 6, 86, 176
Cherbourg 7, 89, 118, 133
Colonial Infantry 30, 94, 100–8, 121, 132, 183
  4th and 37th 6, 38, 102, 104
  21st 3, 5, 88, 102, 104
  112th and 143rd 6
colonialism 2, 18, 57, 84, 89, 106–8, 131, 149
  Algeria 2, 101, 103–5, 152, 154, 184
  Indochina 107, 131, 149, 151
Comité des Marins (Sailors' Committee) 9, 149, 163
Communist International (Comintern) 3, 10, 84, 93, 107
Condorcet (Danton-class battleship) 7, 27, 57, 58, 62, 70, 91, 97, 104, 117, 118, 122, 135
Confédération Générale du Travail (CGT, General Confederation of Labour) 41, 131, 147, 165
Confédération Générale du Travail Unitaire (CGTU, United General Confederation of Labour) 125, 148

d'Anselme, General Philippe 4, 177
Dehorter (torpedo boat) 6, 33
Démocratie (Republic-class battleship) 6, 42, 59
D'Estrées (cruiser) 8
Diderot (Danton-class battleship) 6, 8
Du Chayla (Chanzy-class battlecruiser) 5, 87, 90
Duclos, Jacques 149, 150, 155, 158, 163
Dunois (destroyer) 7

emotions 3, 12–13, 15–16, 18, 54–82, 174–6, 181–3
  activation 68, 81, 117, 120
  anger 18, 55, 61–4, 67–9, 75
  despair 18, 54, 69, 74, 75, 124–5, 175, 182, 184
  emotional community 16
  emotional exchanges 72
  emotional self-emancipation 75
  emotional sequences 18, 29, 44, 71–2, 175
  emotionology 16, 18, 54–5, 61, 68, 175
  emotive 16, 65, 66
  fear 18, 32, 38, 54, 55, 61–8
  hope 69, 71, 72, 75, 116, 124–5
  managed emotion 66, 67
Ernest Renan (Ernest Renan-class battleship) 6, 12, 33, 36, 42, 85, 92, 127

Fauconneau (torpedo boat) 6
Fauxbras, César vi, 142, 184
France (Jean Bart-class battleship) vi, 5, 28–36, 40, 42–6, 56–9, 62–7, 69–74, 85–7, 91–2, 97, 103, 117, 124–5, 127–8, 131, 134, 137, 146, 157, 166, 167, 168
Franchet d'Espèrey, General Louis 27, 55, 61, 124
Francs-Tireurs et Partisans (FTP, Sharpshooters and Partisans, the military-wing of the Communist resistance movement) 148–50

Galați (Galatz) 5, 27, 86, 95, 104, 183
Gramsci, Antonio vi, 14
  contradictory consciousness 15, 181
Guichen (cruiser) 7, 10, 35, 41, 88, 91, 104–5, 116, 117, 119, 120, 123, 133, 148, 152, 154, 157, 160, 161, 166

Intrépide (torpedo boat) 7

Jean Bart (Jean Bart-class battleship) 5, 6, 28–30, 32, 35, 38, 43, 44, 56–7, 61, 65, 68, 71–4, 86, 94, 96, 105, 116, 175
Justice (Republic-class battleship) 4, 5, 30, 35, 40, 42, 44, 56, 57, 60, 67, 72, 73, 85, 86, 90, 92, 93, 97, 98, 147

Kertch 6
Kherson 3, 4
  evacuation 42, 132
  mutiny 4, 118
  naval bombardment 58, 86

Labourbe, (Marie) Jeanne 4, 68, 75, 86, 97, 100, 117, 127, 135, 158, 160, 163, 176–80, 183
Lefebvre, Henri 14, 15, 83
Leygues, Georges 6, 8, 11, 179
Lorient 7, 89

Mameluk (torpedo boat) 6
Mangin, General Charles Emmanuel Marie 101–3, 107
memory
  associative 116, 119, 120, 122
  autobiographical and personal 115–28
  commemoration 19, 104, 107–8, 120, 128, 146, 148, 152, 158, 163
  composure and discompose 123
  emotional intensity 123
  forgetting 118, 121, 133, 137, 138, 146

group or collective 8, 33, 115, 121, 129, 135, 147
imaged and narrative 131–2
mementos 98, 126–8
pathology 136–7
recognition-recall distinction 118, 119
Mirabeau (Danton-class battleship) 5, 44, 134
Morskaia Road 'ambush' 5, 9, 33, 67, 70, 72, 86, 99, 117, 176
Murmansk 5
mutineers
Alquier, Henri (*Voltaire*) 7, 116
Ascoet, René 116
Badina, Louis (*Protet*) 50, 61, 88, 125, 133, 145, 183, 185, 187
Barillon, Alex 63, 65, 125
Basset, François (*Justice*) 147, 151, 153–66
Benoist, Roger 58, 98, 99, 118
Brest, Désiré (Brest Depot) 136, 152
Buffet, Émile (1917 and Odessa) 67
Camille, Jean (*Du Chayla*) 42, 68, 95, 97, 98, 122, 127
Cannone, Alphonse (*France*) 125
Carrière, Jean (*Jean Bart*) 29, 55, 105, 116
Champale, Gustave (*Voltaire*) 50, 133
Chenevaz, Joseph (*Guichen*) 150, 152–6, 166
Cornier, Albert (*Condorcet*) 27, 31, 55, 57, 58, 62, 70, 100, 118, 122
Cyrille, Marius Jules (*Ernest Renan*) 12, 42, 92, 127
Daniel, Edouard (Brest depot) 133
Daucros, Frédéric (*France*) 97, 127, 161
Decorps, Georges (*Justice*) 85, 93
Douvrin, Germaine (*Guichen*) 119–20, 152, 165
Dubreuil, Lucien (85th Heavy Artillery) 151, 154, 156, 158–61, 163
Dufour, Raymonde 58, 94

Duport, Ernest (*France*) 12–13, 29, 32–3, 43, 55, 57, 59, 63–7, 71–3, 85, 124–5, 127–8, 131
Dupuit, Denis (*Guichen*) 91, 123
Espagnet, Louis (2nd Mountain Artillery) 97, 173
Foucault, Maurice (58th Infantry) 151, 153
Fracchia, Marius (*France*) 31, 91, 125, 133, 161, 179
Gillé, Emmanuel (*France*) 136, 146, 151, 156
Godin, Lucien (*Bruix*) 12, 33, 56, 58, 60, 68, 128
Hiarel, L. (*Démocratie*) 42, 59
Huret, Léon (*France*) 71
Joseph, R. (301st Tank) 118, 122, 124, 132
Lachurie (*Vergniaud*) 33, 44–5, 99, 124, 128
Lagaillarde, Léo (*France*) 128, 185
Lavieu, André (*Waldeck-Rousseau*) 146, 147, 161, 166
Layarde, J. (*Justice*) 42, 98
Le Bras (*Voltaire*) 7
Le Coze, Théo (*Guichen*) 105, 116–17, 148
Lefebvre (176th Infantry) 95–6, 118
Lefort, Eugène (*Jean Bart*) 56, 61–3, 86, 91, 94–6, 103, 118–19, 122
Le Ramey, Jean (*France*) 11, 29, 42–4, 66–7, 71–2, 120, 146–7, 149, 151–9, 161, 163, 166–8
Le Roux, Pierre (*France*) 10, 34, 151
Leva (*Patrie*) 29, 55, 57, 68, 119
Marty, André (*Protet*)
anti-colonialism 102, 104, 107
Association Fraternelle des Anciens de la Mer Noire 146–55, 159–60, 163–6
court martial 5–6, 29, 56, 59, 61, 91, 117
grief 66–7
historian vi, 5, 8–14, 40–1, 65, 72, 75, 100, 115–16, 120, 127–8, 138, 178–9

incarceration and campaign to
 free 70, 87, 88, 129, 145, 185
photographic record 132–3,
 135, 159
Protet conspiracy 5, 69, 85, 95,
 183–4
regret 126
song 128–31
Mauence, François (*Justice*) 40, 56,
 60, 61, 73, 86, 97
Millerin (*Guichen*) 133
Monribot, Marcel (*Condorcet*)
 135, 150, 165
Morvan, Raymond Firmin
 (*Vergniaud*) 5, 179–80
Notta (*France*) 29, 33, 35, 43,
 59, 63, 65, 72, 85, 86,
 128, 176
Nouveau, R. (*Waldeck-Rousseau*)
 29, 35, 60, 62, 85, 90, 128, 175
Poisson, Paul (*Mirabeau*) 134
Riballet, Jean (175th Infantry) 124
Ribot, Eugène (1st RMA) 33, 34,
 38, 66, 70, 71, 75, 92, 98, 123,
 125, 127
Ricros, Antonin (*France*) 31, 35,
 71, 128
Rolland, Roger (*Voltaire*) 116
Térion, Lucien (7th Engineers) 161
Tillon, Charles (*Guichen*) 10–11,
 13, 35, 41–2, 88, 91, 104, 105,
 116–20, 123, 127–8, 133–8,
 147–68
Tondut, Marcel (58th Infantry) 26,
 91, 128, 136, 147, 151, 153–5,
 158–63, 165–6
Vergua, Marcel (4th and 37th
 Colonial) 38, 102
Vottero, Pierre (*Voltaire*) 7, 11, 36,
 55, 70–1, 120, 124, 127, 133,
 160, 166, 168
Vuillemin, Virgle (*France*) 59, 60,
 62, 71, 72, 137, 146, 147, 150,
 152, 160, 161, 163–8
Wallet, Georges (*Voltaire*) 7,
 69, 116
Mykolaiv (Nikolaev) 3, 4, 5, 97, 98

Nantes 7
nationalism 2, 18, 83, 84, 93, 129,
 153, 174
 methodological 3, 83
 Ukrainian 3

Odessa 3, 5, 7, 28, 29, 33, 36, 40, 42,
 64, 75, 85, 89, 90, 96–9, 118,
 125, 128, 129, 131, 132, 134,
 135, 163, 165, 173, 177, 179

Parti Communiste Française (PCF,
 French Communist Party) 1,
 8, 9, 11, 12, 69, 107, 123, 126,
 135, 145–68, 180
Patrie (Republic-class battleship) 29,
 55, 57, 68, 119
place 90–2
 Frenchness 28, 83, 91–2
 regional identity 91
Protet (Bisson-class destroyer) 5, 69,
 85, 95, 183–4
Provence (Provence-class battleship) 6

race riots 1, 2, 89
Robez-Pagillon, Jules-Aimé
 (Commander of the *France*)
 30, 57, 59, 62–3, 70, 74, 92
Rochefort 6, 89
rumour 4, 10, 20, 31, 36, 42, 63, 67,
 68, 85–6, 95, 129, 162, 173,
 178, 180

Sadoul, Jacques 97, 149, 151
*Section Française de l'Internationale
 Ouvrière* (SFIO, French
 Section of the Worker's
 International) 155
Section Russe (SR, Russian Section of
 French military intelligence)
 177
Senegalese riflemen 7, 101–5, 117
senses 17–18, 25–46, 174–5
 hearing 31–46
 historiography 25–6
 Proust effect 131

INDEX 209

ratio 27
sight 28–31
smell 26, 27
taste 27–8
touch 27
Service Historique de la Defence,
    Vincennes (SHD) 75, 168
Sevastopol vi, 3, 5, 6, 10, 30, 34, 35,
    44, 45, 61, 62, 63, 65, 66, 68,
    69, 70, 72, 73, 85, 86, 89, 92,
    93, 94, 96, 99, 101, 105, 118,
    119, 124, 129, 131, 132, 134,
    153, 176, 179
social movement theory 15–16
    frame alignment 31, 43
    moral shock/injustice frame 4,
        20, 86
    protest cycle 35, 42, 44, 67–9
    repertoire of action 44, 182
song 14, 18, 30, 31, 33, 34, 36, 39–45,
    52, 93, 98, 115, 121, 127, 128,
    129, 147, 154, 174, 182
    Chanson des Fayots 37–9, 40, 41,
        45, 73
    *Glory to the Sailors of the Black
        Sea* 69, 129–31
    Odessa Waltz 40, 44, 52, 173–4
strikes 1, 2, 27, 41, 89, 90, 103, 147

Tendra 6, 7
Thorez, Maurice 146, 149, 151, 157,
    160, 165
time
    conjuncture of 1919 vi–vii, 1–3, 10,
        12, 14, 18–19, 84–90, 107, 125,
        135, 146–8, 152, 162, 174, 178,
        183–5
    events of 1968 156, 161–2, 167–8,
        180, 185

generational 19, 41, 115, 121, 123,
    136–8, 145, 153, 165, 168, 180,
    181, 184
Tiraspol 4, 122, 152
Touareg (torpedo boat) 8
Toulon 6, 7, 30, 55, 58, 70, 73, 87–8,
    90–1, 119, 148, 157
transnationalism
    circulation 84–90
    disease 89–90
    fraternisation 18, 84–100, 104,
        107–8, 145, 159, 175, 183
    ideas 84–8
    port cities 89
Trousson, Colonel 4, 101

Ukraine 4, 88, 95, 96

Vergniaud (Danton-class battleship)
    5, 33, 44, 55, 99, 124, 128, 179
Vladivostok 8
Voloshinov, Valentin 14, 36–7, 95
Voltaire (Danton-class battleship) vi,
    7, 36, 55, 69, 70, 71, 86, 87, 124,
    127, 133, 160
Vygotsky, Lev 14, 15, 37, 88, 181

Waldeck-Rousseau (Ernest Renan-
    class battlecruiser) 5, 6, 29,
    32, 34, 35, 36, 60, 62, 63, 65,
    70, 85, 86, 87, 90, 91, 97, 117,
    125, 128, 129, 135, 146, 147,
    175, 180
women 1, 2, 51, 58, 84, 86, 98, 106,
    107, 183, 187

Zak, William vi–vii

EU authorised representative for GPSR:
Easy Access System Europe, Mustamäe tee 50,
10621 Tallinn, Estonia
gpsr.requests@easproject.com

www.ingramcontent.com/pod-product-compliance
Lightning Source LLC
Chambersburg PA
CBHW070238240426
43673CB00044B/1841